Abstract
Machines
and Grammars

Little, Brown Computer Systems Series

Gerald M. Weinberg, *Editor*

Basso, David T., and Ronald D. Schwartz
Programming with FORTRAN/WATFOR/WATFIV

Chattergy, Rahul, and Udo W. Pooch
Top-down, Modular Programming in FORTRAN with WATFIV

Coats, R.B., and A. Parkin
Computer Models in the Social Sciences

Conway, Richard, and David Gries
An Introduction to Programming: A Structured Approach Using PL/1 and PL/C

Conway, Richard, and David Gries
Primer on Structured Programming: Using PL/1, PL/C, and PL/CT

Conway, Richard, David Gries, and E. Carl Zimmerman
A Primer on Pascal, Second Edition

Cripps, Martin
An Introduction to Computer Hardware

Easley, Grady M.
Primer for Small Systems Management

Finkenaur, Robert G.
COBOL for Students: A Programming Primer

Freedman, Daniel P., and Gerald M. Weinberg
Handbook of Walkthroughs, Inspections, and Technical Reviews: Evaluating Programs, Projects, and Products

Graybeal, Wayne, and Udo W. Pooch
Simulation: Principles and Methods

Greenfield, S.E.
The Architecture of Microcomputers

Greenwood, Frank
Profitable Small Business Computing

Healy, Martin, and David Hebditch
The Microcomputer in On-Line Systems: Small Computers in Terminal-Based Systems and Distributed Processing Networks

Lias, Edward J.
Future Mind: The Microcomputer — New Medium, New Mental Environment

Lines, M. Vardell, and Boeing Computer Services Company
Minicomputer Systems

Mills, Harlan D.
Software Productivity

Monro, Donald M.
Basic BASIC: An Introduction to Programming

Mosteller, William S.
Systems Programmer's Problem Solver

Nahigian, J. Victor, and William S. Hodges
Computer Games for Businesses, Schools, and Homes

Nahigian, J. Victor, and William S. Hodges
*Computer Games for Business, School, and Home for TRS-80
Level II BASIC*

Orwig, Gary W., and William S. Hodges
The Computer Tutor: Learning Activities for Homes and Schools

Parikh, Girish
Techniques of Program and System Maintenance

Parkin, Andrew
Data Processing Management

Parkin, Andrew
Systems Analysis

Pizer, Stephen M., with Victor L. Wallace
Numerical Computing: Concepts and Strategies

Pooch, Udo W., William H. Greene, and Gary G. Moss
Telecommunications and Networking

Reingold, Edward M., and Wilfred J. Hansen
Data Structures

Savitch, Walter J.
Abstract Machines and Grammars

Shneiderman, Ben
*Software Psychology: Human Factors in Computer and
Information Systems*

Walker, Henry M.
Problems for Computer Solutions Using FORTRAN

Walker, Henry M.
Problems for Computer Solutions Using BASIC

Weinberg, Gerald M.
Rethinking Systems Analysis and Design

Weinberg, Gerald M.
Understanding the Professional Programmer

**Weinberg, Gerald M., Stephen E. Wright, Richard Kauffman, and
Martin A. Goetz**
High Level COBOL Programming

Abstract Machines and Grammars

Walter J. Savitch

University of California
San Diego

Little, Brown and Company
Boston   Toronto

Library of Congress Cataloging in Publication Data

Savitch, Walter J., 1943-
    Abstract machines and grammars.

    Bibliography: p. 206
    Includes indexes.
    1. Machine theory.   2. Formal languages.
I. Title.
QA267.S29   511   81-16136
ISBN 0-316-771619   AACR2

Library of Congress Catalog Card No. 81-16136

ISBN 0-316-771619

9 8 7 6 5 4 3 2 1

VB

Published simultaneously in Canada
by Little, Brown & Company (Canada) Limited

Printed in the United States of America

To My Parents

Preface

Computability theory is concerned primarily with determining what tasks can be accomplished by idealized computer programs. Formal language theory deals primarily with the ability of certain grammars to express the syntax of various types of languages. Both fields are branches of formal mathematics. The former theory has its roots in mathematical logic, the latter in mathematical linguistics which includes the mathematical theory of compiler design. In recent years, these two subjects have been studied extensively by computer scientists and have interacted to the point where, from the perspective of a computer scientist, they are frequently viewed as a single unified subject. As such, they have become a standard course topic in many computer science curricula. This book contains an introduction to these two interrelated subjects. It is suitable for an introductory course at either the advanced undergraduate or beginning graduate level. It also can be read and understood, without the aid of an instructor, by anybody who has either a background in theoretical mathematics or a reasonable amount of programming experience and some exposure to mathematical proofs.

The present text grew out of notes used in both graduate and undergraduate courses at the University of California at San Diego. These courses were designed for students with a good deal of experience in the areas of computer programming and systems, but with limited exposure to formal mathematics. This explains the slightly unorthodox arrangement of the material in this book. In teaching these courses it was found that the notion of a context-free grammar was easily understood by students who have had a fair amount of programming experience. In fact it proved to be the one notion in the course that they were most comfortable with. Primarily for this reason, the book presents context-free grammars first and uses these grammars as the central focus of the book. This approach, while it may not be the traditional way to structure the material, has proved to be pedagogically sound. It has also proved to be a sound and efficient approach mathematically, since context-free grammars turn out to be a convenient and efficient vehicle for presenting a number of other key notions in computability and formal language theory.

There are some points to keep in mind when using this book as a text. In reading this book you will find that a number of details are left as exercises. These exercises should be done by the student. They are usually not difficult, but they do insure that the student is an active participant in the development of the material presented. Occasionally these exercises, although routine, are lengthy. These instances are noted in the text and, for these exercises, a quick mental review of what is involved should be sufficient for understanding the material. The material presented has proved to be a bit too much for a one-quarter course, and it may be too much for a one-semester undergraduate course. It is possible to choose a subset of the sections as a shorter course. Sections marked with a star may be omitted without missing results needed later on in the book.

In preparing this book I have sought and received helpful comments from a number of people. I would like to especially thank the following people for their helpful comments on earlier versions of the text: K. Apt, P. W. Dymond, M. L. Fredman, J. Goldstine, B. Levergood, G. Rozenberg, M. J. Stimson, D. Vermeir, P. M. B. Vitanyi, and most especially the students who suffered through and helped correct mistakes in earlier versions of this text. I would also like to thank Sue Sullivan for her expert assistance in typesetting and preparing the manuscript.

W.J.S.

Contents

Chapter Six

Universal Turing Machines and the Halting Problem   125

Chapter Seven

Turing Machines as Accepting Devices   140

Chapter Eight

*Nondeterministic Turing Machines   150

Chapter One

Introduction

The term *machine* in the title of this book refers to computers. A more descriptive title would be "computing machines and grammars." Much of the formal development of the subject will be stated in terms of machines or computers. However, the primary object of study will not be computers so much as computer programs. We assume that the reader has a general idea of what a computer program is. It is a set of instructions for a computer to follow. Of course, the instructions could be carried out by a human being instead of a computer. In this context, you might consider a human being to be a computer. In any event, the set of instructions describe a process to be carried out and the set of instructions can be given even if no computer is available. Such sets of instructions are frequently called *effective procedures* or, in certain circumstances, *algorithms*. If you interpret the term "computer program" loosely enough, then an effective procedure is approximately the same thing as a computer program. Later on we will give formal definitions of what we mean by effective procedures and algorithms. In this chapter we will give an intuitive idea of what effective procedures and algorithms are. For this intuitive discussion, it is best to think of the instructions as being given to a human being in an informal but still completely precise way. After this intuitive discussion, we go on to describe some of the mathematical notation we will use.

PROCEDURES AND ALGORITHMS

An *effective procedure* is a finite set of instructions that can be carried out by a computing device, or a human being, in an effective, deterministic, step-by-step manner. Usually, the procedure has some input and produces some output. So, an effective procedure is usually a set of instructions for computing a function from inputs to outputs. However, an effective procedure need not

1

necessarily compute a function. To qualify as an effective procedure, the instructions must be completely unambiguous and there must be a method for unambiguously determining the order in which the instructions are carried out. The instructions must also be carried out in a discrete, deterministic way. There must not be any resorting to continuous methods or analog devices. There must not be any resorting to random methods or devices. Usually, an effective procedure has access to facilities for storing and retrieving intermediate calculations.

Programs for digital computers are examples of effective procedures. Since an effective procedure need not be written in a programming language for any particular computer, the notion of an effective procedure is slightly more general than that of a computer program. However, the added generality is slight and we will not go too far astray if we think of an effective procedure as a computer program. When thinking of an effective procedure as a computer program, we must not think of our programs as being limited by any time or machine size constraints. We will not require that the procedure terminate in a "reasonable" amount of time. Also, we will assume that the storage facilities available have no size limitation. At any point in time the procedure will use only a finite amount of such storage. However, we will assume that the storage facilities always have room to hold more information. In particular, if we think in terms of computer programs, we will assume the machine is so large that we never run out of storage and never get an integer overflow or other type of termination due to a size limit of the machine. This may seem unreasonable to some computer programmers. However, it is a reasonable first step in developing a theory of computer programs. More advanced texts refine these notions and develop theories for programs that run realistically efficiently.

An effective procedure need not end. For example, a computer program may contain an infinite loop. If an effective procedure has the property that, for all inputs, the computing process eventually terminates, then the procedure is called an *algorithm.*

One final word of warning is in order. Later on we will generalize the notion of an effective procedure and consider things called nondeterministic procedures. These nondeterministic procedures are mathematically useful and interesting. However, they do not correspond exactly to our intuitive notion of an effective procedure and some of the above remarks do not apply to such nondeterministic procedures.

SETS, RELATIONS, AND FUNCTIONS

We will use standard set theory notation and assume familiarity with the elementary notions of set theory. In this section we will briefly describe most of the set theory notation employed in this text. This section need only be skimmed through rapidly and then used as a reference if necessary.

Finite sets will usually be denoted by listing their elements (members) enclosed in brackets. For example, {1, 3, 5} denotes the set which contains exactly the three elements 1, 3, and 5. This notation is extended in the usual way to obtain a notation which describes the set in question by some property that holds for exactly those elements in the set. For example, $\{x \mid x$ is an integer and $1 \leqslant x \leqslant 3\} = \{1, 2, 3\}$ and $\{x \mid x$ is an even positive integer$\} = \{2, 4, 6, 8, ...\}$. When part of the description of a set is clear from context, we will omit it. For example, if it is clear from context that we are discussing integers, then $\{x \mid 1 \leqslant x \leqslant 3\} = \{1, 2, 3\}$.

The symbols $\in$, $\notin$, $\cup$, $\cap$, $-$, $\subseteq$, and $\subset$ denote membership, non-membership, set union, set intersection, set difference, set inclusion and set proper inclusion respectively. So, for example, $1 \in \{1, 2\}$, $3 \notin \{1, 2\}$, $\{1, 2\} \cup \{2, 3\} = \{1, 2, 3\}$, $\{1, 2\} \cap \{2, 3\} = \{2\}$, $\{1, 2\} - \{2, 3\} = \{1\}$, $\{1, 2\} \subseteq \{1, 2, 3\}$, $\{1, 2\} \subseteq \{1, 2\}$, $\{1, 2\} \subset \{1, 2, 3\}$ but it is not true that $\{1, 2\} \subset \{1, 2\}$. The symbol $\varnothing$ will denote the empty set. Thus, for example, $\{1, 2\} \cap \{3, 4\} = \varnothing$.

Ordered tuples will be denoted in the usual way. For example, $(1, 2, 2)$ is the ordered three-tuple with the three elements 1, 2 and 2 in that order. Note that the order is important and so an element may occur more than once in an ordered tuple. The sign $\times$ will denote Cartesian product. If A and B are sets, then by definition $A \times B = \{(a, b) \mid a \in A$ and $b \in B\}$. For example, $\{1, 2\} \times \{3, 4\} = \{(1, 3), (1, 4), (2, 3), (2, 4)\}$.

A *binary relation* R on a set A is defined as a set of ordered pairs (two-tuples) of elements of A. If $(a, b) \in R$, then we will write "aRb" instead of "$(a, b) \in R$." Intuitively, a relation is a condition on pairs of elements and we will usually define relations by describing a condition on pairs. For example, we may define aRb to mean a and b are integers and b is the square of a. So, with this definition of R, $2R4$ and $4R16$ hold but it is not true that $1R2$ or $4R2$ hold. A more formal definition of this particular relation is $R = \{(a, b) \mid a$ and b are integers and $a^2 = b\}$. However, we will seldom use this formal set-theory type of definition.

A *function* f from a set X to a set Y is a subset of $X \times Y$ such that: for each $x \in X$ there is at most one $y \in Y$ such that $(x, y) \in f$. Rather than writing "$(x, y) \in f$," we will follow standard notation and write "$f(x) = y$." To make the above definition look more familiar, read "$f(x) = y$" in place of "$(x, y) \in f$." If f is a function from X to Y, we may denote this by writing $f : X \rightarrow Y$. The set X is called the *domain* of f and the set Y is called the *range* of f.

Note that we have not required that the following condition hold:

1. for each $x \in X$, there is a $y \in Y$ such that $f(x) = y$.

If, for some particular $x \in X$, no such y exists, then we say that $f(x)$ is *undefined* at x. If f does satisfy condition (1), then f is said to be a *total function*. We will use the terms *function* and *partial function* as exact synonyms. The adjective "partial" is to remind ourselves that condition (1) might possibly not hold. To prevent confusion, we will avoid using the unmodified term "function."

The following condition may or may not be satisfied by a partial function:

2. for each $y \in Y$, there is an $x \in X$ such that $f(x) = y$.

If f is a partial function from X to Y and f satisfies (2), then we sometimes say that f is a function from X *onto* Y. If (2) is possibly not satisfied, we say that f is a function from X *into* Y. Actually, any function from X to Y can be said to be a function from X into Y, even if (2) is satisfied. However, the term "into" is usually used when (2) does not hold or at least is not definitely known to hold.

The words *function* and *mapping* are exact synonyms. The only reason for using both words is that it introduces some variety and that they are both standard terms.

We conclude this section with some simple examples of functions in order to clarify our terminology. Let Q denote the set of rational numbers and let I denote the set of integers and let N denote the set of natural numbers (non-negative integers). Define $f : I \rightarrow N$ by $f(x) = x^2$. Then f is a total function. Define $g : N \rightarrow Q$ by $g(x) = 1/x$, provided x is not zero. Then g is a partial function. The function g is not total, since $g(0)$ is undefined. It is correct to call f a partial function. The term *partial function* means a function which is not necessarily total. However, if we know f is a total function, we will usually call it that. We will sometimes encounter situations where we do not know whether or not a function is total. In these cases, the function will be referred to as a partial function.

ALPHABETS AND LANGUAGES

The notions of symbol and string of symbols are central to what we will be doing. The input and output to procedures and algorithms will usually consist of strings of symbols and we will represent many aspects of the computing process itself as strings of symbols. We now review our notation for handling strings and symbols.

The notion of a *symbol* is a primitive notion which we will not define. It corresponds to the common use of this notion. So, for example, it is true that the English alphabet can be thought of as having 26 symbols. If we consider both upper- and lower-case letters, then it contains 52 symbols. The word "*pop*" contains two symbols, "p" and "o." It contains three *occurrences* of symbols, two occurrences of "p" and one occurrence of "o." It is common practice to use the word "symbol" rather loosely to mean either symbol or occurrence of a symbol. Whenever we do so, the intended meaning should be clear from the context. *Word* is another primitive notion. Intuitively, a word is a finite string of symbols or, more correctly, a string of occurrences of symbols. In fact, we will use the words *string* and *word* interchangeably. A symbol is a special kind of word. It is a word with only one occurrence of a symbol. There is also a word with zero occurrences of symbols. This is the *empty word* and will be denoted by the upper-case Greek letter Λ. For example, if asked to find the word between the symbols "*x*" and "*y*" in the words "*xabley*" and "*xy*," the correct answers are "*able*" and Λ. (At the back of this book there is an appendix which gives the names of the Greek letters.)

The last primitive notion we will need is that of *concatenation*. The concatenation of two strings α and β is the string obtained by writing β after α. The concatenation of α and β is denoted $\alpha\beta$. For example, if α is the string "*aba*" and β is the string "*bab*," then $\alpha\beta$ is the string "*ababab*."

SUMMARY OF NOTATION

The following is a tabulation of the notation we will use for handling symbols and strings. Give it a quick reading now and then use it as a reference. The terms are assimilated best through usage and we will be using them frequently.

1.1 Definition

1.1.1 An *alphabet* is a finite set of symbols.

1.1.2 A *language* is a set of words.

1.1.3 If L_1 and L_2 are languages, then L_1L_2 denotes the product of the two languages. The product L_1L_2 is the set of all strings of the form $\alpha\beta$ where α is a string in L_1 and β is a string in L_2. For example, if $L_1 = \{a, bb\}$ and $L_2 = \{ab, c\}$ then $L_1L_2 = \{aab, ac, bbab, bbc\}$.

1.1.4 Λ denotes the empty string.

1.1.5 If α is a string and n is a non-negative integer, then α^n denotes n occurrences of α concatenated together. By convention, $\alpha^0 = \Lambda$. For example, if $\alpha = $ "*abc*," then $\alpha^3 = $ "*abcabcabc*."

From now on, we will usually not bother with quotes. We will write $\alpha = abc$ instead of $\alpha = $ "*abc*." This can produce some ambiguity and we will have to rely on context to clear up this ambiguity. For example, if $\alpha = 2$, then $\alpha^2 = 22$, when 2 denotes the symbol "2" and $\alpha^2 = 4$ when 2 denotes the number two. In what follows we will always be careful to ensure that the intended meaning is clear from context.

1.1.6 If L is a language, then L^n denotes the product of L with itself n times. L^n can be defined recursively as follows:

$$L^0 = \{\Lambda\}$$

$$L^{n+1} = L^n L$$

1.1.7 If L is a language, then L^* is called the *star closure* of L. It consists of all finite concatenations of strings from L. That is,

$$L^* = \bigcup_{n=0}^{\infty} L^n$$

For example, if L contains just the two symbols 0 and 1, then L^* consists of all binary numerals with any number of leading zeros.

1.1.8 If L is a language, then L^+ denotes the language defined as follows:

$$L^+ = \bigcup_{n=1}^{\infty} L^n$$

So, in particular, if Σ is an alphabet, then $\Sigma^+ = \Sigma^* - \{\Lambda\}$.

1.1.9 If α denotes a string, then $\text{length}(\alpha)$ denotes the length of α. More precisely, $\text{length}(\alpha)$ is the number of occurrences of symbols in α. For example, $\text{length}(abc) = 3$, $\text{length}(aabb) = 4$ and $\text{length}(\Lambda) = 0$.

In order to make the text more readable, we will follow a number of conventions on symbol usage. Upper-case Greek letters Σ, Γ, ..., will usually range over alphabets. Lower-case Roman letters near the beginning of the alphabet, $a, b, c, ...$, will usually range over individual symbols. Lower-case Greek letters, $\alpha, \beta, \gamma, ...$, will usually range over strings of symbols. The one notable exception to this rule is δ, which will always denote a function. Upper-case Roman letters, $A, B, C, ...$, will be used to denote sets and to denote some special kinds of symbols. Since languages are sets, they are denoted by upper-case Roman letters, usually by L. Upper-case Roman letters will also be used to denote machines. In fact, we will usually use M for machines. The other conventions are standard to most all fields of mathematics. The letters, i, j, and k are usually indices or integers; l, m, and n inevitably stand for integers; f, g and h inevitably denote functions and of course, x, y and z are variables that might range over anything.

Frequently, we will want an entire word to be treated as a single symbol. We indicate this by enclosing the word in angular brackets. Thus "even" is a word with four occurrences of symbols while "<even>" is just one single symbol. The reason for doing this is to make the mathematics more readable. We could use e or X or α in place of $<even>$. However, if we want a symbol to use in recording the fact that some count is even, then $<even>$ has obvious advantages over x. It even has advantages over e which may already stand for something. Sometimes we will use boldface type instead of angular brackets. So **even** denotes a single symbol just as $<even>$ does.

EXERCISES

1. Let J, K, and L be languages. Prove the following:
   a. $(JK)L = J(KL)$
   b. $J(K \cup L) = JK \cup JL$
   c. If $J \subseteq K$, then $J^* \subseteq K^*$
   d. $(L^*)^* = L^*$

2. Give examples of languages to show that the following statements are false.
   a. $J(K \cap L) = JK \cap JL$
   b. $L^+ = L^* - \{\Lambda\}$

3. Give an effective procedure that takes an arbitrary natural number as input and gives the square root of the number as output, provided the square root is itself a natural number.

Chapter
Two

Context-Free
Grammars

Many common programming languages have a syntax that can be described, either completely or partially, by a set of rewrite rules called context-free productions. The set of such productions that defines the syntax of a particular language is called a *context-free grammar*. Context-free grammars are also frequently referred to as BNF grammars, but we will always use the term context-free grammar.

An informal example will help to introduce the notion of a context-free grammar. Suppose we want to describe the syntax of all well-formed arithmetic expressions involving the variables x and y and the operation $+$. We can do this by a set of productions or rewrite rules which describe how a specified start symbol can be transformed to such an arithmetic expression. Specifically, we can let S be the start symbol and use the following productions: $S \rightarrow (S+S)$, $S \rightarrow V$, $V \rightarrow x$ and $V \rightarrow y$. The production $S \rightarrow (S+S)$, for example, means S can be rewritten as $(S+S)$. So one possible sequence of rewritings is: S is rewritten as $(S+S)$ using the production $S \rightarrow (S+S)$, then $(S+S)$ is rewritten as $(V+S)$ using the production $S \rightarrow V$, then $(V+S)$ is rewritten as $(V+V)$ using the production $S \rightarrow V$ again and finally, in two steps, $(V+V)$ is rewritten as $(x+y)$ using the productions $V \rightarrow x$ and $V \rightarrow y$. We can abbreviate this rewriting process by $S \Rightarrow (S+S) \Rightarrow (V+S) \Rightarrow (V+V) \Rightarrow (x+V) \Rightarrow (x+y)$. Another possible sequence of rewritings is: $S \Rightarrow (S+S) \Rightarrow ((S+S)+S) \Rightarrow ((V+S)+S) \Rightarrow ((V+V)+S) \Rightarrow ((V+V)+V) \Rightarrow ((x+V)+V) \Rightarrow ((x+y)+V) \Rightarrow (((x+y)+x)$. The symbols x, y, $+$, $)$ and $($ are called *terminal symbols*, since they cannot be rewritten. The symbols S and V are called *nonterminals* or *sentential variables*. It should be clear that the set of all strings of terminal symbols that can be obtained in this way is exactly equal to the set of all well-formed, parenthesized arithmetic expressions involving the terminal symbols. We now make these notions more formal.

8

DEFINITIONS AND EXAMPLES

2.1 Definition

2.1.1 A *context-free grammar* (*cfg*) is a quadruple $G = (N, T, P, S)$ where

1. N is a finite set of symbols called *nonterminals*.
2. T is a finite set of symbols called *terminals* and is such that $N \cap T$ is empty.
3. S is an element of N called the *start symbol*.
4. P is a finite set of strings of the form $A \rightarrow \alpha$ where A is in N and α is a string in $(N \cup T)^*$. These strings in P are called *productions*. Productions are sometimes also called *rewrite rules*.

We must be able to distinguish between the four elements of G. We choose to do this by the usual mathematical trick. We make the four elements into an ordered four-tuple. Then, by convention, the first entry is the set of nonterminals, the second is the set of terminals, and so forth. This trick requires an arbitrary convention that is hard to remember and is, after all, an arbitrary convention. It does not really matter that N is the first entry. What matters is that N is the entry that is the set of nonterminals. So as not to have to remember this arbitrary convention, we will use more suggestive notation than first entry, second entry, and so forth. The nonterminals of G will be denoted by Nonterminals(G). The next three entries will be denoted by Terminals(G), Productions(G), and Start(G) respectively. So Nonterminals(G) $= N$, Terminals(G) $= T$, Productions(G) $= P$, and Start(G) $= S$. In mathematical terminology, Nonterminals() is a projection that maps each context-free grammar onto its first coordinate, Terminals() maps it onto its second coordinate, and so forth. The important thing to remember is that if G is a context-free grammar, then Nonterminals(G) is the set of nonterminals of G and the other three projections yield the things they sound like.

It will sometimes be useful to have a notation for all the symbols of G, both terminals and nonterminals. So we expand the above notation by defining Symbols(G) to be Nonterminals(G) $\cup$ Terminals(G).

2.1.2 The relation $\Rightarrow$ on (Symbols(G))* is defined so that $\beta \Rightarrow \gamma$ holds provided β and γ can be expressed as $\beta = \nu A \mu$ and $\gamma = \nu \alpha \mu$ where $A \rightarrow \alpha$ is in Productions(G) and both ν and μ are strings of symbols. The notation $\overset{*}{\Rightarrow}$ denotes any finite (possibly zero) number of applications of $\Rightarrow$. More precisely, $\beta \overset{*}{\Rightarrow} \gamma$ if $\beta = \gamma$ or if there is an n and there are $\xi_1, \xi_2, ..., \xi_n$ such that: $\xi_1 = \beta$, $\xi_n = \gamma$ and $\xi_i \Rightarrow \xi_{i+1}$ for all $i < n$. If we have more than one grammar under consideration, we will sometimes write $\underset{G}{\Rightarrow}$ and $\underset{G}{\overset{*}{\Rightarrow}}$ to mean $\Rightarrow$ and $\overset{*}{\Rightarrow}$ in the grammar G.

2.1.3 Let w be in (Terminals(G))*. A *derivation* of w in G is a sequence $\xi_0, \xi_1, ..., \xi_n$ of strings in (Symbols(G))* such that $\xi_0 = S$, $\xi_n = w$ and $\xi_i \Rightarrow \xi_{i+1}$ for $i = 0, 1, ..., n-1$.

2.1.4 The *language generated by* G is defined and denoted by $L(G) = \{w \mid S \overset{*}{\Rightarrow} w$ and $w \in (\text{Terminals}(G))^*\}$. A language H is called a *context-free language* (cfl) provided $H = L(G)$ for some cfg G.

2.1.5 Two cfg's G_1 and G_2 are said to be *equivalent* if $L(G_1) = L(G_2)$. Intuitively, two cfg's are equivalent if they describe the same set of syntactically "correct sentences."

2.2 Examples of cfg's

2.2.1 Let $G = (N, T, P, S)$ where $N = \{S\}$, $T = \{a, b\}$, and $P = \{S \to \Lambda, S \to aSb\}$. Then $L(G) = \{a^n b^n \mid n \geqslant 0\}$. A sample derivation in G is $S \Rightarrow aSb \Rightarrow aaSbb \Rightarrow aabb$.

When two or more productions have the same nonterminal on the left-hand side, we may abbreviate the list of productions. For example, $S \to \Lambda$ and $S \to aSb$ would be abbreviated to $S \to \Lambda \mid aSb$.

2.2.2 Let $G = (N, T, P, S)$ where

$$N = \{S, <\text{noun}>, <\text{verbphrase}>, <\text{verb}>\}$$

$T = \{\textbf{man}, \textbf{dog}, \textbf{bites}\}$ and P contains the following productions:

$S \to <\text{noun}> <\text{verbphrase}>$

$<\text{verbphrase}> \to <\text{verb}> <\text{noun}>$

$<\text{verb}> \to \textbf{bites}$

$<\text{noun}> \to \textbf{man} \mid \textbf{dog}$

Then $L(G)$ contains exactly four strings: **dog bites man**, **dog bites dog**, **man bites man**, **man bites dog**. A sample derivation follows:

$S \Rightarrow <\text{noun}> <\text{verbphrase}> \Rightarrow <\text{noun}> <\text{verb}> <\text{noun}> \Rightarrow$

$\quad \textbf{man} <\text{verb}> <\text{noun}> \Rightarrow \textbf{man bites} <\text{noun}> \Rightarrow \textbf{man bites dog}$

Note that we are treating the English words "man," "bites," and "dog" as single symbols. This is quite common in linguistic analysis. The reason is that, for our purposes, the words are basic units that will not be broken down. We will not bother to break "man" down into m-a-n. We could consider "man" as a three-symbol string and redefine G. We get a well-defined cfg either way. However, if we treat "man" as a single symbol, the grammar is easier to handle. Notice that, in this example, the derived terminal strings are sentences. For this reason, elements of context-free languages are sometimes referred to as "sentences." Although it is a little bit confusing, the formal notion of a derived terminal word corresponds to our intuitive notion of a sentence and the formal notion of a terminal symbol corresponds to our intuitive notion of a word.

2.2.3 In this example we define a cfg G for a subset of the well-formed arithmetic expressions using $+$ and $\times$ as operators, x, y, and z as the only variables, and binary numerals as the constants.

Nonterminals $(G) = \{S, <\text{operation}>, <\text{variable}>, <\text{constant}>\}$
Terminals $(G) = \{1, 0, x, y, z, (,), +, \times\}$, Start $(G) = S$

The productions of G are given below:

$S \rightarrow (S <\text{operation}> S) \mid <\text{variable}> \mid <\text{constant}>$
$<\text{variable}> \rightarrow x \mid y \mid z$
$<\text{constant}> \rightarrow 0 \mid 1 \mid 0<\text{constant}> \mid 1<\text{constant}>$
$<\text{operation}> \rightarrow + \mid \times$

A sample derivation is the following:

$S \Rightarrow (S <\text{operation}> S) \Rightarrow (S + S) \Rightarrow (<\text{variable}> + S) \Rightarrow (x + S) \Rightarrow$
$(x + (S <\text{operation}> S)) \Rightarrow (x + (S \times S)) \Rightarrow$
$(x + (<\text{variable}> \times S)) \Rightarrow (x + (y \times S)) \Rightarrow$
$(x + (y \times <\text{constant}>)) \Rightarrow (x + (y \times 1<\text{constant}>)) \Rightarrow (x + (y \times 10))$

PARSE TREES AND AMBIGUITY

A useful observation that can be a great aid to intuition is that derivations can be viewed as trees called *parse trees*. These parse trees can also be helpful when we study the semantics of languages. Since we will usually use trees in an informal sense, we will explain them by examples. We will use them frequently though, so the examples should be thoroughly understood.

2.3 Examples

In these examples of derivations and their corresponding trees, all upper-case letters are nonterminals and all lower-case letters are terminals. S is the start symbol. We only describe as much of the grammar as is needed for the examples.

2.3.1 $S \Rightarrow AB \Rightarrow aAaB \Rightarrow aaaB \Rightarrow aaab$ by the productions $S \rightarrow AB$, $A \rightarrow aAa$, $A \rightarrow a$, $B \rightarrow b$. The parse tree is given in Figure 2.1(a).

2.3.2 $S \Rightarrow AB \Rightarrow Ab \Rightarrow aAab \Rightarrow aaab$ by the productions $S \rightarrow AB$, $B \rightarrow b$, $A \rightarrow aAa$, $A \rightarrow a$. The parse tree for this derivation is also the tree in Figure 2.1(a). So two distinct derivations can yield the same parse tree.

2.3.3 $S \Rightarrow AB \Rightarrow aAB \Rightarrow aB \Rightarrow ab$ by the productions $S \rightarrow AB$, $A \rightarrow aA$, $A \rightarrow \Lambda$, $B \rightarrow b$. The parse tree is given in Figure 2.1(b).

The parse tree for a string generated by a context-free grammar often has much to do with the meaning of the sentence. For example, the parse trees for the sentences in Example 2.2.2 describe the grammatical structure of the strings as sentences in the English language. Each of the sentences in that example has only one parse tree. If some sentence had two parse trees and if the grammar

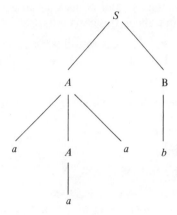

Figure 2.1(a)

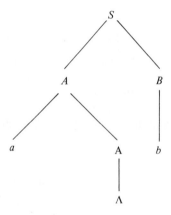

Figure 2.1(b)

contained clues to the meaning, then the meaning of the sentence could be ambiguous. For example, it is not hard to construct a context-free grammar that generates a subset of English, mirrors our intuitive notion of English grammar, and yields two parse trees for the following sentence: "They are flying planes." The two parse trees are diagrammed in Figure 2.2. The diagram in Figure 2.2(a) would explain the structure of the sentence if it were the answer to the question "What are those people doing?" The diagram in Figure 2.2(b) would explain the structure of the sentence if it were the answer to the question "What are those things in the sky?"

A classic example of ambiguity that can arise in designing grammars for programming languages has to do with the optional **ELSE** in the **IF-THEN-ELSE** construction.

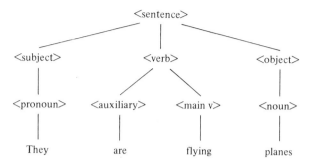

Figure 2.2(a)

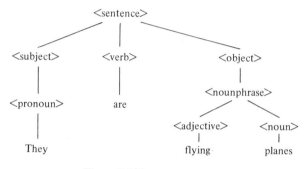

Figure 2.2(b)

2.4 Example

Let $G = (N, T, P, S)$ be the context-free grammar with

$$N = \{S, B\}, \ T = \{\mathbf{IF}, \mathbf{THEN}, \mathbf{ELSE}, b_1, b_2, a_1, a_2\}$$

and P consisting of the following productions:

$$S \rightarrow \mathbf{IF}\ B\ \mathbf{THEN}\ S\ \mathbf{ELSE}\ S \,|\, \mathbf{IF}\ B\ \mathbf{THEN}\ S \,|\, a_1 \,|\, a_2$$

$$B \rightarrow b_1 \,|\, b_2$$

Intuitively, b_1 and b_2 are the only Boolean expressions; a_1 and a_2 are the only "atomic" statements. The statement

$$\mathbf{IF}\ b_1\ \mathbf{THEN}\ \mathbf{IF}\ b_2\ \mathbf{THEN}\ a_1\ \mathbf{ELSE}\ a_2$$

has two parse trees, as shown in Figure 2.3. The problem is that there is no way to tell which **IF-THEN** the **ELSE** should be associated with.

It is common practice to draw parse trees as we have done in Figures 2.1 and 2.2. To see why they are called trees, turn the page upside down. The branching structure will then resemble a tree. This will also make the following standard terminology seem more reasonable. The node corresponding to the occurrence of the start symbol that begins the derivation (the node labeled S

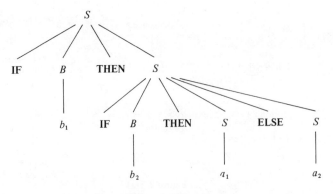

Figure 2.3(a)

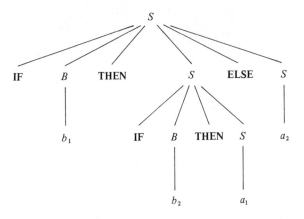

Figure 2.3(b)

in Figure 2.1(a) and Figure 2.1(b) and the node labeled <sentence> in Figure 2.2(a) and Figure 2.2(b)) is called the *root* node. The nodes labeled by either a terminal symbol or by a Λ are called *leaf* nodes or *leaves.* (In Figure 2.2, the individual words of the sentence are each considered to be single terminal symbols.)

2.5 Definition

2.5.1 A context-free grammar G is called *ambiguous* if there is some string w in $L(G)$ such that w has two different parse trees in G. G is said to be *unambiguous* if it is not ambiguous, that is, if every string in $L(G)$ has just one parse tree. A language L is said to be *unambiguous* if $L = L(G)$ for some unambiguous grammar G.

2.5.2 A context-free language L is said to be *inherently ambiguous* if every context-free grammar for L is ambiguous; that is, if whenever $L = L(G)$, then G is ambiguous.

2.6 Example

The language $L = \{a^i b^j c^k \mid i = j \text{ or } j = k\}$ is an inherently ambiguous context-free language. The intuitive reason for this is that any grammar for L must have two kinds of parse trees: one kind to get $i = j$, another kind to get $j = k$. Thus any string with both $i = j$ and $j = k$ will have two parse trees. This is just an intuitive idea though. A formal proof that L is inherently ambiguous is quite difficult and will not be given until we have had a lot more material on context-free grammars.

LEFTMOST DERIVATIONS

As Examples 2.3.1 and 2.3.2 indicate, two distinct derivations can yield the same parse tree. It is sometimes useful to have a method of associating a unique derivation with each parse tree. One way of accomplishing this is to consider only leftmost derivations. The leftmost derivations are a special subclass of all derivations and, as we shall see, they have the nice property that every parse tree yields a unique leftmost derivation. So parse trees and leftmost derivations are in some sense equivalent notions.

2.7 Definition

Let $G = (N, T, P, S)$ be a context-free grammar. A derivation $S = \xi_1 \Rightarrow \xi_2 \Rightarrow \dots \Rightarrow \xi_n$ is said to be a *leftmost derivation* provided the following holds for all $i < n$: $\xi_i = xA\beta$ and $\xi_{i+1} = x\alpha\beta$ for some x in $(\text{Terminals}(G))^*$, A in $\text{Nonterminals}(G)$, β in $(\text{Symbols}(G))^*$, and $A \to \alpha$ in $\text{Productions}(G)$. In less formal terms, a derivation is leftmost provided that, at each step of the derivation, the leftmost occurrence of a nonterminal is rewritten.

2.8 Example

Let G be the cfg of Example 2.2.2. The following is a leftmost derivation:

> S ⇒ <noun> <verbphrase> ⇒
> **dog** <verbphrase> ⇒
> **dog** <verb> <noun> ⇒
> **dog bites** <noun> ⇒
> **dog bites man**

The following derivations are not leftmost:

> S ⇒ <noun> <verbphrase> ⇒
> <noun> <verb> <noun> ⇒
> **dog** <verb> <noun> ⇒
> **dog bites** <noun> ⇒
> **dog bites man**

$$S \Rightarrow <\text{noun}> <\text{verbphrase}> \Rightarrow$$
$$\mathbf{dog} \ <\text{verbphrase}> \Rightarrow$$
$$\mathbf{dog} \ <\text{verb}> \ <\text{noun}> \Rightarrow$$
$$\mathbf{dog} \ <\text{verb}> \ \mathbf{man} \Rightarrow$$
$$\mathbf{dog \ bites \ man}$$

It is not difficult to see that every parse tree yields a unique leftmost derivation. Hence there is a natural one-to-one correspondence between parse trees and leftmost derivations. Hence an equivalent way of stating Definition 2.5 is to say: A context-free grammar G is called ambiguous if there is some string w in $L(G)$ such that w has two different leftmost derivations. Similarly, the rest of Definition 2.5 could be rewritten with the term "leftmost derivation" substituted for "parse tree" and we would obtain equivalent, alternate definitions of unambiguous context-free grammars and inherently ambiguous context-free languages.

CHOMSKY NORMAL FORM

It is frequently useful to know that a context-free grammar is in a particularly simple form. There are a number of results that show that every context-free grammar is equivalent to a context-free grammar of a particular type. (Recall that two cfg's, G_1 and G_2, are said to be equivalent if $L(G_1) = L(G_2)$.) In this section we consider one example of a special type of context-free grammars, called *Chomsky normal form grammars*, and show that every context-free grammar is equivalent to a grammar in Chomsky normal form. Intuitively, a grammar is in Chomsky normal form if all parse trees have binary branching at all points except the ends of the tree.

2.9 Definition

2.9.1 A cfg is said to be *nonerasing* provided (1) the start symbol does not occur on the right-hand side of any production and (2) there are no productions of the form $A \rightarrow \Lambda$, except possibly the production $S \rightarrow \Lambda$ where S is the start symbol.

Clause (1) of this definition deserves some explanation. Intuitively, a nonerasing cfg should be one that has no productions of the form $A \rightarrow \Lambda$. This presents a problem if we wish to have the empty string in the language generated. It will turn out that we will have need for a notion of nonerasing cfg which still allows us to derive the empty string. So we made a special case of the empty string and allowed the possibility of including the production $S \rightarrow \Lambda$, where S is the start symbol. In order to keep to the spirit of our intuitive notion of nonerasing cfg, we want to insist that if the production $S \rightarrow \Lambda$ is included in the grammar, then it is only used to derive the empty string. Clause (1) of the definition ensures that the production $S \rightarrow \Lambda$ is not used for any purpose other than a one-step derivation of the empty string.

2.9.2 A cfg is said to be in *Chomsky normal form* if it is nonerasing and has only three types of productions:

1. Productions of the form $A \rightarrow BC$, where A, B, and C are nonterminals
2. Productions of the form $A \rightarrow a$, where A is a nonterminal and a is a terminal
3. If the empty string is in the language, then the grammar includes the production $S \rightarrow \Lambda$, where S is the start symbol.

2.10 Examples

2.10.1 Let G_1 be the cfg defined by setting $\text{Start}(G_1) = S$, $\text{Nonterminals}(G_1) = \{S, A\}$, $\text{Terminals}(G_1) = \{a, b\}$, and letting the productions of G_1 be

$$S \rightarrow \Lambda \mid ab \mid aAb \qquad\qquad A \rightarrow aAb \mid ab$$

Then $L(G_1) = \{a^n b^n \mid n \geq 0\}$ and G_1 is nonerasing.

2.10.2 Let G_2 be the cfg defined by setting $\text{Start}(G_2) = S$, $\text{Nonterminals}(G_2) = \{S, A, B, X, Y\}$, $\text{Terminals}(G_2) = \{a, b\}$, and letting the productions of G_2 be

$$S \rightarrow \Lambda \mid AB \mid XB$$
$$X \rightarrow AY$$
$$Y \rightarrow AB \mid XB$$
$$A \rightarrow a$$
$$B \rightarrow b$$

Then $L(G_2) = \{a^n b^n \mid n \geq 0\}$ and G_2 is in Chomsky normal form. The grammars G_1 and G_2 are equivalent and are equivalent to the grammar G of Example 2.2.1.

In order to prove that every cfg is equivalent to a cfg in Chomsky normal form, we need to make some preliminary observations about cfg's. One fact that we will frequently use is that if $A \overset{*}{\Rightarrow} w$ in some cfg and $A \rightarrow C_1 C_2 ... C_n$ is the first production used, then we can decompose w and write $w = w_1 w_2 ... w_n$ where $C_i \overset{*}{\Rightarrow} w_i$. This is, in fact, the essence of the notion of a cfg. What C_i does is independent of what its neighbors do; that is, it is independent of context. We now proceed to develop a series of theorems that lead to showing that every cfg is equivalent to a cfg in Chomsky normal form.

2.11 Theorem There is an algorithm which can determine, for any cfg G and any nonterminal A of G, whether or not $A \overset{*}{\Rightarrow} \Lambda$ in G.

PROOF First notice that if $A \overset{*}{\Rightarrow} \Lambda$ in G, then there is always a derivation $A \overset{*}{\Rightarrow} \Lambda$ such that, in the corresponding parse tree, no path from root to tip has more than $k + 1$ nodes, where k is the number of nonterminals in G. To see this, notice that if $A \overset{*}{\Rightarrow} \Lambda$ and the parse tree has a path of length greater than $k + 1$ from root to tip, then some nonterminal B must be repeated on this path. So if we "prune" out the tree below the higher B and "graft" on the tree below the

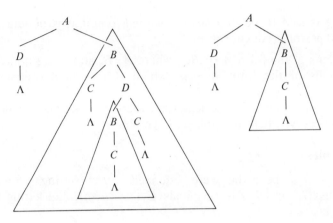

Figure 2.4

lower B, we still get a valid parse tree for $A \overset{*}{\Rightarrow} \Lambda$. (An example is given in Figure 2.4). Now the parse tree is smaller. We can continue to make it smaller until no path from root to tip contains more than $k+1$ nodes. What this means is that in order to check if $A \overset{*}{\Rightarrow} \Lambda$ in G, we need only check those derivation trees in which the longest path from root to tip has length at most $k+1$. The algorithm to test if $A \overset{*}{\Rightarrow} \Lambda$ would first produce all such trees (there are only finitely many of them) and then check if any one of these corresponds to $A \overset{*}{\Rightarrow} \Lambda$. This is not a formal proof, but can be converted to a formal proof. However, since the formal proof would be much longer and much less intuitive, we will stop here. □

2.12 Theorem There is an algorithm which, given an arbitrary cfg, will produce an equivalent nonerasing cfg.

PROOF Let $G_1 = (N_1, T_1, P_1, S_1)$ be an arbitrary cfg. We will first define a cfg G_2 such that in G_2 the start symbol never occurs on the right-hand side of a production and such that $L(G_2) = L(G_1)$. We then define a nonerasing cfg G_3 such that $L(G_3) = L(G_2) = L(G_1)$.

$G_2 = (N_2, T_2, P_2, S_2)$ where S_2 is a new symbol, $N_2 = N_1 \cup \{S_2\}$, $T_2 = T_1$, and P_2 contains the production $S_2 \to S_1$ plus all productions in P_1. Clearly, $L(G_2) = L(G_1)$.

$G_3 = (N_3, T_3, P_3, S_3)$ where $N_3 = N_2$, $T_3 = T_2$, $S_3 = S_2$, and P_3 contains the productions described in (1) and (2) below. By Theorem 2.11 we know that for any A in N_2 we can tell whether or not $A \overset{*}{\Rightarrow} \Lambda$ in G_2.

1. If $S_2 \overset{*}{\Rightarrow} \Lambda$ in G_2, then $S_3 \to \Lambda$ is in P_3.
2. If $A \to \alpha_0 B_1 \alpha_1 B_2 \alpha_2 ... B_n \alpha_n$ is in P_2, where each $B_i \overset{*}{\Rightarrow} \Lambda$ in G_2 and where each α_i does not contain any B such that $B \overset{*}{\Rightarrow} \Lambda$ in G_2, then all productions of the following form are in P_3:

$$A \to \alpha_0 X_1 \alpha_1 X_2 \alpha_2 ... X_n \alpha_n$$

where each X_i is either Λ or B_i and $\alpha_0 X_1 \alpha_1 X_2 \alpha_2 ... X_n \alpha_n \neq \Lambda$.

Clause (2) of this definition needs to be read carefully to see exactly what the relationship between P_2 and P_3 is. Except for possibly the production $S_3 \to \Lambda$ mentioned in clause (1), P_3 contains no productions of the form $A \to \Lambda$. This is because clause (2) explicitly excludes all such productions from P_3. So a production $A \to \Lambda$ in P_2 gives rise to no productions in P_3. If $A \to \xi$ is a production in P_2, ξ is not the empty string, and ξ contains no nonterminals B such that $B \overset{*}{\Rightarrow} \Lambda$, then $A \to \xi$ is in P_3 and this is the only production in P_3 which we get from $A \to \xi$ using clause (2). In this case, $\alpha_0 = \xi$ and $n = 0$. That is, there are no B_i's. If $A \to \xi$ in P_2 and ξ does contain some nonterminal B such that $B \overset{*}{\Rightarrow} \Lambda$, then $A \to \xi$ gives rise to a number of different productions in P_3. In the last case, $A \to \xi$ is in P_3 and there are also a number of productions $A \to \eta$ in P_3, where η is obtained from ξ by deleting some nonterminals B such that $B \overset{*}{\Rightarrow} \Lambda$. In fact, by clause (2), $A \to \xi$ in P_2 causes P_3 to contain all such productions $A \to \eta$, with the single exception that $\eta = \Lambda$ is not allowed.

Clearly, G_3 is nonerasing. By inspecting the algorithm to obtain G_3 from G_2, we see that if $A \overset{*}{\Rightarrow} w$ in G_3, then $A \overset{*}{\Rightarrow} w$ in G_2. So $L(G_3) \subseteq L(G_2)$. In order to show that G_3 and G_2 are equivalent, it remains to show that $L(G_2) \subseteq L(G_3)$. To establish this, we will show by induction on the number of steps in the derivation that if A is a nonterminal, w is a nonempty string of terminals, and $A \overset{*}{\Rightarrow} w$ in G_2, then $A \overset{*}{\Rightarrow} w$ in G_3. (By the definition of G_3, we know that the empty string is in $L(G_2)$ if and only if it is in $L(G_3)$.) For one-step derivations, the result is immediate. Let $k > 1$ and assume the result is true for all A, all $w \neq \Lambda$, and all derivations of fewer than k steps. Suppose $A \overset{*}{\Rightarrow} w$ in G_2 in k steps for some A, and suppose $w \neq \Lambda$. Let $A \to C_1 C_2 ... C_l$ be the first production used. We can set $w = w_1 w_2 ... w_l$ where $C_i \overset{*}{\Rightarrow} w_i$ in G_2 in fewer than k steps. (Some of the C_i may be terminals. If C_i is a terminal, then $w_i = C_i$.) Now P_3 contains the production $A \to Y_1 Y_2 ... Y_l$ where $Y_i = C_i$ if $w_i \neq \Lambda$ and where $Y_i = \Lambda$ if $w_i = \Lambda$. Also, by induction hypothesis, if $w_i \neq \Lambda$, then $C_i \overset{*}{\Rightarrow} w_i$ in G_3. So $A \Rightarrow Y_1 Y_2 ... Y_l \overset{*}{\Rightarrow} w_1 w_2 ... w_l = w$ in G_3. Thus $A \overset{*}{\Rightarrow} w$ in G_3 as desired. □

2.13 Theorem There is an algorithm which, given an arbitrary cfg, will produce an equivalent grammar that is nonerasing and has no productions of the form $A \to B$, where A and B are nonterminals.

PROOF Let $G = (N, T, P, S)$ be an arbitrary cfg. We know by Theorem 2.12 that we can find an equivalent nonerasing cfg. Thus G can always be replaced by a nonerasing cfg. We assume that G is nonerasing. We first show that there is an algorithm to determine for any two nonterminals A and B, whether or not $A \overset{*}{\Rightarrow} B$. We then use this algorithm as a subroutine in producing an equivalent cfg G' of the desired form.

The algorithm to tell whether or not $A \overset{*}{\Rightarrow} B$ is as follows. We keep a list of nonterminals. Initially, only A is on the list. We then add to the list all nonterminals C such that $A \to C$ is in P. We then add to the list all nonterminals D (not already on the list) such that $C \to D$ is in P and C is already on the list. We repeat this last step until there are no more nonterminals to add to the list. $A \overset{*}{\Rightarrow} B$ if and only if B is on the final list.

To see that this algorithm works, first note that it always terminates. This is because there are only finitely many symbols that can be added to the list. Secondly, note that since G is nonerasing, $A \overset{*}{\Rightarrow} B$ if and only if there are $C_1, C_2, ..., C_n$ such that $A = C_1$, $B = C_n$, and $C_i \to C_{i+1}$ for all $i < n$. So $A \overset{*}{\Rightarrow} B$ if and only if there are such $C_1, C_2, ..., C_n$ on the final list produced by the algorithm. But B is on the list if and only if such $C_1, C_2, ..., C_n$ are on the list. So $A \overset{*}{\Rightarrow} B$ if and only if B is on the list. Thus the algorithm works.

To get a cfg G' that is equivalent to G and has no productions of the form $A \to B$, proceed as follows: $G' = (N', T', P', S')$ where $N' = N$, $T' = T$, $S' = S$, and P' is the set of all productions of the form $A \to \alpha$ where, for some B,

1. $B \to \alpha$ is in P
2. $A \overset{*}{\Rightarrow} B$ and
3. α is not a single nonterminal

(Recall that $A \overset{*}{\Rightarrow} A$. Therefore, A is one of the B's.)

Another way of describing P' is as follows: Start with P; throw out all productions of the form $A \to B$; for each production $B \to \alpha$, throw in $A \to \alpha$ for each A such that $A \overset{*}{\Rightarrow} B$. The resulting set is P'.

G' is of the correct form since if $A \to \alpha$ is a production, then α is not a single nonterminal. If $A \to \alpha$ in G', then $A \overset{*}{\Rightarrow} \alpha$ in G. So $L(G') \subseteq L(G)$. It remains to show that $L(G) \subseteq L(G')$. To see this, note that a derivation in G can be converted to a valid derivation of the same terminal string in G' by the following method: Pick a rule $A \to B$ that is applied some place in the derivation and is such that B is not rewritten by a rule of the form $B \to C$. Omit the step that uses $A \to B$. At the subsequent place that $B \to \alpha$ is used to rewrite this B (α is not a single nonterminal), use $A \to \alpha$ instead. Do this again and again until there are no steps left that use a $A \to B$ type rule. The result is a valid G' derivation and uses no rules of the form $A \to B$. □

2.14 Theorem There is an algorithm which, given an arbitrary cfg, will produce an equivalent cfg in Chomsky normal form.

PROOF Given a cfg G_0, we will obtain an equivalent cfg G' in Chomsky normal form. First find a grammar G_1 such that G_1 is nonerasing, has no rules of the form $A \to B$ where A and B are nonterminals, and is equivalent to G_0. This is possible by Theorem 2.13. Next, obtain a grammar G_2 such that G_2 is nonerasing, is equivalent to G_1, and has only three types of productions:

1. Possibly $S \to \Lambda$ where S is the start symbol
2. $A \to a$, where a is a terminal
3. $A \to B_1 B_2 ... B_n$ where the B_i are nonterminals and $n \geqslant 2$

To get G_2 from G_1, proceed as follows. Let $G_1 = (N_1, T_1, P_1, S_1)$. Define $G_2 = (N_2, T_2, P_2, S_2)$, where $T_2 = T_1$, $S_2 = S_1$, and N_2 contains all symbols in N_1 plus a new nonterminal for each terminal in $T_1 = T_2$. If a is in $T_1 = T_2$, then $<$pseudo-$a>$ will denote the new nonterminal corresponding to a. P_2 is the set of all productions of the following forms:

4. $S_2 \rightarrow \Lambda$ provided $S_1 \rightarrow \Lambda$ is in P_1
5. $<$pseudo-$a> \rightarrow a$
6. $A \rightarrow a$ provided $A \rightarrow a$ is in P_1
7. $A \rightarrow X_1' X_2' \ldots X_n'$ provided $A \rightarrow X_1 X_2 \ldots X_n$ is in P_1 and $X_i' = $ $<$pseudo-$X_i>$ if X_i is a terminal and $X_i' = X_i$ if X_i is a nonterminal.

Clearly, G_2 has the desired properties.

Finally, G' is obtained from G_2 as follows: $G' = (N', T', P', S')$ where $S' = S_2$, $T' = T_2$, and N' contains all symbols of N_2 plus one new symbol for each string $X_1 X_2 \ldots X_l$ described below ($l \geqslant 2$); $<X_1 X_2 \ldots X_l>$ will denote the new symbol corresponding to $X_1 X_2 \ldots X_l$. P' contains all productions of the following forms:

8. $S' \rightarrow \Lambda$ provided $S_2 \rightarrow \Lambda$ is in P_2
9. $A \rightarrow a$, provided $A \rightarrow a$ is in P_2
10. $A \rightarrow BC$, provided $A \rightarrow BC$ is in P_2
11. If $A \rightarrow X_1 X_2 \ldots X_n$ is in P_2 and $n > 2$, then all of the following are in P':
    a. $A \rightarrow <X_1 X_2 \ldots X_{n-1}> X_n$
    b. $<X_1 X_2 \ldots X_{l+1}> \rightarrow <X_1 X_2 \ldots X_l> X_{l+1}$ provided $l \geqslant 2$
    c. $<X_1 X_2> \rightarrow X_1 X_2$

G' is easily seen to be in Chomsky normal form. If we show that $L(G') = L(G_2)$, then $L(G') = L(G_2) = L(G_1) = L(G_0)$ and so G' and G_0 are equivalent. It remains to show that $L(G') = L(G_2)$. The proof of this fact is left as an exercise. $\square$

2.15 Example

In this example we start with a cfg G_0, carry out the algorithms given in the proofs of Theorems 2.12 through 2.14 and finally produce an equivalent cfg G_c which is in Chomsky normal form and is equivalent to G_0. In all the grammars under discussion, the only terminals will be a and b. In describing the various grammars we will simply give the productions and specify the start symbol. All symbols other than a and b will be nonterminals.

G_0 is the cfg given in Example 2.2.1 and, as we have seen, $L(G_0) = \{a^n b^n \mid n \geqslant 0\}$.

G_0 can be described as follows:

        start symbol $= S$
        productions: $S \rightarrow \Lambda$, $S \rightarrow aSb$

To get a nonerasing cfg, apply the algorithm in the proof of Theorem 2.12. In the proof of Theorem 2.12, take $G_1 = G_0$. The G_2 of Theorem 2.12 is then as follows:

> start symbol $= S_2$
> productions: $S_2 \rightarrow S$, $S \rightarrow \Lambda$, $S \rightarrow aSb$

The G_3 of Theorem 2.12 is then as follows:

> start symbol $= S_2$
> productions: $S_2 \rightarrow \Lambda$, $S_2 \rightarrow S$, $S \rightarrow aSb$, $S \rightarrow ab$

G_3 is a nonerasing cfg equivalent to G_0.

Next, to get a nonerasing cfg with no productions of the form $A \rightarrow B$, apply the algorithm in the proof of Theorem 2.13 with $G = G_3$, where G_3 is the grammar just obtained using Theorem 2.12.

The G' of Theorem 2.13 is then as follows:

> start symbol $= S_2$
> productions: $S_2 \rightarrow \Lambda$, $S \rightarrow aSb$, $S_2 \rightarrow aSb$, $S \rightarrow ab$, $S_2 \rightarrow ab$

G' is a nonerasing cfg with no productions of the form $A \rightarrow B$. G' is equivalent to the G_3 obtained using Theorem 2.12 and so G' is equivalent to G_0.

Finally, to get a cfg in Chomsky normal form, apply the algorithm in the proof of Theorem 2.14. In the proof of Theorem 2.14, set $G_1 = G'$.

The G_2 of Theorem 2.14 is then as follows:

> start symbol $= S_2$
> productions: $S_2 \rightarrow \Lambda$, $<$pseudo-$a> \rightarrow a$, $<$pseudo-$b> \rightarrow b$,
> $\quad S \rightarrow <$pseudo-$a> S <$pseudo-$b>$,
> $\quad S_2 \rightarrow <$pseudo-$a> S <$pseudo-$b>$,
> $\quad S \rightarrow <$pseudo-$a><$pseudo-$b>$,
> $\quad S_2 \rightarrow <$pseudo-$a><$pseudo-$b>$

Before proceeding, let us first simplify the notation by using the symbols A and B in place of $<$pseudo-$a>$ and $<$pseudo-$b>$ respectively. We then get a grammar G'_2 which is clearly equivalent to G_2 and easier to read. G'_2 is described as follows:

> start symbol $= S_2$
> productions: $S_2 \rightarrow \Lambda$, $A \rightarrow a$, $B \rightarrow b$
> $\quad S \rightarrow ASB$, $S_2 \rightarrow ASB$, $S \rightarrow AB$, $S_2 \rightarrow AB$

The G' of Theorem 2.14 can be obtained from G'_2 rather than from G_2. This G' is described as follows:

> start symbol $= S_2$
> productions: $S_2 \rightarrow \Lambda$, $A \rightarrow a$, $B \rightarrow b$, $S \rightarrow <AS>B$,
> $\quad <AS> \rightarrow AS$, $S_2 \rightarrow <AS>B$, $S \rightarrow AB$, $S_2 \rightarrow AB$

The G' obtained in this way using Theorem 2.14 is in Chomsky normal form and is equivalent to all the above grammars, including G_0. This completes the algorithm to find a Chomsky normal form cfg equivalent to G_0.

To make the grammar easier to read, we will go one step further and simplify the notation. In order to get a more readable grammar, start with this last G' and replace $<AS>$ by X, replace S by Y, and then replace S_2 by S. Call the grammar so obtained G_c. G_c can be described as follows:

> start symbol $= S$
> productions: $S \rightarrow \Lambda, A \rightarrow a, B \rightarrow b, Y \rightarrow XB, X \rightarrow AY,$
> $S \rightarrow XB, Y \rightarrow AB, S \rightarrow AB$

If we now group together those productions of G_c that have the same symbol on the left-hand side, we get the following, more compact description of G_c:

> start symbol $= S$
> productions: $S \rightarrow \Lambda \mid AB \mid XB$
> $X \rightarrow AY$
> $Y \rightarrow AB \mid XB$
> $A \rightarrow a, B \rightarrow b$

So G_c is exactly the cfg of Example 2.10.2, which we have already seen to be in Chomsky normal form and equivalent to G_0, the grammar of Example 2.2.1.

This example worked out particularly well. In general, the Chomsky normal form grammar produced by this algorithm need not be so clean. It can turn out to have many more productions than are needed and can even have productions that are useless. The grammar produced will always be in Chomsky normal form though and will always be equivalent to the grammar we started out with. If a simple grammar is desired, it is often necessary to perform some additional transformations on the grammar obtained by simply applying the algorithm.

The next result shows that a cfg description of a language can be converted to an effective procedure for testing strings to see whether or not they are in the language.

2.16 Theorem If G is a cfg, then there is an algorithm that can tell for any string w whether or not w is in $L(G)$.

PROOF This is left as an exercise. *Hint*: First find a Chomsky normal form grammar G' equivalent to G. Then compute a bound on the size of the parse tree for a string of length n. Use this to show that for any length n, we can compute a finite number of derivations such that if w has length n and w is in $L(G')$, then a derivation of w is in this set. $\square$

THE PUMPING LEMMA

Our next result provides a method whereby, given a suitably long string in a cfl, we can produce infinitely many other strings which are also in the language.

This does not mean that all cfl's are infinite. If the cfl is finite, then there will not be any suitably long strings. This result will be useful in a number of contexts. One of its most common applications is to use it to show that certain languages are not cfl's.

2.17 Theorem (Pumping Lemma for CFL's). For each context-free language L, we can find an integer k, depending only on L, and such that the following holds: If z is in L and length$(z) > k$, then z may be written as $z = uvwxy$ where

1. length $(vwx) \leqslant k$
2. at least one of v and x is nonempty, and
3. $uv^i wx^i y$ is in L for all $i \geqslant 0$

PROOF Since L is a context-free language, there is a context-free grammar G such that $L = L(G)$. By Theorem 2.14, we may assume that G is in Chomsky normal form. First note that, since G is in Chomsky normal form, we can derive a relationship between the length of a string z in $L(G) = L$ and the longest path from S to a terminal symbol in a parse tree for z. Specifically,

Claim 1a: If the longest path contains at most m nodes $(m-1$ arcs), then z has length at most 2^{m-2}.

To see this, note that the longest string is obtained if all paths are as long as the longest path. In that case, we start with one node; that node produces two nodes, each of those produce two nodes, and so forth. After $m-2$ iterations of this doubling, we have produced a tree with 2^{m-2} nodes at the growing ends. To get a terminal string, each of these 2^{m-2} nonterminal nodes must produce a terminal node. So, after $m-1$ arcs we can, in this way, produce a terminal string of length 2^{m-2}. Clearly, this is the longest string we can produce under the constraint that no path has more than $m-1$ arcs. Another way of stating this relationship is as follows:

Claim 1b: If the length of a terminal string z is greater than 2^n, then some path in the parse tree must contain at least one more than $n+2$ nodes.

Let $k = 2^n$, where n is the number of nonterminals of G and suppose length$(z) > k$. Consider a fixed parse tree for z. By Claim 1b, some path, from S to a terminal, has $n+2$ or more nodes. Consider the longest such path. Going from S to a terminal along this path, we pass through all the nodes of this path. Consider the last $n+2$ such nodes. One is labeled with a terminal and $n+1$ are labeled with nonterminals. There are only n nonterminals; therefore, two such nodes must be labeled with the same nonterminal. Call this nonterminal A. The situation is diagrammed in Figure 2.5(a). One way to write a derivation corresponding to this tree is

4. $S \overset{*}{\Rightarrow} uAy \overset{*}{\Rightarrow} uvAxy \overset{*}{\Rightarrow} uvwxy = z$

where the two A's shown are the ones under consideration. Consider the sub-tree for $A \overset{*}{\Rightarrow} vAx \overset{*}{\Rightarrow} vwx$. Since the first A was chosen to be among the last $n+2$ nodes of the longest path, it follows that no path from the first A to a terminal has length greater than $n+2$. So, by Claim 1a, the string derived, namely vwx, has length at most 2^n. So we have

5. $\text{length}(vwx) \leqslant 2^n = k$

Now, by 4, it follows that for all $i \geqslant 0$,

6. $S \overset{*}{\Rightarrow} uAy \overset{*}{\Rightarrow} uv^i Ax^i y \overset{*}{\Rightarrow} uv^i wx^i y$

This is diagrammed in Figure 2.5(b), for the case of $i = 2$.

Finally, it remains only to show that either x or v is nonempty. Again, consider the subtree $A \overset{*}{\Rightarrow} vAx \overset{*}{\Rightarrow} vwx$. Since the grammar is in Chomsky normal form, it can be written as $A \Rightarrow BC \overset{*}{\Rightarrow} vAx \overset{*}{\Rightarrow} vwx = z_1 z_2$, where B and C are nonterminals such that $B \overset{*}{\Rightarrow} z_1$ and $C \overset{*}{\Rightarrow} z_2$. Since all Chomsky normal form grammars are nonerasing, it follows that both z_1 and z_2 are nonempty. Now the second A must be derived from either the B or the C. If it is derived from the B, then z_2 lies completely to the right of w. So z_2 is a substring of x and so x is nonempty. This situation is diagrammed in Figure 2.5(a). If A is derived from C, then a similar argument shows that, in this case, v is nonempty. In any case, either x or v is nonempty and the proof is complete. □

We conclude this section with two applications of the pumping lemma. When applying the pumping lemma, it is important to remember that, while we know for certain that any z satisfying the hypothesis of the pumping lemma can be written as $z = uvwxy$ and that this decomposition has the properties listed in the pumping lemma, we do not get to choose how z is divided into u, v, w, x, and y. We only know that there is at least one such decomposition. It is also important to note that we can "pump down" as well as "pump up." In the notation of the pumping lemma, we can take $i = 0$ and conclude that uwy is in L. So we can use the pumping lemma to produce either longer or shorter strings which are in the given cfl.

2.18 Theorem $L = \{a^n b^n c^n \mid n \geqslant 0\}$ is not a context-free language.

PROOF Suppose L were a cfl. We will derive a contradiction. Let k be as in the pumping lemma for cfl's. The string $a^k b^k c^k$ is in L. By the pumping lemma $a^k b^k c^k = uvwxy$, where

1. $uv^2 wx^2 y$ is in L and
2. either v or x (or both) are nonempty

First note that v must be either all a's, all b's, or all c's. Otherwise, $uv^2 wx^2 y$ would not have only a's followed by b's followed by c's, and so would not be in L. Similarly, x must be all a's, all b's, or all c's. Say v is all a's and x is all b's (the other cases are similar). If v is nonempty, then $uv^2 wx^2 y$ contains more a's than c's. If x is non-empty, then it contains more b's than c's. In any case, we conclude that uv^2wx^2y is not of the form $a^nb^nc^n$, and so we have contradicted (1). $\square$

2.19 Theorem There is an algorithm to determine if a given context-free grammar generates a finite or infinite number of words.

PROOF Let G be a cfg, let $L = L(G)$, and let Σ be an alphabet such that L is a subset of Σ^*. We will first give an algorithm that produces a finite set F of words such that L is infinite if and only if there is some word w in both F and L. Then to test if L is infinite, we test whether or not w is in L for each w in F. If any such w is in L, then L is infinite. If no such w is in L, then L is finite. Let $F = \{z \mid z \in \Sigma^* \text{ and } k < \text{length}(z) \leqslant 2k\}$, where k is the constant associated with G by the pumping lemma 2.17. The next claim tells us that this F is just the sort of set we need for our plan.

Claim 1: L is infinite if and only if there is some word z in F which is also in L.

In order to prove Claim 1, it will suffice to prove two things: (1) If there is a z in $L \cap F$, then L is infinite and (2) if L is infinite then $L \cap F$ is not empty. We first prove (1). Suppose z is in $L \cap F$. Then $\text{length}(z) > k$. By the pumping lemma, $z = uvwxy$ where $vx \neq \Lambda$ and uv^iwx^iy is in L for all $i = 0, 1, 2, \dots$. So there are an infinite number of strings in L, namely, the uv^iwx^iy. Thus (1) is shown.

Next we show (2). Suppose L is infinite. We must show that $L \cap F$ is not empty. Since L is infinite, it follows that there are arbitrarily long strings in L. So there must be some string z in L such that $\text{length}(z) > k$. Now if $\text{length}(z) \leqslant 2k$, then z is in F. Thus z is $L \cap F$ and (2) is true. Unfortunately, all we know is that $\text{length}(z) > k$. It could be true that $\text{length}(z) > 2k$. Assume the worst, namely, that $\text{length}(z) > 2k$. We will find another word z' such that z' is in L and $k < \text{length}(z') \leqslant 2k$. The string z' is obtained from z by using the pumping lemma. By the pumping lemma, $z = uvwxy$ where $vx \neq \Lambda$ and $\text{length}(vwx) \leqslant k$ and uwy is in L. Now $\text{length}(z) > 2k$ and, since $\text{length}(vwx) \leqslant k$, $\text{length}(uwy) \geqslant \text{length}(z) - k$. Therefore, $\text{length}(uwy) > k$. But $vx \neq \Lambda$. Thus uwy is shorter than z. So, starting with any z such that z is in L and $\text{length}(z) > 2k$, we can produce a string t, namely, $t = uwy$, such that $\text{length}(t) > k$ and $\text{length}(t) < \text{length}(z)$. If $\text{length}(t) \leqslant 2k$, then set $z' = t$ and we have our z' in $F \cap L$. If $\text{length}(t) > 2k$, then just as we produced a shorter string in L from z, we can produce a shorter string in L from t. We repeat this process again and again, and get a list of strings in L each shorter than the previous one. We continue to do this so long as the strings produced are greater than $2k$. Since each string produced is shorter than the previous string, we eventually get a string z' in L such that $\text{length}(z') \leqslant 2k$ and, by the way we are producing these strings, we also know $\text{length}(z') > k$. Therefore, z' is in $F \cap L$. Thus $F \cap L$ is nonempty and (2) is proven.

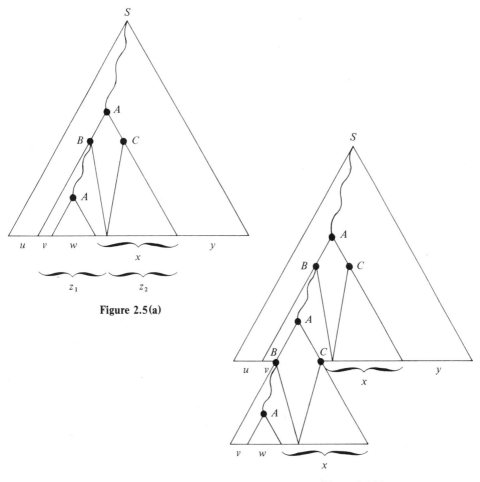

Figure 2.5(a)

Figure 2.5(b)

Procedure 2.1

Algorithm to tell if L is finite or infinite.

1. Produce $F = \{z \mid k < \text{length}(z) \leqslant 2k\}$.
2. For each z in F, test if z is in L.
3. If one such test gives an affirmative answer output, "L is infinite."
4. If all tests in 2 give a negative answer output, "L is finite."

The algorithm is now easy to state. Procedure 2.1 is the algorithm. By Theorem 2.16, we know we can write a subroutine to test if an arbitrary string is in L. So step 2 can be converted to an algorithm. It is easy to write a subroutine to do step 1, namely, to generate F. Steps 3 and 4 require no subroutines. Thus the thing we called an "algorithm" can indeed be converted to an algorithm. $\square$

EXERCISES

1. Write cfg's for each of the following languages:
   a. $\{\alpha\alpha^R \mid \alpha \in \{a, b\}^*\}$, where $\alpha^R = \alpha$ written backward. For example, $(abb)^R = bba$.
   b. $\{a^i b^j c^k \mid i = j \text{ or } j = k\}$.
   c. The set of all well-formed parenthesis strings. For example, $(())$, $()()$, and $(()(()))$ are well formed. $(()))$ and $)($ are not.

2. Prove that:
   a. If L_1 and L_2 are cfl's, then $L_1 \cup L_2$ is a cfl.
   b. If L_1 and L_2 are unambiguous cfl's and $L_1 \cap L_2$ is empty, then $L_1 \cup L_2$ is an unambiguous cfl.

3. Give an example of two cfl's L_1 and L_2 such that $L_1 \cap L_2$ is not a cfl.

4. Prove that every finite language is a cfl.

5. Prove that the following are not cfl's:
   a. $\{a^n b^{2n} c^{3n} \mid n \geqslant 0\}$
   b. $\{\alpha\alpha \mid \alpha \in \{a, b\}^*\}$
   c. $\{a^i \mid i \text{ a prime}\}$
   d. $\{a^i \mid i = n^2, \text{ for some positive integer } n\}$
   e. $\{a^n b^n c b^n a^n \mid n \geqslant 1\}$

6. Give an example of a cfl L and an alphabet Σ such that $\Sigma^* \supseteq L$ and $\Sigma^* - L$ is not a cfl.

7. Complete the proof of Theorem 2.14 by proving the claim that $L(G') = L(G_2)$.

8. Prove Theorem 2.16.

9. Use the algorithm given in the proof of Theorem 2.12 to find a nonerasing cfg equivalent to the following cfg:
   $$G = (N, T, P, S) \text{ where}$$
   $$N = \{S, X\}, \quad T = \{a, b\}$$
   $$P = \{S \rightarrow XS, \quad S \rightarrow \Lambda, \quad X \rightarrow aXb, \quad X \rightarrow \Lambda\}$$

10. What is $L(G)$? G as in 9.

11. For each cfg G below, use the algorithm given in Theorem 2.14 to find a cfg in Chomsky normal form that is equivalent to G.
   a. $G = (N, T, P, S)$ where $N = \{S, A, B, C\}$, $T = \{a, b, c\}$.
      $P = \{S \rightarrow ABC, A \rightarrow aA, A \rightarrow a, B \rightarrow bB, B \rightarrow b, C \rightarrow cC, C \rightarrow c\}$.
   b. $G = (N, T, P, S)$ where $N = \{S, A, B, C\}$, $T = \{a, b, c\}$.
      $P = \{S \rightarrow ABC, C \rightarrow A, A \rightarrow a, B \rightarrow b, C \rightarrow c\}$.
   c. G as in 9.

12. For each G in 11, describe $L(G)$.

13. Give an algorithm that will determine for any cfg G whether or not $L(G)$ is empty, that is, whether or not it is possible to generate any terminal string from the start symbol. (*Hint*: It is much like the algorithm given in the proof of Theorem 2.19.)

Chapter
Three

Finite-State Acceptors

In this chapter we present a formal model for digital computers. Later on we will consider other models which capture more details of the computing process, but this model will always play a central role in our considerations. The model is called a *finite-state acceptor*. A finite-state acceptor is nothing but a digital computer with some restrictions on how it processes input and output. Any digital computer that satisfies these input and output restrictions can be modeled by the mathematics of finite-state acceptors. By digital computer we mean any piece of hardware that is finite and that proceeds in discrete steps. There is a first instance of time, then the machine changes its configuration and is in a new configuration at the second instance of time, then the machine changes its configuration and is in another configuration at the third instance of time, and so forth. The total machine configuration (position of cogs and wheels or orientation of the magnetic field of cores or current in a VLSI chip or whatever) is the state of the machine. If the machine is a real machine, it will be finite and so have only a finite number of configurations or states. While we will place some restrictions on input and output processing, we will place absolutely no restrictions on how the device computes except that it be finite and discrete (digital). The input/output conventions are that it receives its input as a string of symbols, that it only gets one left-to-right scan of this input, and that, immediately after reading the input, it must give one of two outputs which we will refer to as "acceptance" and "rejection." Thus these devices can only answer questions that admit yes/no answers. The set of possible input strings is partitioned into two subsets, those accepted and those rejected. We are modeling the entire computer configuration as a single state. If it is a "hardware-programmed" special-purpose computer, then it is the hardware that is being modeled. If it is a programmable computer we are modeling, then we are modeling both the hardware and a single, fixed program. Every time we change the program we get a new finite-state model. We are really emphasizing programs at least as much as hardware. In fact, this text is only concerned with programming, but the mathematics does in some gross sense model the hardware as well. Many people find it a help to their intuition to consider finite-state acceptors as hardware devices. For this reason, we sometimes refer to a finite-state acceptor as a finite-state machine. A finite-state acceptor is neither hardware nor exactly a program but a formal mathematical construct that can model both of these. We now describe the working of this abstract mathematical device in more detail and then give a formal mathematical definition for finite-state acceptors.

CONCEPTUAL DESCRIPTION

A finite-state acceptor consists of a device that can exist in only a finite number of different states. There is an input alphabet associated with the device. Any string of symbols from this alphabet may be given to the machine as input. The finite-state acceptor operates in discrete steps. There is a first instant of time, a second instant of time, and so forth, until the end of the computation. The device reads one symbol of the input during each unit of time. On the basis of its state and this symbol, it changes to a new state. This constitutes a single move. It is then ready to perform another move with the next input symbol and this new state. This process continues until the entire input string is read. After reading all the input, the machine either accepts or rejects the input. That is, it somehow outputs a bit of information which indicates either acceptance or rejection of the input. Thus these devices may be viewed as checking to see whether or not the input has some special property.

In this text a finite-state acceptor will be defined as an abstract mathematical object consisting of five distinguishable items: a finite set of states, an input alphabet, a designated start state, a next state or transition function which maps each state/input symbol combination into some other state, and a partitioning of the states into the categories of accepting states and rejecting states. More formally, a finite-state acceptor is a five-tuple $(S, \Sigma, \delta, s, Y)$ where the five elements are the states, input alphabet, next-state function, start state and accepting states respectively. These five elements must satisfy certain properties in order for this five-tuple to be a finite-state acceptor. S must be a finite set of things which we will call *states*. The states may be any well-defined mathematical object. So S may be a set of symbols or a set of numbers or a set of labels or a mixture of some of each or any other mathematical entities. S may even be a set of sets. Σ must be a finite set of symbols which we call the *input alphabet*. The element δ must be a function from $S \times \Sigma$ into S. That is, δ is a function of two arguments: the first is a state from S; the second is a symbol from Σ. If p is in S and a is in Σ, then $\delta(p, a)$ must be a state in S. (We will merely require that δ be a partial function. So $\delta(p, a)$ is either a state in S or is undefined, but this point need not concern us yet.) If $\delta(p, a) = q$, then this has the following intuitive meaning. If the machine is in state p about to read a as the next symbol in the input string, then the machine will read the a and enter state q. The fourth entry s will be called the *start state*. It must be an element of the set S of all states. The last entry Y must be a subset of S. If, after reading an input string, the machine is in a state in Y, then we say the input is accepted. If, after reading the input string, the machine is in a state which is not in Y, then we say that the machine rejects the input. States in Y are called *accepting states*.

A simple example of a finite-state acceptor is diagrammed in Figure 3.1. There are two states: one labeled <even> and one labeled <odd>. The input alphabet consists of the two digits 0 and 1. The start state is the one labeled <even>. The next state function is represented by the arrows in the diagram. Given input 1, the machine changes state. This is indicated by the arrows labeled 1. Given input 0, the machine remains in the same state. This is indicated by the arrows labeled 0. The state labeled <odd> is an accepting state. The state labeled <even> is a rejecting state. (The rejecting state is not labeled in the figure.) Given input 11010, for example, the machine would go through the following states in order: <even>, <odd>, <even>, <even>, <odd>, <odd>. Since the last state, <odd>, is an accepting state, the string 11010 is accepted. This machine will accept those strings of zeros and ones which contain an odd number of ones and rejects those strings of zeros and ones which contain an even number of ones. In terms of the mathematical formalism, this machine is a five-tuple $(S, \Sigma, \delta, s, Y)$ where $S = \{$<even>, <odd>$\}$, $\Sigma = \{0, 1\}$, $s = $ <even>, $Y = \{$<odd>$\}$, and δ is defined by the following equations: $\delta($<even>$, 0) = $ <even>, $\delta($<even>$, 1) = $ <odd>, $\delta($<odd>$, 0) = $ <odd>, and $\delta($<odd>$, 1) = $ <even>.

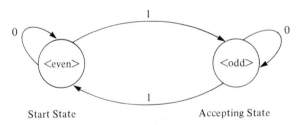

Figure 3.1

It can be argued that this model is too restricted to correspond to an arbitrary computer. For example, the machine only gets to read the input once. Given an input string of length n, it must, in fact, complete its computation in n steps. We will eventually show that this restriction does not at all restrict the computing power of these machines. Also, these machines have very restricted output. There are only two possible outputs: either the input is accepted or it is rejected. In the next section we will extend this model to allow arbitrary strings of symbols as output. These obvious objections to the finite-state model turn out to be without substance.

There is, however, one serious shortcoming of the finite-state acceptor model. The model is too restricted to capture the notion of an effective procedure in its full generality. Every finite-state acceptor is an effective procedure. However, there are some effective procedures which cannot be carried out by finite-state acceptors. This will be proven formally later in this book. The intuitive reason for this is easy to see. We said that an effective procedure could have access to a storage facility to hold intermediate results and that there should be no limit to the size of this storage facility. A finite-state acceptor can use its states to, in effect, store intermediate results, but there is a limit to how many intermediate results it can hold. This limitation turns out to be a real limitation. Later on we will define computer models that do not have this limitation and we will see that these models can do more than finite-state acceptors. For this reason we will eventually argue for a different model of the computing process. However, we should not dismiss the finite-state model as being wrong. After all, it can model any real computer with real size restrictions. The only real shortcoming of the finite-state acceptor model is that it is not detailed enough to capture all the concepts we wish to investigate, but it will serve as our first approximation for modeling digital computers. It will also turn up again as a subpart of other more sophisticated models.

NONDETERMINISTIC MACHINES

The model we described above will be called a deterministic finite-state acceptor. We will also use a more general concept than this. Machines of this more general type are called nondeterministic finite-state acceptors. We refer to them as though they were machines. They do not, however, correspond in an obvious way to physical machines. It is possible to build physical machines that closely mirror the operation of abstract deterministic finite-state acceptors. However, for many nondeterministic finite-state acceptors, there may be no obvious sense in which they can be physically realized by the common types of physical machines. They are a purely abstract concept. There are physical machines which can accomplish the same task as a given nondeterministic acceptor. However, they might not mirror the step-by-step operations of the nondeterministic acceptor very closely.

Since they do not correspond closely to physical machines, one may wonder why we bother to study nondeterministic machines at all. The answer is that there is only a small amount of extra effort involved in carrying along the added generality of nondeterminism and that nondeterminism has proven to be a fruitful concept in a number of areas of computer science. At first these nondeterministic machines may seem a bit peculiar but once the formal mathematics becomes well understood and routine, it should become clear that they usually do not complicate the formalism very much and do sometimes simplify proofs greatly. (Exercise 3-6 is a good example of how they can simplify a proof.) The one point that should become clear early on is that it is frequently much easier to design a nondeterministic finite-state acceptor to accomplish a given task than it is to design a deterministic finite-state acceptor to accomplish the same task. Other reasons for studying nondeterminism will appear later on in this text and in subject matter beyond the scope of this text. One clear example of how nondeterminism arises naturally has to do with context-free languages. Much later on in this text we will see that the context-free languages can be characterized by a type of nondeterministic machine called a pushdown automaton. We will also see that the deterministic version of this machine definitely is not adequate to characterize the context-free languages. It may take some time to see the true fruitfulness of this concept of nondeterminism but, with a little effort, one can quickly see that it is at least natural and not too difficult.

A nondeterministic finite-state acceptor differs from a deterministic one in that it may have more than one possible next state for some situations. In other words, its transition function is multiple valued. It maps each symbol-state pair into a finite set of states rather than just one state. Suppose $a_1 a_2 ... a_n$ is an input string where the a_i are individual symbols. If the acceptor is deterministic, then the computation proceeds as follows. In the start state, it will read a_1 and go to some state q_1, then it will read a_2 and go to some state q_2, then read a_3 and go to some state q_3, and so on. After it reads $a_1 a_2 ... a_n$, it will be in a unique state q_n. It accepts if q_n is one of the states designated as accepting states. If the machine is nondeterministic, then there may not be a unique computation associated with the input $a_1 a_2 ... a_n$. Instead, there may be many computations. In the start state reading a_1, it may have a choice of next states. Each of these states may lead to a different computation or computations. A nondeterministic machine may have many computations associated with the same input. The input is said to be accepted if at least one of these computations processes the entire input and terminates in an accepting state.

One way to think of these nondeterministic machine computations is the following. Whenever a state-symbol pair is mapped onto one single new state, then the computation proceeds just as it does for deterministic acceptors. Whenever a state-symbol pair is mapped into some number $m \geqslant 2$ of next states, then m copies of the machine are created, one corresponding to each state. Each copy of the machine is placed in its corresponding one-out-of-the-m possible new states. These m machines proceed in parallel to process the rest of the input. If any of these parallel computations reaches a state-symbol pair which yields more than one next-state, then that computation branches into a set of machines running in parallel. The input is accepted if at least one out of all these parallel computations manages to process the entire input string and to end up in an accepting state. For example, suppose the input string were *abcbd*, and the acceptor always has two new states whenever it reads a *b*, but only one new state when it reads any other symbol. The resulting parallel computations can be diagrammed as in Figure 3.2. The acceptor starts in the start state q_0. It reads the first symbol, an *a*. The state symbol pair (q_0, a) is mapped into one single next state, q_1. The machine goes to state q_1. It reads

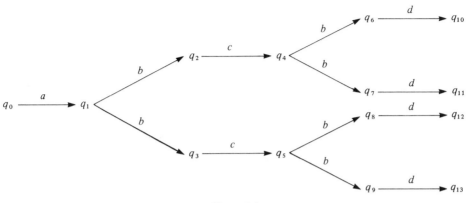

Figure 3.2

the next symbol, which is b. The state symbol pair (q_1, b) is mapped into the two states q_2 and q_3. The computation branches. Two copies of the machine are created. One is placed in state q_2. The other is placed in state q_3. Each of these machines processes the rest of the input. The machine in state q_2 reads c. The pair (q_2, c) maps onto a single state q_4 and so this copy of the machine goes to q_4. In parallel, the machine in state q_3 reads the same c and goes into some state , q_5. At the next step, both computations branch. The input $abcbd$ is accepted if at least one of the end states q_{10}, q_{11}, q_{12}, or q_{13} is an accepting state. Notice that the nodes of the tree in Figure 3.2 do not necessarily receive unique labels. It could, for example, turn out that $q_6 = q_9 = q_2$. (It is easy to show that, for suitably large inputs, the tree must necessarily have some non-unique labeling of nodes.)

A few paragraphs back we said that nondeterministic machines do not correspond in an obvious way to physical machines. When we said this we had in mind a machine that, in some intuitive sense, could do only one thing at a time. We had in mind what is commonly called a serial machine. If we expand our intuitive notion of a machine to include parallel processing machines, then nondeterministic machines can be realized as physical machines. However, it is perhaps more natural to think of such parallel processing machines as a network of machines rather than as a single machine.

Let us consider a specific example. Suppose we wish to design a finite-state acceptor which accepts exactly those inputs of the following form: a string of 0's and 1's such that the total number of 1's is odd followed by a second string of alternating 1's and 0's beginning with a 1 and ending with a 0. For example, 10111010 is to be accepted because 1011 has an odd number of 1's and 1010 is a string of alternating 1's and 0's. We already discussed an acceptor which recognizes strings which contain an odd number of ones. It is represented in Figure 3.1. A finite-state machine to recognize strings of alternating ones and zeros is also easy to construct. So it should be possible to realize a suitable machine by somehow hooking up these two machines. The machine to recognize an odd number of ones is run until it accepts some initial segment of the input. The other acceptor is then run to see if it accepts what is left of the input. There is a problem though. Consider the string 101110. The initial segments 10 and 1011 both contain an odd number of ones. Should we switch to the second machine after 10 or after 1011? If we switch after 10, the input is rejected. If we switch after 1011, the input is accepted. Remember that the decision of what to do after processing 10 must be made before the rest of the input is read. There are a number of solutions to this problem. We wish to give an example of a nondeterministic machine. So we will solve the problem by putting the two acceptors together to form a nondeterministic machine. The resulting machine, in some sense, "guesses" at when it should switch from one routine to the other. The resulting nondeterministic machine is shown in Figure 3.3. This machine is nondeterministic because in state <odd> with 1 as the next symbol, there are two states that the machine may change to. It can change to state <even> or it can change to state <one>. The input 101110, for example, gives rise to three different computations.

$$\begin{array}{ccccccc} 1 & 0 & 1 & 1 & 1 & 0 \end{array}$$

1. <even> <odd> <odd> <even> <odd> <even> <even>
2. <even> <odd> <odd> <even> <odd> <one> <zero>
3. <even> <odd> <odd> <one> and then no next move is specified so the computation ends

Figure 3.4 is a diagram of the situation. It is read in the same way as Figure 3.2. One computation terminates in a nonaccepting state, one computation terminates in an accepting state, and one computation terminates before the entire input is processed. For a nondeterministic machine, we say the machine accepts if at least one computation processes the entire input and ends in an accepting state. Thus 101110 is accepted by this machine. Notice that the notion of rejection has been lost for nondeterministic acceptors. If one computation does not end in an accepting state, it does not mean the input is rejected. Instead of thinking of the states as accepting and rejecting states, think of them as accepting and "no decision" states. We now turn to the formal development of these concepts.

FORMAL DEFINITIONS AND BASIC RESULTS

3.1 Definition

3.1.1 A (*nondeterministic*) *finite-state acceptor* is a five-tuple $M = (S, \Sigma, \delta, s, Y)$ where S is a finite set of things called *states*, Σ is a finite set of *input symbols*, δ is a function from $S \times \Sigma$ into subsets of S and is called the *transition function*, s is an element of S called the *start state*, and Y is a subset of S called the set of *accepting states*.

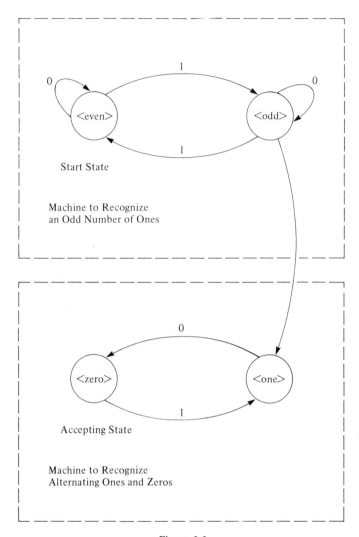

Figure 3.3

Suppose q is a state of M, a is an input symbol, and $\delta(q, a) = \{p_1, p_2, ..., p_n\}$. This means that whenever M is in state q and a is the next symbol of the input string to be read, then M may read a and change from state q to any one of the states $p_1, p_2, ..., p_n$.

We must be able to distinguish the five elements of M. We choose to do this by expressing M as an ordered five-tuple. This requires remembering the convention that the states are the first entry, the input alphabet is the second, and so forth. In order to avoid having to use this rather arbitrary convention, we will adopt the following notation: States$(M) = S$, Symbols$(M) = \Sigma$,

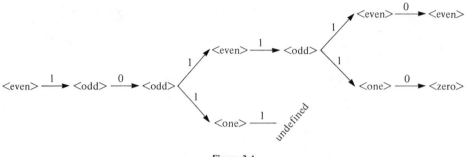

Figure 3.4

Instructions$(M) = \delta$, Start$(M) = s$, and Accepting-states$(M) = Y$.

3.1.2 An *instantaneous description* (*id*) of M is a pair (p, β), where p is a state in S and β is a string in Σ^*. Or, to rephrase things in our more suggestive notation, p is in States(M) and β is in [Symbols(M)]*.

The intuitive interpretation of (p, β) is that M is in state p and is about to read the string β of input symbols. It is important to note that β is not necessarily the entire input string but only that portion of the input which has not yet been read.

3.1.3 The *next step relation* $\vdash_M$ is a binary relation on the *id*'s of M and is defined as follows. For any string β in Σ^*, any symbol a in Σ, and any states p and q in S, $(p, a\beta) \vdash_M (q, \beta)$ holds provided q is an element of $\delta(p, a)$. The informal interpretation of $(p, a\beta) \vdash_M (q, \beta)$ is that M can change from id $(p, a\beta)$ to id (q, β) in one step. If, for example, in reading a, M can go from state p to any of the three states q_1, q_2, and q_3, then $(p, a\beta) \vdash_M (q_1, \beta)$, $(p, a\beta) \vdash_M (q_2, \beta)$, and $(p, a\beta) \vdash_M (q_3, \beta)$ all hold.

If M can change from id (p, β) to id (q, α) in some finite number of steps, then we write $(p, \beta) \vdash_M^* (q, \alpha)$. More precisely, $(p, \beta) \vdash_M^* (q, \alpha)$ if there is a positive integer n, there are symbols $a_1, a_2, ..., a_n$ in Σ, and there are states $p_1, p_2, ..., p_{n+1}$ in S such that $\beta = a_1a_2...a_n\alpha$, $p = p_1$, $q = p_{n+1}$, and $(p, \beta) = (p_1, a_1a_2...a_n\alpha) \vdash_M (p_2, a_2a_3...a_n\alpha) \vdash_M ... \vdash_M (p_n, a_n\alpha) \vdash_M (p_{n+1}, \alpha) = (q, \alpha)$. We adopt the convention that $(p, \beta) \vdash_M^* (p, \beta)$, for all id's (p, β). The intuition for this convention is that M can go from id (p, β) to id (p, β) in zero steps.

When no confusion can result, we will omit the subscript M and write $\vdash$ and $\vdash^*$ rather than $\vdash_M$ and $\vdash_M^*$.

3.1.4 The machine M is said to be a *deterministic* finite-state acceptor provided $\delta(q, a)$ contains at most one element for every q in S and a in Σ. If M is deterministic and $\delta(q, a) = \{p\}$, then we will usually omit the braces and write $\delta(q, a) = p$. If $\delta(q, a)$ is the empty set, we will sometimes indicate this by saying "$\delta(q, a)$ is undefined." There is a technical difference between $\{p\}$ and p. Sometimes this difference can be very important. However, in this context we can identify the two things without causing any problems. The informal description of deterministic finite-state acceptors that opened this chapter assumed $\delta(p, a)$ had values in States(M). Technically, by our definition it has values in $\{\{p\} \mid p \text{ is in States } (M)\}$, but there is an obvious way of identifying this set with States(M).

Note that a deterministic finite-state acceptor is a special kind of non-deterministic finite-state acceptor. To say a machine is nondeterministic does not mean that it is not a deterministic machine. It just means that it is not necessarily a deterministic machine. For this reason, the unqualified term "finite-state acceptor" will always mean nondeterministic finite-state acceptor. (Some authors differ on this usage and one should take care to check definitions carefully when using other sources.)

3.1.5 A *computation* of M on the input α is a sequence of id's $(q_0, \beta_0), (q_1, \beta_1), \ldots, (q_n, \beta_n)$ such that

1. $(q_0, \beta_0) = (s, \alpha)$, where $s = \text{Start}(M)$.
2. $(q_i, \beta_i) \mid_{\overline{M}} (q_{i+1}, \beta_{i+1})$ for $i = 0, 1, 2, \ldots, n-1$.
3. (q_n, β_n) is a *halting* id. That is, either $\beta_n = \Lambda$ or else $\beta_n = a\gamma$ for some string γ and some symbol a such that $\delta(q_n, a)$ is empty.

In order to emphasize condition (2), we will usually use $\vdash$ rather than a comma to punctuate the sequence. Thus we will usually write computations in the form $(q_0, \beta_0) \vdash (q_1, \beta_1) \vdash \ldots \vdash (q_n, \beta_n)$.

A computation on the input α represents one possible sequence of actions for the machine with input α. If the machine is deterministic, then each input will give rise to exactly one computation. If the machine is nondeterministic, then the machine will typically have many different computations on a single input string. To illustrate the concept, suppose that *abcbd* is the input string in question and that the machine is nondeterministic. To be specific, let us assume that the transition function δ yields exactly two instructions for each argument pair which has b as the symbol and yields exactly one instruction for all other arguments. In the discussion that preceded this definition, we noted that the action of such a machine, on the input *abcbd*, could be diagrammed by the tree in Figure 3.2. Recall that the nodes are labeled by states and that the arcs represent transitions from one state to another. A computation of the finite state acceptor on the input *abcbd* corresponds to a path through this tree from root to tip (that is, from left to right). For example, one path passes through the nodes q_0, q_1, q_2, q_4, q_7 and q_{11} in that order. This path corresponds to the computation

$$(q_0, abcbd) \vdash (q_1, bcbd) \vdash (q_2, cbd) \vdash (q_4, bd) \vdash (q_7, d) \vdash (q_{11}, \Lambda)$$

As another illustration, consider Figure 3.4. This represents the action of another machine on the input 101110. In this case, there are three computations corresponding to the three paths through the tree. Notice that one computation does not use up all the input string. This is the computation:

$$(<\text{even}>, 101110) \vdash (<\text{odd}>, 01110) \vdash (<\text{odd}>, 1110) \vdash (<\text{one}>, 110)$$

The computation ends before using up all the input because the transition function yields the empty set as the set of instructions for the state-symbol pair $(<\text{one}>, 1)$.

3.1.6 M is said to *accept* an input string α in $[\text{Symbols}(M)]^*$ provided: $(s, \alpha) \vdash_M^* (p, \Lambda)$ for some state p in Accepting-states(M). Recall that s is the designated start state and Λ denotes the empty string. Notice that this definition requires that M be in an accepting state after the entire input is read. If M enters an accepting state before all the input is read, that does not indicate acceptance of the input.

The *language accepted* by M, denoted $A(M)$, is defined to be the set of all strings α accepted by M. A set of strings L is called a *finite-state language* if $L = A(M)$ for some nondeterministic finite-state acceptor M.

3.2 Examples of Finite-State Acceptors

3.2.1 We will describe a finite-state acceptor M in two different but equivalent ways: one in terms of an ordered five-tuple and one in our more intuitive notation.

Definition (1): Let $M = (S, \Sigma, \delta, s, Y)$ where $S = \{<\text{even}>, <\text{odd}>\}$, $\Sigma = \{0, 1\}$, $s = <\text{even}>$, $Y = \{<\text{odd}>\}$, and δ is defined by the equations below.

Definition (2): Let M be defined so that States$(M) = \{<\text{even}>, <\text{odd}>\}$, Symbols$(M) = \{0, 1\}$, Start$(M) = <\text{even}>$, Accepting-states$(M) = \{<\text{odd}>\}$ and Instructions$(M) = \delta$ where δ is defined by the equations below.

Equations describing δ:

$$\delta(<\text{even}>, 0) = \{<\text{even}>\}$$
$$\delta(<\text{even}>, 1) = \{<\text{odd}>\}$$
$$\delta(<\text{odd}>, 0) = \{<\text{odd}>\}$$
$$\delta(<\text{odd}>, 1) = \{<\text{even}>\}$$

M is a deterministic finite-state acceptor and $A(M)$ consists of all strings of 0's and 1's which contain an odd number of 1's. M is, in fact, the machine diagrammed in Figure 3.1.

3.2.2 Let M be defined so that Symbols$(M) = \{0, 1\}$, States$(M) = \{<\text{even } 0>, <\text{even } 1>, <\text{odd } 0>, <\text{odd } 1>, <\text{start}>\}$, Start$(M) = <\text{start}>$, Accepting-states$(M) = \{<\text{odd } 0>, <\text{odd } 1>\}$, and Instructions$(M) = \delta$ where δ is defined by:

$$\delta(<\text{start}>, 0) = \{<\text{even } 1>, <\text{odd } 0>\}$$
$$\delta(<\text{start}>, 1) = \{<\text{even } 0>, <\text{odd } 1>\}$$
$$\delta(<\text{even } x>, x) = \{<\text{odd } x>\} \text{ for } x = 0 \text{ or } 1$$
$$\delta(<\text{even } x>, y) = \{<\text{even } x>\} \text{ for } x = 0 \text{ or } 1 \text{ and } y \neq x$$
$$\delta(<\text{odd } x>, x) = \{<\text{even } x>\} \text{ for } x = 0 \text{ or } 1$$
$$\delta(<\text{odd } x>, y) = \{<\text{odd } x>\} \text{ for } x = 0 \text{ or } 1 \text{ and } y \neq x$$

Then M is a nondeterministic finite-state acceptor and $A(M)$ consists of all strings of 0's and 1's which contain either an odd number of 1's or an odd number of 0's. A diagram for M is given in Figure 3.5.

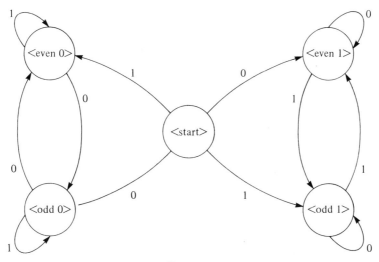

Figure 3.5

The following sequence of id's shows the complete accepting computation of M on input 010.

$$(<\text{start}>, 010) \vdash (<\text{even } 1>, 10) \vdash (<\text{odd } 1>, 0) \vdash (<\text{odd } 1>, \Lambda)$$

The following sequence of id's shows another complete computation of M on input 010.

$$(<\text{start}>, 010) \vdash (<\text{odd } 0>, 10) \vdash (<\text{odd } 0>, 0) \vdash (<\text{even } 0>, \Lambda)$$

Note that this second computation is not an accepting computation because the last state $<\text{even } 0>$ is not an accepting state. So M with input 010 has one computation which ends in an accepting state and one computation which ends in a nonaccepting state. A nondeterministic acceptor is said to accept an input if there is at least one accepting computation. Therefore, 010 is in $A(M)$.

Our next result shows that finite-state acceptors can at least perform the simple task of checking to see if its input is on a fixed finite list.

3.3 Theorem If L is any finite set of strings, then we can find a deterministic finite-state acceptor M such that $L = A(M)$.

PROOF Let L be a finite language. We will construct a deterministic finite-state acceptor M such that $A(M) = L$. Let l be the maximal length of any word in L. On an intuitive level, we can think of M as having a table of all words of length at most l. Those words which are in L will be marked in this table. Given any input, M compares this input to the table. M accepts if the input is short enough to be on the table and is marked to indicate that it is in L.

More formally, define M so that Symbols(M) is the set of all symbols that occur in any string in L, States(M) contains all strings in [Symbols(M)]* which have length at most l, and States(M) also contains an additional state t which will serve as a "trap" state. In set theoretic notation, States$(M) = \{\alpha \mid \alpha \in$ [Symbols(M)]* and length$(\alpha) \leqslant l\} \cup \{t\}$, where t is anything which is not in [Symbols(M)]*, Start$(M) = \Lambda$ (recall that Λ denotes the empty string), Accepting-states$(M) = L$, and Instructions$(M) = \delta$ where δ is specified by the equations:

1. $\delta(\alpha, a) = \{\alpha a\}$, for all a in Symbols(M) and all strings α of length strictly less than l.
2. $\delta(\alpha, a) = \{t\}$, for all a in Symbols(M) and all strings α of length l.
3. $\delta(t, a) = \{t\}$, for all a in Symbols(M).

With this definition of δ and with s defined by $s = \Lambda = $ Start(M), the following statements are true:

1. If the length of α is greater than l and $(s, \alpha) \vdash^* (p, \Lambda)$, then $p = t$.
2. If the length of α is at most l, then $(s, \alpha) \vdash^* (\alpha, \Lambda)$.

By (1), (2), and the definition of accepting states, it follows that $A(M) = L$. $\square$

The acceptor M, defined in the above proof, has the property that for every state-symbol pair (p, a), the value of the transition function $\delta(p, a)$ is nonempty. Intuitively, this means that the only thing that can force a computation of M to terminate is running out of input symbols. Not every acceptor has this property. The acceptor in Figure 3.3 has an empty instruction set for the state-symbol pairs $(<$one$>, 1)$ and $(<$zero$>, 0)$. So, on the input 101110, there is one computation which terminates after reading only the first three symbols (see Figure 3.4). The next lemma says that every finite-state acceptor is equivalent to a finite-state acceptor with nice properties. One of the nice properties is that the transition function is always defined to be a nonempty set of instructions. This is a purely technical result, with little intuitive content. It does, though, simplify a number of proofs.

3.4 Lemma Given any finite-state acceptor M and any alphabet Σ_2 containing Symbols(M), we can find another finite-state acceptor M_2 such that Symbols$(M_2) = \Sigma_2$, $A(M) = A(M_2)$, and, for any state-symbol pair (p, a) in

States(M_2) × Symbols(M_2), $\delta_2(p, a)$ is nonempty, where δ_2 denotes Instructions(M_2). Furthermore, if M is deterministic, then M_2 will also be deterministic.

PROOF M_2, defined as follows, clearly has the desired properties. States(M_2) consists of all the states in States(M) plus one additional state t, which intuitively serves as a trap state. M_2 has the same start state as M and the same accepting states as M. Let δ = Instructions(M) and define Instructions(M_2) to be δ_2, where δ_2 is defined in three parts. For any state-symbol pair (p, a) in States(M) × Symbols(M_2), let $\delta_2(p, a) = \delta(p, a)$, provided $\delta(p, a)$ is nonempty. If $\delta(p, a)$ is empty, then $\delta_2(p, a) = \{t\}$. For all a in Symbols(M_2), $\delta_2(t, a) = \{t\}$. □

3.5 Theorem If L_1 and L_2 are finite-state languages, then $L_1 \cup L_2$, $L_1 \cap L_2$, and $L_1 L_2$ are also finite-state languages.

PROOF Let M_1 and M_2 be nondeterministic finite-state acceptors such that $L_1 = A(M_1)$ and $L_2 = A(M_2)$. First, notice that we may assume that M_1 and M_2 have the following properties:

1. M_1 and M_2 have the same input alphabet.
2. Let δ_1 = Instructions(M_1) and δ_2 = Instructions(M_2). For any pair (p, a) in States(M_1) × Symbols(M_1), $\delta_1(p, a)$ is nonempty. Similarly, $\delta_2(p, a)$ is nonempty for any pair (p, a) in States(M_2) × Symbols(M_2).

Lemma 3.4 guarantees that we can find M_1 and M_2, which satisfy assumptions (1) and (2).

The theorem is proven by defining a finite-state acceptor to accept each of the languages in question. First we define $M_\cup$, which accepts $L_1 \cup L_2$. States$(M_\cup)$ = States(M_1) × States(M_2), Symbols$(M_\cup)$ = Symbols(M_1) = Symbols(M_2). The transition function δ of $M_\cup$ is just δ_1 and δ_2 applied to the two coordinates. That is, for all p_1 in States(M_1), all p_2 in States(M_2), and all a in Symbols$(M_\cup)$, define $\delta_\cup((p_1, p_2), a) = \{(q_1, q_2) \mid q_1$ is in $\delta_1(p_1, a)$ and q_2 is in $\delta_2(p_2, a)\}$. Set Start$(M_\cup)$ = (Start(M_1), Start(M_2)) and Accepting-states$(M_\cup)$ = $\{(p, q) \mid p$ is an accepting state of M_1 or q is an accepting state of $M_2\}$. $M_\cup$ is just M_1 and M_2 run in parallel and so, with these accepting states,

$$A(M_\cup) = A(M_1) \cup A(M_2) = L_1 \cup L_2$$

If $M_\cap$ is defined exactly as $M_\cup$ except that $M_\cap$ has final states Accepting-states(M_1) × Accepting-states(M_2), then

$$A(M_\cap) = A(M_1) \cap A(M_2) = L_1 \cap L_2$$

Next we show that $L_1 L_2$ is a finite-state language. First, consider the special case where Λ is neither in L_1 nor in L_2. Without loss of generality, we will assume that States(M_1) and States(M_2) are disjoint. If they are not disjoint, we can always make them so by replacing each state of M_1 by a state which is not in States(M_2). Define a nondeterministic finite-state acceptor M_P by setting States(M_P) = States(M_1) ∪ States(M_2),   Symbols(M_P) = Symbols(M_1) = Symbols(M_2),   Start(M_P) = Start(M_1),   Accepting-states(M_P) = Accepting-states(M_2), and Instructions(M_P) = δ_p, where δ_p is defined as follows. For any symbol a and any state q_1 of M_1, $\delta_p(q_1, a) = \delta_1(q_1, a)$ provided $\delta_1(q_1, a)$ does not contain an accepting state; $\delta_p(q_1, a) = \delta_1(q_1, a)$ ∪ $\{s_2\}$ provided $\delta_1(q_1, a)$ does contain an accepting state. Here s_2 is the start state of M_2. For any symbol a and any state q_2 of M_2, $\delta_p(q_2, a) = \delta_2(q_2, a)$. We claim that $A(M_P) = A(M_1)A(M_2) = L_1L_2$. To see this, note that the following statements are equivalent.

1. ξ is in $A(M_P)$.
2. There are strings α and β such that $\xi = \alpha\beta$ and $(s_1, \xi) = (s_1, \alpha\beta) \mathbin{\vert^*_{M_p}}$ $(s_2, \beta) \mathbin{\vert^*_{M_p}} (q_f, \Lambda)$ where s_1 is the start state of M_1, s_2 is the start state of M_2, and q_f is in Accepting-states(M_P) = Accepting-states(M_2).
3. There are strings α and β such that $\xi = \alpha\beta$, $(s_1, \alpha\beta) \mathbin{\vert^*_{M_1}} (\bar{q}_f, \beta)$ and $(s_2, \beta) \mathbin{\vert^*_{M_2}} (q_f, \Lambda)$, where $\bar{q}_f$ is an accepting state of M_1 and s_1, s_2, q_f are as in (2).
4. There are strings α and β such that $\xi = \alpha\beta$, $(s_1, \alpha) \mathbin{\vert^*_{M_1}} (\bar{q}_f, \Lambda)$,   and $(s_2, \beta) \mathbin{\vert^*_{M_2}} (q_f, \Lambda)$, where s_1, s_2, $\bar{q}_f$, and q_f are as in (3).
5. There are strings α and β such that $\xi = \alpha\beta$, α is in $A(M_1) = L_1$, and β is in $A(M_2) = L_2$.
6. ξ is in L_1L_2.

Hence $A(M_P) = L_1L_2$ and so L_1L_2 is a finite-state language, at least in the case where Λ is in neither L_1 nor L_2.

A careful rereading of the above proof will reveal that it is valid even if Λ is in L_2. In order to see this, try $\beta = \Lambda$ and $s_2 = q_f$. Hence we know that L_1L_2 is a finite-state language provided L_1 and L_2 are both finite-state languages and Λ is not in L_1.

Finally, consider the case where L_1 and L_2 are finite-state languages and Λ is in L_1. With M_P defined as above, $A(M_P) = (L_1 - \{\Lambda\})L_2$. So $(L_1 - \{\Lambda\})L_2$ is a finite-state language. Also, $L_1L_2 = (L_1 - \{\Lambda\})L_2 \cup L_2$. From these two facts it follows that L_1L_2 is the union of two finite-state languages. Hence, by the first part of this proof, L_1L_2 is a finite-state language in this case as well. Since we have now considered all cases, we know that L_1L_2 is a finite-state language whenever both L_1 and L_2 are finite-state languages. □

Using Theorems 3.3 and 3.5 and the examples, we see that many languages are finite-state languages. Later on we will present additional operations that allow us to produce even more finite-state languages. However, there are still many interesting languages that are not accepted by any finite-state acceptor. Our next result puts an upper bound on how complex a finite-state language can be. It cannot be any more complex than a context-free language. Further on in this chapter we will see that this upper bound is strict. That is, there are context-free languages that are not finite-state languages.

3.6 Theorem If L is a finite-state language, then L is a context-free language.

PROOF Let M be a nondeterministic finite-state acceptor such that $A(M) = L$. Without loss of generality, we may assume that the states of M are symbols of some sort and that States$(M) \cap$ Symbols(M) is empty; if M does not have these properties, we can easily replace M by an equivalent machine which does have these properties. We will define a context-free grammar G such that $L(G) = A(M) = L$. Let $G = (N, T, P, S)$ where Nonterminals$(G) = N =$ States(M), Terminals$(G) = T =$ Symbols(M), start symbol of $G = S =$ start state of M, and P consists of all productions which are of form (1) or form (2) below:

1. $A \rightarrow aB$ provided B is in $\delta(A, a)$, where δ is the transition function of M.
2. $A \rightarrow \Lambda$ where A is an accepting state of M.

The relationship of M and G is given by the next claim.

Claim 1: For any A, B in N, and any α in T^*, $A \overset{*}{\Rightarrow} \alpha B$ if and only if $(A, \alpha) \overset{*}{\underset{M}{\vdash}} (B, \Lambda)$.

The claim is proven by induction on the length of α. For the base of the induction, note that if length$(\alpha) =$ zero, then $\alpha = \Lambda$. In this case, $A \overset{*}{\Rightarrow} \alpha B$ if and only if $A = B$ which, in turn, is equivalent to saying $(A, \Lambda) \overset{*}{\underset{M}{\vdash}} (B, \Lambda)$. For the induction step, suppose length(α) is at least one and that the claim is true for all shorter strings and all elements in N. In this case, $\alpha = a\beta$ where a is a single symbol. The following statements are equivalent.

1. $A \overset{*}{\Rightarrow} \alpha B$.
2. $A \Rightarrow aC \overset{*}{\Rightarrow} a\beta B$, for some C in N and some β in T^*.
3. There is some C such that C is in $\delta(A, a)$ and $C \overset{*}{\Rightarrow} \beta B$.
4. $(A, a\beta) \vdash (C, \beta)$ and $(C, \beta) \overset{*}{\vdash} (B, \Lambda)$, for some C.
5. $(A, \alpha) \overset{*}{\vdash} (B, \Lambda)$.

Statements (3) and (4) are equivalent by the induction hypothesis and the definitions involved. All other adjacent statements are equivalent by the definitions involved. Thus Claim 1 is proven.

To see that $L(G) = L$, note that, by Claim 1 and the definitions involved, we can show the following chain of statements to be equivalent: α is in $L(G)$; $S \overset{*}{\Rightarrow} \alpha$; $S \overset{*}{\Rightarrow} \alpha B$, for some accepting state B; $(S, \alpha) \overset{*}{\vdash} (B, \Lambda)$, for some accepting state B; α is in $A(M)$. $\square$

EQUIVALENCE OF DETERMINISTIC AND NONDETERMINISTIC ACCEPTORS

At first glance it may appear that nondeterministic finite-state acceptors are more powerful than deterministic finite-state acceptors. It is sometimes the case that there is no obvious way to define a deterministic finite-state acceptor for a given language, yet there is a very simple nondeterministic finite-state acceptor that accepts that language. The next result says that deterministic finite-state acceptors are just as powerful as nondeterministic finite-state acceptors.

3.7 Theorem If M is a nondeterministic finite-state acceptor, then we can find a deterministic finite-state acceptor M_D such that $A(M) = A(M_D)$.

PROOF Let M be a nondeterministic finite-state acceptor. We will define a deterministic finite-state acceptor M_D such that $A(M_D) = A(M)$. Before giving a formal construction for M_D, we will describe M_D in a very informal way. Given an input $\alpha = a_1 a_2 ... a_n$, M_D will keep a list of the possible states that M could enter in a computation on α. After reading $a_1 a_2 ... a_i$, this list will contain exactly those states which M could possibly be in after reading $a_1 a_2 ... a_i$. M_D accepts α if, after scanning all of α, this list contains at least one of the accepting states of M. In effect, M_D is simulating all possible computations of M on α. Clearly, this is adequate to determine if M accepts α. These lists are to be nonredundant. That is, each state occurs at most once on any list. Since M has only a finite number of states, there are only a finite number of lists and so M_D has only a finite number of states. For example, Figure 3.4 diagrams the computation of a nondeterministic machine on the input 101110. The corresponding deterministic machine, with the same input, goes through states: {<even>}, {<odd>}, {<odd>}, {<even>, <one>}, {<odd>}, {<even>, <one>} and finally {<even>, <zero>}. In this construction we consider the objects like {<even>, <one>} to be single states of M_D, even though they happen to be sets of states of M. The formal construction M_D from M is given in the next two paragraphs.

M_D has the same input alphabet as M. States(M_D) is the set of all subsets of States(M). The start state of M_D is $\{s\}$, where s is the start state of M. Note that the notion of state depends on the machine in question. Each set of M states is a single M_D state. Each single state of M_D is a set of M states. An element of States(M_D) is an accepting state if it contains at least one accepting state of M.

Let δ denote the transition function of M. The transition function, δ_D, of M_D is defined so that $\delta_D(H, a)$ contains the one state J defined by

$$J = \{p \mid p \text{ is in } \delta(q, a), \text{ for some } q \text{ in } H\}$$

for all H in States(M_D) and all input symbols a. An equivalent definition of this J is:

$$J = \bigcup_q \delta(q, a),$$

where the union is taken over all states q in H. M_D clearly is a deterministic finite-state acceptor. So it remains to show that $A(M_D) = A(M)$. This follows immediately once the following claim is demonstrated. The claim is quite obvious and for many readers it may not require any proof. However, we will include a formal inductive proof so as to have the practice of doing a fairly easy inductive proof in preparation for other more difficult proofs.

Claim: For all H in States(M_D), and all strings α, β in Σ^*: $(s_D, \alpha\beta) \vdash^*_{M_D}$ (H, β) if and only if $H = \{p \mid (s, \alpha\beta) \vdash^*_M (p, \beta)\}$, where $s = \text{Start}(M)$, $s_D = \text{Start}(M_D)$, and Σ denotes the common input alphabet of M and M_D.

The claim is proven by induction on the length of α. Recall that $s_D = \{s\}$. If α is the empty word, then $(s_D, \alpha\beta) \vdash^*_{M_D} (H, \beta)$ if and only if $H = s_D = \{s\} = \{p \mid (s, \alpha\beta) = (s, \beta) \vdash^*_M (p, \beta)\}$. Hence, the base case of the inductive argument is proven. If α is at least one symbol in length, then $\alpha = \gamma a$, where a is a single symbol. In this case, we see that the following statements are equivalent:

1. $(s_D, \gamma a\beta) \vdash^*_{M_D} (H, \beta)$.
2. There is some J in States(M_D) such that $(s_D, \gamma a\beta) \vdash^*_{M_D} (J, a\beta)$ and $(J, a\beta) \vdash^*_{M_D} (H, \beta)$.
3. There is some J in States(M_D) such that $J = \{q \mid (s, \gamma a\beta) \vdash^*_M (q, a\beta)\}$, and $(J, a\beta) \vdash^*_{M_D} (H, \beta)$.
4. There is some J in States(M_D) such that $J = \{q \mid (s, \gamma a\beta) \vdash^*_M (q, a\beta)\}$ and $H = \{p \mid (q, a\beta) \vdash_M (p, \beta)$ for some q in $J\}$.
5. $H = \{p \mid (s, \gamma a\beta) \vdash^*_{M_D} (p, \beta)\}$.

Statements (1) and (2) are equivalent by definition of $\vdash^*_{M_D}$; (2) and (3) are equivalent by the induction hypothesis, since length$(\gamma) < $ length(α); (3) and (4) are equivalent by definition of δ_D, and (4) and (5) are equivalent by definition of $\vdash^*_M$. Finally, we combine this chain of equivalences to conclude that (1) is equivalent to (5). This demonstrates the inductive step and concludes the proof of the claim.

To see that $A(M) = A(M_D)$, note that α is in $A(M)$ if and only if $(s, \alpha) \vdash^*_M (p, \Lambda)$ for some M accepting state p. Also, by the claim, $(s, \alpha) \vdash^*_M (p, \Lambda)$ for some M accepting state p if and only if $(s_D, \alpha) \vdash^*_{M_D} (H, \Lambda)$ for some H containing an M-accepting state. But H is an M_D-accepting state if and only if H contains an M-accepting state. So α is in $A(M)$ if and only if α is in $A(M_D)$. $\square$

Using the previous theorem, it is easy to show that the class of finite-state languages is closed under complement. To show this, we simply note that any given finite-state language is accepted by a well-behaved, deterministic finite-state machine. Then, to obtain a machine accepting the complement of the given language, we need only interchange the notions of accepting and non-accepting states.

3.8 Theorem If L is a finite-state language and Σ is an alphabet such that $\Sigma^* \supseteq L$, then $\Sigma^* - L$ is a finite-state language.

PROOF Suppose L is a finite-state language. By Theorem 3.7 we know that $L = A(M)$, where M is a deterministic finite-state acceptor. By Lemma 3.4, we may assume that $\Sigma = \text{Symbols}(M)$ and that the transition function of M defines a next state for every state/symbol pair of M. Let M_c be the same finite-state acceptor as M except that M_c has a different set of accepting states from M. The accepting states of M_c are all the states which are not accepting states of M. Clearly, M_c accepts a string α in Σ^* if and only if M does not accept α. So $A(M_c) = \Sigma^* - L$ and $\Sigma^* - L$ is thus a finite-state language. $\square$

THE PUMPING LEMMA AND LANGUAGES WHICH ARE NOT FINITE-STATE

Before proceeding to our next result, we need to discuss a simple property of finite-state acceptors. This property is an immediate consequence of the definitions involved. Suppose M is a finite-state acceptor, α, β, and γ are strings of input symbols for M and both p and q are states of M. Suppose further that $\beta \neq \gamma$. In proofs, we will frequently show that $(p, \alpha\beta) \vdash_M^* (q, \beta)$ and then conclude that $(p, \alpha\gamma) \vdash_M^* (q, \gamma)$. This is perfectly valid, since the relation $\vdash_M^*$ does not depend on the input that is not read. The fact that the relation $(p, \alpha\beta) \vdash_M^* (q, \beta)$ holds depends on M, p, q and α but has nothing to do with β. So, if we substitute γ for β, it is still true. This point is quite obvious. The only reason we are belaboring it is that we will use it often and we do not want to stop to justify it each time. So we are now discussing it once and for all.

The next results show that there are context-free languages which are not finite-state languages. So the class of finite-state languages is a proper subclass of the context-free languages.

3.9 Theorem $L = \{a^n b^n \mid n \geqslant 1\}$ is not a finite-state language.

PROOF We wish to show that there is no finite-state acceptor M such that $A(M) = L$. By Theorem 3.7, it will suffice to consider only deterministic acceptors. Hence, it suffices to establish the following claim.

Claim: If M is a deterministic finite-state acceptor and M accepts every string in L, then M will also accept some string which is not in L.

Suppose M is as described in the hypothesis of the claim. M has only a finite number of states but there are infinitely many strings of a's. So it follows that there are two different strings of a's which leave M in the same state. That is, there are i and j such that $i \neq j$ and, for some single state p, both $(s, a^i) \vdash^* (q, \Lambda)$ and $(s, a^j) \vdash^* (p, \Lambda)$, where s is the start state of M. Hence, if q is the unique state such that $(s, a^i b^i) \vdash^* (p, b^i) \vdash^* (q, \Lambda)$, then $(s, a^j b^i) \vdash^* (p, b^i) \vdash^* (q, \Lambda)$. Now $a^i b^i$ is in L and, by our hypothesis, M accepts all strings in L. So q is an accepting state of M. But $(s, a^j b^i) \vdash^* (q, \Lambda)$. So $a^j b^i$ is accepted by M. Finally, recall that $j \neq i$, and so $a^j b^i$ is a string which is not in L but is accepted by M. This establishes the claim. $\square$

Our next result is a pumping lemma for finite-state languages which is rather like the pumping lemma for context-free languages. Since finite-state languages are simpler than cfl's the proof is simpler and the result is, in a sense, simpler. In this case, we are guaranteed that there is a substring, called

β in this pumping lemma, which can be "pumped up." As in the cfl case, we do not get to choose β. We only know that there is some such β. However, we do get to choose any substring, ξ, and, provided ξ is sufficiently long, we at least know that β lies somewhere within ξ.

3.10 Theorem (The Pumping Lemma for Finite-State Acceptors). Let M be a nondeterministic finite-state acceptor with k states. Suppose ζ is in $A(M)$ and $\zeta = \mu\xi\nu$, where length$(\xi) \geqslant k$ and μ, ν are any (possibly empty) strings. It then follows that ξ can be written in the form $\xi = \alpha\beta\gamma$ where $1 \leqslant$ length$(\beta) \leqslant k$ and where $\mu\alpha\beta^i\gamma\nu$ is in $A(M)$ for all $i \geqslant 0$.

PROOF (The proof is a little easier to follow if you assume M is a deterministic machine. You may find it helpful to make this assumption in your first reading of this proof.)

Let M and k be as in the statement of the theorem. Suppose $\zeta = \mu\xi\nu$ is in $A(M)$ and length$(\xi) \geqslant k$. Consider any one fixed accepting computation of M on $\mu\xi\nu$: $(s, \mu\xi\nu) \overset{*}{\vdash} (p_1, \xi\nu) \overset{*}{\vdash} (p_2, \nu) \overset{*}{\vdash} (p_3, \Lambda)$, where s is the start state and p_3 is an accepting state. M takes at least k steps in the partial computation $(p_1, \xi\nu) \overset{*}{\vdash} (p_2, \nu)$. So it must enter at least $k+1$ states in this partial computation. But M only has k states. So it must enter some state twice in this computation. That is, $\xi = \alpha\beta\gamma$ where β is nonempty and

1. $(p_1, \xi\nu) = (p_1, \alpha\beta\gamma\nu) \overset{*}{\vdash} (q, \beta\gamma\nu) \overset{*}{\vdash} (q, \gamma\nu) \overset{*}{\vdash} (p_2, \nu)$ for some state q.

Choose the decomposition $\xi = \alpha\beta\gamma$ so that (1) is true, β is nonempty, and, within these constraints, β is as short as possible. In the partial computation (1), M goes from state q to state q in processing β. If $\beta\beta$ is inserted in place of β, then M can go from state q to state q in processing the first β and then again go from state q to state q in processing the second β. Whether M gets $\mu\xi\nu = \mu\alpha\beta\gamma\nu$ or $\mu\alpha\beta\beta\gamma\nu$ as input, it can still end up in the final state p_3. That is,

$$(s, \mu\alpha\beta\beta\gamma\nu) \overset{*}{\vdash} (p_1, \alpha\beta\beta\gamma\nu) \overset{*}{\vdash}$$
$$(q, \beta\beta\gamma\nu) \overset{*}{\vdash} (q, \beta\gamma\nu) \overset{*}{\vdash} (q, \gamma\nu) \overset{*}{\vdash} (p_2, \nu) \overset{*}{\vdash} (p_3, \Lambda)$$

Similarly, for any $i \geqslant 0$, $(s, \mu\alpha\beta^i\gamma\nu) \overset{*}{\vdash} (q, \beta^i\gamma\nu) \overset{*}{\vdash} (q, \gamma\nu) \overset{*}{\vdash} (p_3, \Lambda)$.

It remains to show that length$(\beta) \leqslant k$. But β was chosen to be as short as possible and still both be nonempty and satisfy (1). Suppose length$(\beta) > k$. We will derive a contradiction. Namely, we will show that there is a nonempty β' such that β' is shorter than β and still satisfies (1). Since length$(\beta) > k$, M enters at least $k+2$ states in processing β. So $\beta = \alpha'\beta'\gamma'$ where $1 \leqslant$ length$(\beta') <$ length(β) and $(q, \beta) = (q, \alpha'\beta'\gamma') \overset{*}{\vdash} (q_2, \beta'\gamma') \overset{*}{\vdash} (q_2, \gamma') \overset{*}{\vdash} (q, \Lambda)$, for some state q_2. Therefore, (1) is still true if we replace β by β', α by $\alpha\alpha'$, γ by $\gamma'\gamma$ and q by q_2. This contradicts the fact that β has been chosen to have minimal length. $\square$

The pumping lemma imposes rather severe constraints on finite-state languages and is very useful in proving that certain sets are not finite-state languages. As an example, we present the next theorem.

3.11 Theorem $L = \{a^n \mid n \text{ is a prime}\}$ is not a finite-state language.

PROOF Assume $L = A(M)$ for some finite-state acceptor M. We will derive a contradiction. Let n be a prime which is larger than the number of states of M plus two. Apply the pumping lemma with $\xi = a^n$ and both μ and ν empty. Then $a^n = a^h a^i a^j$, where $i \neq 0$, $h + j > 1$, and $a^h a^{mi} a^j$ is in $A(M)$ for all $m \geqslant 0$. In particular, $a^h a^{(h+j)i} a^j$ is in $A(M)$. But $h + (h+j)i + j = (h+j)(i+1)$ is not a prime. So $A(M)$ contains at least one string of the form a^n, where n is not a prime. This is the desired contradiction. $\square$

Using the pumping lemma, we can show that there are algorithms to test if a given finite-state acceptor accepts any input at all and to test if it accepts a finite or infinite number of input strings. The next theorem shows that, in order to test these properties, we need only test whether or not the finite-state acceptor will accept some word from a suitable finite list of words. The algorithms for these properties then consist of testing whether or not the given finite-state acceptor does indeed accept any of the strings on this finite list. To test if a finite-state acceptor accepts a string, simply try all possible computations on this string; or else use Theorem 3.7 to obtain an equivalent deterministic machine and then run the deterministic machine with this string as input.

3.12 Theorem Let M be a finite-state acceptor with k states.

1. $A(M)$ is nonempty if and only if M accepts a word of length less than k.
2. $A(M)$ is infinite if and only if M accepts some word of length n with $k \leqslant n < 2k$.

Hence, there is an algorithm to determine for any finite-state acceptor M whether M accepts zero, a finite number, or an infinite number of inputs.

PROOF **1.** If M accepts a word of length less than k, then $A(M)$ is obviously nonempty. Conversely, suppose $A(M)$ is nonempty. We will show that $A(M)$ accepts some input of length less than k. Let ξ be a word in $A(M)$. If ξ is of length less than k, we are done. Suppose ξ is of length greater than k. By 3.10, the pumping lemma, $\xi = \alpha\beta\gamma$ where β is nonempty and $\alpha\gamma$ is in $A(M)$. If $\alpha\gamma$ is of length less than k, we are done. If $\alpha\gamma$ is of length k or more, we apply the pumping lemma to $\alpha\gamma$ and get a still shorter word in $A(M)$. Proceeding in this way, we eventually find a word in $A(M)$ of length less than k.

2. Suppose $A(M)$ contains a word ξ such that $k \leqslant \text{length}(\xi) < 2k$. By the pumping lemma, $\xi = \alpha\beta\gamma$ where β is nonempty and $A(M)$ contains $\alpha\beta^i\gamma$ for all i. So $A(M)$ is infinite.

Conversely, suppose $A(M)$ is infinite. Then $A(M)$ contains one word ξ of length at least k. If ξ is of length less that $2k$, we are done. Suppose ξ is of length at least $2k$. Again we apply the pumping lemma and set $\xi = \alpha\beta\gamma$, where $1 \leqslant \text{length}(\beta) \leqslant k$ and $\alpha\gamma$ is in $A(M)$. Since $\text{length}(\xi) \geqslant 2k$ and $\text{length}(\beta) \leqslant k$, we know $\text{length}(\alpha\gamma) \geqslant k$. If $\alpha\gamma$ is of length less than $2k$, we are done. If not, we again apply the pumping lemma to $\alpha\gamma$ and get a still shorter word which is in $A(M)$. Proceeding in this way, we eventually find a word in $A(M)$ whose length is between k and $2k$. $\square$

*REGULAR EXPRESSIONS

In this section we will give an alternate characterization of finite-state languages. The characterization will also give us a succinct notation for describing finite-state languages. This notation is called regular expression notation. It will turn out that the finite-state languages are exactly the languages which can be described by regular expressions.

Intuitively, a regular expression is a description of a set of words. This description is itself a string made up from individual letters; the symbol *; the symbol $\vee$, meaning "or"; parentheses; and two additional special symbols. For example, $(a \vee b)$ is read as "a or b" and describes the language $\{a, b\}$. The expression $(a \vee b)^*$ is read "a or b star" and describes the language $\{a, b\}^*$. We will use juxtaposition to denote the product of languages. For example, $(a \vee b) (c \vee d)$ will be a regular expression denoting the language $\{a, b\}\{c, d\} = \{ac, ad, bc, bd\}$. We will also use the symbols $\varnothing$ and Λ to denote the empty set and the empty string respectively. For example, $(\Lambda \vee a)$ will be a regular expression denoting the language $\{\Lambda, a\}$ and $(\varnothing \vee a)$ will be a regular expression denoting the language $\{a\}$. A formal definition of regular expressions can be given in terms of a context-free grammar.

3.13 Definition

3.13.1 Let Σ be an alphabet. The set of *regular expressions* over Σ is the context-free language generated by the context-free grammar G defined as follows:

> $\text{Terminals}(G) = \Sigma \cup \{(,), \vee, *, \Lambda, \varnothing\}$
> $\text{Nonterminals}(G) = \{S\}$
> $\text{Start}(G) = S$ and $\text{Productions}(G)$ consist of exactly the productions given below:

1. $S \rightarrow \varnothing, S \rightarrow \Lambda$
2. $S \rightarrow a$, for each a in Σ
3. $S \rightarrow (SS)$
4. $S \rightarrow (S \vee S)$
5. $S \rightarrow S^*$

(We are, of course, assuming that the symbols Λ and $\varnothing$ are not in Σ.)

3.13.2 With each regular expression r, we associate a language, denoted $L(r)$. The definition of $L(r)$ is by induction. The induction follows the pattern of the parse tree for r and is as follows:

1. $L(\varnothing) = \varnothing$, $L(\Lambda) = \{\Lambda\}$.
2. $L(a) = \{a\}$, for each a in Σ.
3. If r is $(r_1 r_2)$, then $L(r) = L(r_1) L(r_2)$.
4. If r is $(r_1 \lor r_2)$, then $L(r) = L(r_1) \cup L(r_2)$.
5. If r is r_1^*, then $L(r) = (L(r_1))^*$.

A language H is called a *regular language* if $H = L(r)$, for some regular expression r.

3.14 Examples

3.14.1 a, $(a \lor b)$, $((ab)c)$, $\varnothing$, and Λ are regular expressions describing the languages $\{a\}$, $\{a, b\}$, $\{abc\}$, $\varnothing$, and $\{\Lambda\}$, respectively.

3.14.2 $r = ((a \lor b)(c(de)))$ is a regular expression. The parse tree for r is given in Figure 3.6. Using the parse tree, you can easily construct $L(r)$. For each subtree of the form $S \rightarrow x$, where x is a letter, replace this occurrence of S by $\{x\}$. Then work your way up the tree replacing each S by the language determined by the languages at the nodes just below this S. The method of obtaining $L(r)$ from the parse tree is illustrated in Figure 3.7. In this figure all S's have been replaced by a language obtained from languages below by applying the appropriate operation. $L(r)$ is at the root node. So $L(r) = \{acde, bcde\}$.

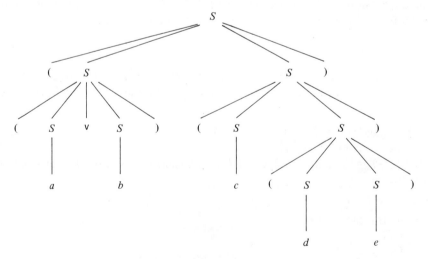

Figure 3.6

3.14.3 $r' = (((a \lor b)c)^* \lor ((de)f))$ is a regular expression and $L(r') = ((\{a\} \cup \{b\})\{c\})^* \cup (\{de\}\{f\}) = (\{a, b\}\{c\})^* \cup \{def\} = \{ac, bc\}^* \cup \{def\}$.

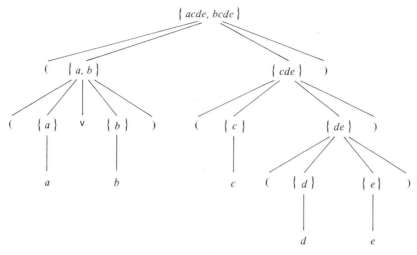

Figure 3.7

In order to prove that regular languages are the same as finite-state languages we will need one lemma. Since the lemma follows easily from the definition of regular languages, we will leave its proof as an exercise.

3.15 Lemma If L_1 and L_2 are regular languages, then so are $L_1 L_2$, $L_1 \cup L_2$ and L_1^*.

3.16 Theorem L is a regular language if and only if L is a finite-state language.

PROOF We will show that all regular languages are finite-state languages and conversely. To see that all regular languages are finite-state languages, just note that, by Theorem 3.3, $\varnothing$, $\{\Lambda\}$, and $\{a\}$ are finite-state languages where a is a single symbol. If L_1 and L_2 are finite-state languages, then so are $L_1 \cup L_2$, $L_1 L_2$ and L_1^* (Theorem 3.5 and Exercise 3-6). The fact that all regular languages are finite-state languages then follows by induction.

To show that every finite-state language is a regular language, we also proceed by induction. This time we perform induction on the number of states in a finite-state acceptor. Specifically, we will show that all languages accepted by one-state, finite-state acceptors are regular languages. After that we will show that if all languages accepted by n state finite-state acceptors are regular, then so are all languages accepted by $n + 1$ state finite-state acceptors.

Consider a one-state, finite-state acceptor, M. If this one state is not an accepting state, then $A(M) = \varnothing$, a regular language. If this one state is an accepting state, then $A(M) = \{a \mid (q, a) \vdash (q, \Lambda)\}^*$, where q is the unique start and accepting state. Hence, $A(M)$ consists of all words made up from a finite list of symbols, $a_1, a_2, ..., a_m$. Let $r = (a_1 \lor a_2 \lor ... \lor a_m)^*$, where we have deleted some parentheses in order to make r more readable. Then $A(M) = L(r)$, a regular language. So we have shown the base case of our induction.

Suppose M is an $n+1$ state finite-state acceptor and assume, inductively, that for any n state finite-state acceptor M', $A(M')$ is a regular language. We must show that $A(M)$ is a regular language. Let q be an arbitrary accepting state of M and let M_q be the finite-state acceptor which is identical to M, except that M_q has q as the only accepting state. (If M has no accepting states, then $A(M) = \varnothing$, a regular language.) We will show that $A(M_q)$ is a regular language. It will then follow that $A(M)$ is a regular language. This is because $A(M) = A(M_{q_1}) \cup A(M_{q_2}) \cup ... \cup A(M_{q_l})$, where $q_1, q_2, ..., q_l$ are the accepting states of M, and because the union of finitely many regular languages is itself a regular language. We now turn to the task of showing that $A(M_q)$ is a regular language.

Let x, y and z be states of M_q. Let R_{xy}^z be the set of all words α such that $(x, \alpha) \overset{*}{\vdash} (y, \Lambda)$ on M_q and no state in the computation is z, except possibly the first state x and possibly the last state y. ($x = y = z$ is allowed, and it is possible that the computation takes zero steps.) If s is the start state of M_q and $s \neq q$, then $A(M_q) = (R_{ss}^s)^* R_{sq}^s$. What all this says is that any accepting computation starts in s, passes through s some finite number of times, and then goes from the last occurrence of s to the final state q. If q is the start state as well as the final state of M_q, then $A(M_q) = (R_{qq}^q)^*$. Hence we know that $A(M_q)$ can be obtained from languages of the form R_{xy}^z using product and star operations. Thus, applying Lemma 3.15, we see that in order to prove that $A(M_q)$ is a regular language, it will suffice to show that R_{xy}^z is a regular language for any states x, y and z. In order to show this, we need to consider one additional construct.

Again, let x, y and z be states of M_q. Let K_{xy} be the set of all symbols a such that $(x, a) \vdash (y, \Lambda)$ on M_q. K_{xy} is a finite set of symbols. Hence K_{xy} can be described by a regular expression consisting of these finite symbols connected by $\vee$ and suitable parentheses. So K_{xy} is a regular language. We now proceed to show that all languages of the form R_{xy}^z are regular languages.

If neither d nor e is equal to z, then $R_{de}^z = A(M')$ where M' is obtained from M by deleting the state z, changing the start state to d and changing the accepting states so that e is the only accepting state. M' has only n states. So, by induction hypothesis, R_{de}^z is a regular language, provided that neither d nor e is equal to z. To see that, in general, R_{xy}^z is a regular language, note that R_{xy}^z is the union of K_{xy} and all sets of the form $K_{xd} R_{de}^z K_{ey}$, where d and e are states other than z. If $x = y$ then, in addition, we need to union this set with $\{\Lambda\}$, which is regular. Thus R_{xy}^z is obtained from regular languages by taking finite products and unions. Hence, by Lemma 3.15, R_{xy}^z is a regular language. This completes the proof since, as outlined above, R_{xy}^z regular implies $A(M_q)$ is regular which, in turn, implies $A(M)$ is regular. $\square$

*TWO-WAY FINITE-STATE ACCEPTORS

One can argue that our definition of finite-state acceptors is too restricted, since the machine only gets to read the input once. We now lift this input restriction. A two-way finite-state acceptor is just like an ordinary (one-way) finite-state acceptor, except that it may back up through the input string. It is helpful to think of the input as being written on a tape and to think of the acceptor as having some reading device referred to as a *head*, which can be positioned at any one symbol of input. At any point in time, the acceptor is in some state and the head is positioned at some symbol. On the basis of this state-symbol pair, the acceptor changes state and moves the head a maximum of one symbol in either direction. Since we do not want the head to leave the input string, we place end markers at each end of the input. Two-way acceptors can be either deterministic or nondeterministic. We will consider only the deterministic case and leave the nondeterministic case as an exercise.

3.17 Definition

3.17.1 A *two-way deterministic finite-state acceptor with end markers* is a seven-tuple $M = (S, \Sigma, \delta, s, Y, \text{¢}, \$)$ where S, Σ, s, and Y are a finite set of states, an input alphabet, a start state, and set of accepting states, respectively. These items are the same as they are in an ordinary finite-state acceptor. The ¢ and \$ are two symbols not in Σ. They are called the *left* and *right end markers* respectively. The transition function δ is a partial function from $S \times (\Sigma \cup \{\text{¢}, \$\})$ into $S \times \{\rightarrow, \leftarrow, \downarrow\}$ such that, for all q in S, $\delta(q, \text{¢}) \neq (p, \leftarrow)$ for any p in S, and $\delta(q, \$) \neq (p, \rightarrow)$ for any p in S. By analogy to one-way finite-state acceptors, we write States(M) for S, Symbols(M) for Σ, Instructions(M) for δ, Start(M) for s, Accepting-state(M) for Y, Left-end(M) for ¢ and Right-end(M) for \$.

The intuitive meaning of δ is as follows. If $\delta(q, a) = (p, x)$, then when M is in state q scanning symbol a, it will change to state p and shift the tape head either left or right or leave it stationary, depending on whether x is $\leftarrow$, $\rightarrow$, or $\downarrow$ respectively. Our machines have the rather atypical property of having a fixed input tape and a read head that moves on the tape. This may explain any confusion you have about distinguishing between $\leftarrow$ and $\rightarrow$. The arrow points in the direction of head movement, not tape movement. One can argue that a stationary head and a moving tape is more realistic. However, our convention is certainly mathematically equivalent to a moving tape and is standard notation. Think of the head as a pointer which points to the scanned symbol. The pointer moves. The tape remains stationary.

3.17.2 An *id* of M is a pair $(p, \alpha \triangleright \beta)$, where p is a state of M, $\alpha\beta$ is a string in $\text{¢}\Sigma^*\$$, and $\triangleright$ is a symbol not in $\Sigma \cup \{\text{¢}, \$\}$. The intuitive meaning of $(p, \alpha \triangleright \beta)$ is that M is in state p, the entire input (including end markers) is $\alpha\beta$, and M is scanning the first symbol in β.

3.17.3 The *next step relation* $\vert_{\overline{M}}$ is defined as follows. If $\delta(p, a) = (q, \rightarrow)$, then $(p, \alpha \triangleright a\beta) \vert_{\overline{M}} (q, \alpha a \triangleright \beta)$ for all $\alpha a\beta$ in $\not{c}\Sigma^*\$$. If $\delta(p, a) = (q, \downarrow)$, then $(p, \alpha \triangleright a\beta) \vert_{\overline{M}} (q, \alpha \triangleright a\beta)$. If $\delta(p, a) = (q, \leftarrow)$, then $(p, \alpha c \triangleright a\beta) \vert_{\overline{M}}$ $(q, \alpha \triangleright ca\beta)$ for all strings $\alpha ca\beta$ in $\not{c}\Sigma^*\$$ such that c is a single symbol.

If M can get from id (p, μ) to id (q, γ) in some finite number (possibly zero) of steps, then we write $(p, \mu) \vert_{\overline{M}}^* (q, \gamma)$. When M is clear from context, we will omit it from $\vert_{\overline{M}}$ and $\vert_{\overline{M}}^*$.

3.17.4 An id $(q, \alpha \triangleright \beta)$ is called a *halting id* if there is no id $(q', \alpha' \triangleright \beta')$ such that $(q, \alpha \triangleright \beta) \vert_{\overline{M}} (q', \alpha' \triangleright \beta')$. Equivalently, $(q, \alpha \triangleright \beta)$ is a halting id provided $\delta(q, a)$ is undefined, where a is the first symbol of the string β.

3.17.5 A *computation* of M on the input ξ is a (finite or infinite) sequence of id's $(q_0, \alpha_0 \triangleright \beta_0)$, $(q_1, \alpha_1 \triangleright \beta_1)$, $(q_2, \alpha_2 \triangleright \beta_2)$ ... such that:

1. $(q_0, \alpha_0 \triangleright \beta_0) = (s, \triangleright \not{c}\xi\$)$, where s is the start state and $\not{c}$ and $\$$ are the end markers.
2. $(q_{i-1}, \alpha_{i-1} \triangleright \beta_{i-1}) \vert_{\overline{M}} (q_i, \alpha_i \triangleright \beta_i)$, for all $i > 0$ such that $(q_i, \alpha_i \triangleright \beta_i)$ is in the sequence.
3. If the sequence is finite, then the last id is a halting id.

3.17.6 The *language accepted* by M is denoted $A(M)$ and is defined to be the set of all strings ξ in Σ^* such that $(s, \triangleright \not{c}\xi\$) \vert_{\overline{M}}^* (p, \not{c}\xi \triangleright \$)$ for some accepting state p. Recall that s is the start state, $\not{c}$ and $\$$ are the end markers, and $\Sigma = \text{Symbols}(M)$.

Note that two conditions must be satisfied in order for an input to be accepted. The acceptor must be in an accepting state and the tape head must be scanning the right-hand end marker. If the acceptor enters an accepting state with the tape head in any other position, this does not constitute an acceptance of the input. (The acceptor may, of course, go on to accept the input at a later stage of the computation.) One can argue that a more reasonable notion of acceptance is to merely require that an accepting state is entered and to put no conditions on the position of the tape head. However, it is easy to show that a language is accepted by an acceptor using one of these two notions of acceptance if and only if it is accepted by some other acceptor using the other notion of acceptance. So, since Definition 3.17.6 will turn out to be mathematically more convenient, it is the definition we will adopt.

3.18 Example

M, defined as follows, is a two-way deterministic finite-state acceptor with end markers.

$$\text{States}(M) = \{1, 2, 3, 3a, 3b, 4a, 4b, t, y\}$$
$$\text{Symbols}(M) = \{a, b, c\}, \text{Start}(M) = 1$$
$$\text{Accepting-states}(M) = \{y\}$$

Left-end$(M) = ¢$, Right-end$(M) = \$$
Instructions$(M) = \delta$ where δ is defined by Table 3.1

Any (q, x) which do not occur in the table will not arise in any computation. So $\delta(q, x)$ can be anything for these (q, x). We will assume that $\delta(q, x)$ is undefined for these (q, x).

Table 3.1

Comment	q	x	$\delta(q, x)$
Check for c	1	$¢$, a, or b	$1, \rightarrow$
	1	c	$2, \downarrow$
	1	$\$$	$t, \downarrow$
Find left end marker	2	a, b, or c	$2, \leftarrow$
	2	$¢$	$3, \rightarrow$
Is first symbol a or b?	3	a	$3a, \rightarrow$
	3	b	$3b, \rightarrow$
	3	c	$t, \downarrow$
Find right-end marker	$3a$	a, b, or c	$3a, \rightarrow$
remembering a or b	$3b$	a, b, or c	$3b, \rightarrow$
	$3a$	$\$$	$4a, \leftarrow$
	$3b$	$\$$	$4b, \leftarrow$
If last symbol matches	$4a$	a	$y, \rightarrow$
first symbol accept	$4b$	b	$y, \rightarrow$
	$4a$	b or c	$t, \downarrow$
	$4b$	a or c	$t, \downarrow$
t is a "trap" state, y is	y	$\$$	$y, \downarrow$
the accepting state	t	Anything	$t, \downarrow$

$A(M)$ is the set of all strings $x\alpha x$, where $x = a$ or b and α is a string containing at least one c. M first checks if the input contains a c. It then goes back to the beginning of the input, remembers the first symbol of the input, and then shifts right until it finds the right-end marker. It then shifts left one square and checks that the last input symbol equals the first input symbol. A diagram of an accepting computation of M is given in Figure 3.8.

The observant reader will note that we can design another finite-state acceptor which accepts the same language and yet never shifts left. The next theorem says that we can do this for any two-way acceptor.

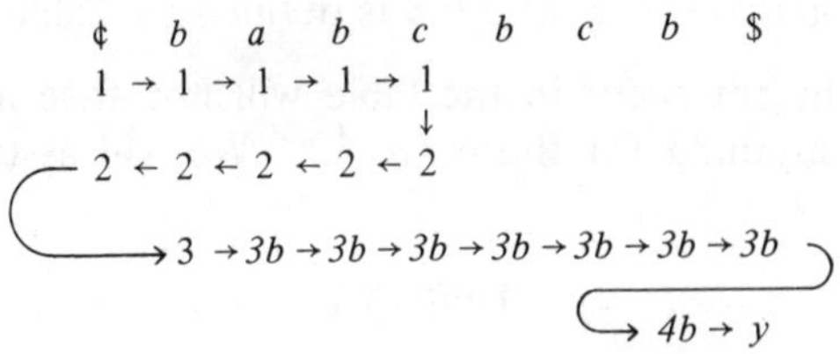

$$\begin{array}{ccccccccc}
\text{¢} & b & a & b & c & b & c & b & \$ \\
1 & \to 1 & \to 1 & \to 1 & \to 1 \\
& & & & \downarrow \\
2 & \leftarrow 2 & \leftarrow 2 & \leftarrow 2 & \leftarrow 2 \\
& \to 3 & \to 3b & \to 3b & \to 3b & \to 3b & \to 3b & \to 3b & \to 3b \\
& & & & & & & \to 4b & \to y
\end{array}$$

Figure 3.8

3.19 Theorem For any language L, the following three statements are equivalent:

1. L is accepted by some two-way deterministic finite-state acceptor with end markers.
2. L is accepted by some (one-way) deterministic finite-state acceptor.
3. L is accepted by some (one-way) nondeterministic finite-state acceptor.

PROOF The equivalence of (2) and (3) was proven in Theorem 3.7. Statement (2) trivially implies (1). In order to establish this theorem, it will suffice to show that (1) implies (2). To accomplish this, we will show that, given a two-way deterministic finite-state acceptor, M, with end markers, we can find a one-way deterministic acceptor M_1 such that $A(M_1) = A(M)$. We first describe M_1 informally and then give a formal set theoretic description of how M_1 is obtained from M.

Given an input $a_1a_2...a_n$, the one-way machine, M_1, will simulate the two-way machine, M, operating on $¢a_1a_2...a_n\$$, where ¢ and \$ are the end markers for M. The difficulty with this plan is that M_1 gets to read through the input only once, while M may move back and forth several times. M_1 overcomes this problem as follows. In scanning the input $a_1a_2...a_n$, it does two things in parallel. While scanning a_i, it will know the state M would be in the first time M scans a_i. It will compute the state M would be in the first time M scans a_{i+1} and it then carries this information with it when it moves on to a_{i+1}. For the two-way acceptor diagrammed in Figure 3.8, this would yield the following sequence of states: 1, 1, 1, 1, 1, 3b, 3b, 3b, 3b. (The first 1 occurs on ¢, which M_1 never gets to see. M_1 actually starts calculating states with the second 1. M_1 also never gets to see the \$. However, it will still compute this last 3b as part of its last state, the state it "falls off the end" in.) While it is scanning a_i, it also computes a function f from States(M) into States(M) $\cup \{R\}$, where R is a new symbol. For any state q, $f(q) = p$ if, when started on a_i in state q, M will eventually shift right to a_{i+1} and the first time that M shifts its head to a_{i+1}, it will be in state p. If M never shifts its head to a_{i+1}, then $f(q) = R$. Consider the machine M in Example 3.18, and the input $babcbcb$. As indicated in Figure 3.9, $f(1) = 3b$ for the second c. The complete definition of f for this symbol occurrence is:

$$f(1) = 3b, \ f(2) = 3b, \ f(3) = R$$
$$f(3a) = 3a, \ f(3b) = 3b$$
$$f(4a) = R, \ f(4b) = R, \ f(t) = R$$
$$f(y) = R$$

These state-function pairs will be the states of M_1. We have not yet said how M_1 will compute these states of M and these functions f. For now, assume that M_1 can somehow compute them. We wish to show that it is possible to define the accepting states of M_1 so that $A(M_1) = A(M)$. In general, when M_1 moves on to a_{i+1} its state consists of the M state for a_{i+1} and the function for a_i. So when M_1 "falls off" the right-hand end of $a_1 a_2 ... a_n$, it is in state

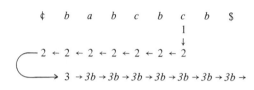

Figure 3.9

(q, f) where q is the state M would be in the first time it moves its head to the right-end marker \$ and where f is the function for a_n. To see if (q, f) is an accepting state, calculate the sequence $p_1, p_2, ..., p_m$ of states that M would be in during each successive time it scans \$. Do this as follows: $p_1 = q$. If $\delta(p_1, \$) = (q_2, \downarrow)$ for some q_2, then $p_2 = q_2$. If $\delta(p_1, \$) = (q_2, \leftarrow)$ for some q_2, then $p_2 = f(q_2)$. In general, if $\delta(p_i, \$) = (q_i, \downarrow)$ for some q_i, then $p_{i+1} = q_i$. If $\delta(p_i, \$) = (q_i, \leftarrow)$, then $p_{i+1} = f(q_i)$. If $\delta(p_i, \$) = (q_i, \leftarrow)$, and $f(q_i) = R$, then the sequence terminates. If $\delta(p_i, \$)$ is undefined, then the sequence terminates. Eventually, either this sequence terminates or else some state is repeated. Once a state is repeated, the sequence will produce no new states but will continually cycle through some fixed sequence of states. Stop this calculation once a repeated state is found. So m will be at most equal to the number of states of M. The two-way machine M would accept the input if one of these states is an accepting state of M. So (q, f) is an accepting state of M_1 if one of these p_i is an accepting state of M.

We still must show how M_1 can update these functions as it shifts from symbol to symbol. If f is the function for a_i, then the function f_+ for a_{i+1} is defined as follows:

(*) Let p be any state of M. $f_+(p) = q$ if there is a sequence $p_1, p_2, ..., p_m$ of states of M such that $p = p_1$, $\delta(p_m, a_{i+1}) = (q, \rightarrow)$ and for each $j < m$, either $\delta(p_j, a_{i+1}) = (p_{j+1}, \downarrow)$ or else there is a state p' such that $\delta(p_j, a_{i+1}) = (p', \cdot)$ and $f(p') = p_{j+1}$.

Note that if there is a sequence $p_1, p_2, ..., p_m$ with the above property, then $p_k \neq p_j$ for $k \neq j$. So m is at most as large as the number of states of M. So there are only a finite number of cases to check in order to compute $f_+(p)$. If no such sequence exists, then $f_+(p) = R$. Also notice that in (*), the description of f_+, does not depend on the numbers i or $i+1$. It only depends on the function f and the symbol a_{i+1}. For example, if a_{i+1} happens to be the symbol c, then to get the definition of f_+ replace a_{i+1} by c in (*). You will then see that both f and c occur in the text of (*) but there is no longer any explicit mention of i or $i+1$ in (*).

We will now give a set theoretic definition of M_1 which follows the above plan. Symbols(M_1) = Symbols(M). The states of M_1 consist of all pairs (p, f), where p is either R or a state of M and f is a total function from States(M) into States$(M) \cup \{R\}$. R may be anything so long as R is not in States(M). The definition of δ_1 = Instructions(M_1) is given in the next paragraph.

For any state (q, f) of M_1 and any symbol a of M_1, $\delta_1((q, f), a) = (g(q), g)$, where g depends on f and a and is defined as follows. For any state p of M, $g(p) = p'$ provided there is a sequence $p_1, p_2, ..., p_m$ of states of M such that $p = p_1$, $\delta(p_m, a) = (p', \rightarrow)$ and for each $j < m$, either $\delta(p_j, a) = (p_{j+1}, \downarrow)$ or else there is a state p'' such that $\delta(p_j, a) = (p'', \leftarrow)$ and $f(p'') = p_{j+1}$. If no such sequence of states exists, then $g(p) = R$. (Recall that δ = Instructions(M).)

The start state of M_1 is $(f_0(s), f_0)$ where s is the start state of M_1 and f_0 is defined in the following way. For any state p of M, $f_0(p) = p'$ provided there is a sequence $p_1, p_2, ..., p_m$ of states of M such that $p = p_1$, $\delta(p_j, \mathcal{c}) = (p_{j+1}, \downarrow)$ for each $j < m$; and $\delta(p_m, \mathcal{c}) = (p', \rightarrow)$. If no such sequence of states exists, then $f_0(p) = R$. The set of accepting states of M_1 is the set of all (q, f) such that there is a sequence $p_1, p_2, ..., p_m$ of states of M with the properties that $p_1 = q$, p_m is an accepting state of M and for each $i < m$, either $\delta(p_i, \$) = (p_{i+1}, \downarrow)$ or else there is a state p' such that $\delta(p_i, \$) = (p', \leftarrow)$ and $f(p') = p_{i+1}$.

The argument to show $A(M_1) = A(M)$ was given in the informal description of M_1. □

EXERCISES

1. Define (one-way) finite-state acceptors to accept each of the following languages:
    a. $\{a^i b^j c^k \mid \text{any } i, j \text{ and } k\}$
    b. $\{(a^3 b^2)^n \mid n \geqslant 0\} \cup \{(a^2 b^3)^n \mid n \geqslant 0\}$
    c. $\{a^n b^n \mid 0 \leqslant n \leqslant 10^{10}\}$

2. Prove: If L is a finite-state language, then L^R is a finite-state language. L^R is the set of all strings α, such that α written backwards is in L. For example, if $L = \{abc, bba\}$, then $L^R = \{cba, abb\}$. (There is an easy proof using a two-way finite-state acceptor but it is more instructive to do the proof using a one-way nondeterministic acceptor.)

3. Prove that the following are not finite-state languages:
   a. $\{a^n b^{2n} \mid n \geq 1\}$
   b. $\{a^n b^m \mid m \geq n \geq 1\} \cup \{a^{2p} \mid p \geq 1\}$
   c. $\{\alpha\alpha^R \mid \alpha \in \{a, b\}^*\}$
      α^R is α written backwards. For example, $(abb)^R = bba$
   d. $\{a^n \mid n = m^2$, for some positive integer $m\}$
   e. $\{\alpha \mid \alpha \in \{a, b\}^*$ and the number of occurrences of a in α is m^2, for some positive integer $m\}$. For example, $abaaba$ is in the language since it has $4 = 2^2$ occurrences of a.
   f. All well-formed parentheses expressions. For example, $()$, $(()())$, and $()()()$ are well-formed $)($, $(())))$, and $(((($ are not well-formed.
   g. All PASCAL programs. (This result is not peculiar to PASCAL but applies to almost any common programming language. Of course, we are assuming that the syntax of any such language allows the possibility of infinitely many programs.)
   h. All English sentences.

4. Prove the following generalization of 3.10, the pumping lemma:
   Theorem. Let M be a (one-way) finite-state acceptor with k states and suppose ξ is in $A(m)$. If any k or more occurrences of symbols in ξ are designated as marked, then ξ can be written in the form $\xi = \alpha\beta\gamma$, where β contains at least one marked occurrence, but no more than k marked occurrences, and where $\alpha\beta^i\gamma$ is in $A(M)$ for all $i \geq 0$.

5. Prove that the following is not a finite-state language (*Hint*: Use Exercise 4): $\{ab^{n_1}ab^{n_2} \ldots ab^{n_m} \mid m = h^2$ for some positive integer h and each $n_i \geq 1\}$.

6. Prove that if L is a finite-state language, then L^* is a finite-state language. (Since this result is used in the proof of Theorem 3.16, it should be proven without using Theorem 3.16.)

7. For any language L, define $\text{Int}(L)$ to be the set of all words x, such that xy is in L, for some word y. Prove that if L is a finite-state language, then so is $\text{Int}(L)$.

8. Show each of the following:
   a. $L((a \vee b)c^*) = L(ac^* \vee bc^*)$
   b. $L(((ac^*)a^*)^*) = L(((aa^*)c^*)^*)$
   c. $L((a^*ab \vee ba)^*a^*) = L((a \vee ab \vee ba)^*)$

9. Define one-way nondeterministic finite-state acceptors to accept each of the languages in Exercise 8.

10. Give regular expressions to describe each of the following languages.
   a. $\{a^i b^j c^k \mid$ any $i, j, k\}$
   b. $\{(a^2b)^n \mid n \geq 0\} \cup \{ab^n \mid n \geq 0\}^*$
   c. $\{a^n \mid n \geq 1\}$

11. Prove Lemma 3.15.

12. As defined in Definition 3.13, regular expressions are fully parenthesized. One can get by with fewer parentheses and still have readability. For example, $(ab)c$ and $((a \lor b) \lor c)$ could be written as abc and $a \lor b \lor c$, respectively, without being misunderstood. Define a cfg that generates all regular expressions as defined in Definition 3.13 plus all "regular expressions" with excess parentheses deleted.

13. Prove that, for every finite-state language L, there is a nondeterministic finite-state acceptor M such that $L = A(M)$ and the state diagram of M (of the type in Figure 3.3) is planar. By planar, we mean that it can be drawn on a piece of paper in such a way that none of the arcs from states to states crosses any other such arcs. (*Hint*: Use the proof of Theorem 3.16.)

14. Let M be a two-way deterministic finite-state acceptor. Define $A'(M)$ to be the set of all strings ξ such that $(s, \rhd \mathrm{\textcent} \xi \$) \mathrel{|\!\!\overset{*}{\underset{M}{}}} (p, \alpha \rhd \beta)$, for some accepting state p and some α, β. Here s is the start state and $\mathrm{\textcent}$, $\$$ are the end markers. Prove that the following two statements are equivalent for any language L: (a) $L = A'(M')$ for some two-way deterministic finite-state acceptor M'; (b) $L = A(M)$ for some two-way deterministic finite-state acceptor M.

15. Give a formal definition of *two-way, nondeterministic finite-state acceptor with end markers*. Prove: If M is a two-way, nondeterministic finite-state acceptor with end markers, then there is a deterministic (one-way) finite-state acceptor M' such that $A(M) = A(M')$. (*Hint*: This is hard but is like other proofs you have seen.)

16. Prove that the set of all finite-state acceptors with states which are natural numbers and with input alphabet $\{0, 1\}$ can be put into one-to-one correspondence with the natural numbers. (*Hint*: This is not really hard but it can be long and tedious.)

17. Let f be a mapping from the set of finite-state acceptors discussed in Exercise 16 onto the natural numbers and such that f is a one-to-one correspondence. Let $(f(M))_2$ denote the binary numeral for the number $f(M)$. Let $L = \{(f(M))_2 \mid M$ is a finite-state acceptor as in Exercise 16 and $(f(M))_2 \notin A(M)\}$. Prove that L is not a finite-state language. (*Hint*: If you identify M with $(f(M))_2$, then L is something like the set of finite-state acceptors which reject themselves. Try a proof by contradiction. The pumping lemma is not likely to be useful here.)

18. Let M be the finite-state acceptor described in Figure 3.3 and let $L = A(M)$. Use the algorithm given in the proof of Theorem 3.6 to obtain a cfg G such that $L(G) = L$.

19. Prove: L is a finite-state language if and only if $L = L(G)$ for some cfg G such that all productions are in one of the following forms: $A \rightarrow aB$, $A \rightarrow a$, $A \rightarrow \Lambda$ where A, B are nonterminals and a is a terminal. (*Hint:* Half of this is proven in Theorem 3.6.)

20. Prove: If L is a cfl, a is a single symbol and $L \subseteq \{a\}^*$, then L is a finite-state language. (*Hint:* Use the pumping lemma for cfl's.)

Chapter Four

Finite-State Transducers

Finite-state acceptors do not have output or, at least, have only very rudimentary output. The acceptance of an input is a type of output but a very restricted type of output. We want to extend the notion of finite-state machines so as to allow them to output a string of symbols. This type of finite-state machine is called a *finite-state transducer*. A finite-state transducer is basically a one-way finite-state acceptor which has the additional feature of being able to output a symbol every time it reads an input symbol. The final output string is the concatenation of all these symbols. A valid intuition is to think of the transducer as a kind of one-way finite-state acceptor with the additional feature of an output tape. Like the acceptor, the transducer operates in discrete time. In a single step, the transducer either reads one input symbol or decides to make that step without reading any input; on the basis of its current state and the symbol read (if any), it changes state and writes at most one symbol on the output tape. The symbols on the output tape are written from left to right as the transducer goes from step to step. Notice that, unlike a one-way finite-state acceptor, the transducer may make a move (change state and write output) without reading any input symbol. When this happens we say the transducer has moved under input Λ, the empty string. If the transducer were not allowed to move under input Λ, then the length of every output string would be bounded by the length of its corresponding input string. Other reasons for allowing these Λ moves will become apparent as the theory progresses. Some special care is required in interpreting the output of these machines. The only computations that are considered successful are those which end in an accepting state. The only output strings which are considered valid are those which come from computations that end in an accepting state. If the computation does not end in an accepting state, the output is discarded. There are several reasons for this feature. It allows the machine to anticipate future input and to abort the computation if the expected input does not arrive. It also allows the transducer to do an additional computation, without input, after it has read the entire input string. Without accepting states, it would be difficult to know when this type of computation has ended. Finally, it should be noted that a finite-state transducer may be a nondeterministic device. Each input can give rise to several different outputs. The accepting states allow the machine to pick out certain of these outputs as valid and reject the rest. Below are the formal details.

DEFINITIONS AND EXAMPLES

4.1 Definition

4.1.1 A (*nondeterministic*) *finite-state transducer* is a six-tuple $M = (S, \Sigma, \Gamma, \delta, s, Y)$, where S is a finite set of *states*, Σ and Γ are finite sets of symbols called the *input* and *output alphabets* respectively, s is an element of S called the *start state*, Y is a subset of S called the set of *accepting states*, and δ is a partial function from $S \times (\Sigma \cup \{\Lambda\})$ into finite subsets of $S \times (\Gamma \cup \{\Lambda\})$. The function δ is called the *transition function* and is constrained so that $\delta(q, \Lambda)$ is empty for all accepting states q. By analogy to finite-state acceptors, we will write States(M) for S, In-symbols(M) for Σ, Out-symbols(M) for Γ, Instructions(M) for δ, Start(M) for s, and Accepting-states(M) for Y.

We think of M as scanning the input strings from left to right, one symbol at a time. If (q, b) is in $\delta(p, a)$, where a is in the input alphabet, then this is to be interpreted to mean that M, when scanning a in state p, may go to state q, output b and advance to the next input. If (q, b) is in $\delta(p, \Lambda)$, then this is to be interpreted to mean that whenever M is in state p it may, no matter what the scanned input symbol is, change to state q, output b and continue to scan the same input symbol.

4.1.2 An *id* of M is a triple (p, β, γ), where p is a state of M, β is in [In-symbols(M)]*, and γ is in [Out-symbols(M)]*. The interpretation of p and β is the same as for a finite-state acceptor. M is in state p and β is that portion of the input that still remains to be scanned. That portion of the output string produced so far is represented by γ.

4.1.3 The *next step relation* $|_{\overline{M}}$ is a binary relation on id's and is defined as follows. For any a in [In-symbols(M)] $\cup \{\Lambda\}$, any states p, q, any string β of input symbols, any string γ of output symbols, and any b in [Out-symbols(M)] $\cup \{\Lambda\}$, the relation $(p, a\beta, \gamma) |_{\overline{M}} (q, \beta, \gamma b)$ holds provided (q, b) is in $\delta(p, a)$. The relation $|_{\overline{M}}^{*}$ holds between two id's if M can go from the first to the second id in some finite (possibly zero) number of steps.

Computations of transducers are defined by exact analogy to computations of one-way finite-state acceptors. A *computation* of M on the input α is a finite or infinite sequence of id's such that (s, α, Λ) is the first id, the relation $|_{\overline{M}}$ holds between consecutive id's, and, if the sequence is finite, then the last id is a halting id. An id is called a *halting id* if there is no next id under the relation $\vdash_{\overline{M}}$. Unlike one-way finite-state acceptors, transducers can move without consuming an input symbol. So, unlike one-way finite-state acceptors, transducers can have infinitely long computations.

4.1.4 M is said to be *deterministic* provided that the following two conditions hold for every state p:

1. $\delta(p, a)$ contains at most one element for each a in [In-symbols(M)] $\cup$ $\{\Lambda\}$.
2. If $\delta(p, \Lambda)$ is nonempty, then $\delta(p, a)$ is empty for each input symbol a.

If we did not insist on (2), then there would be situations in which two instructions apply, one for Λ and one for the input symbol scanned.

If M is deterministic and $\delta(p, a) = \{(q, b)\}$, we will omit the braces and write $\delta(p, a) = (q, b)$.

Notice that a deterministic finite-state transducer is a special type of nondeterministic finite-state transducer. The situation and the usage of the modifiers *deterministic* and *nondeterministic* are exactly analogous to those of finite-state acceptors.

4.1.5 Let α be a string of input symbols and γ a string of output symbols. We say that γ is a *valid output* for the input string α provided that $(s, \alpha, \Lambda) \vdash_{\overline{M}}^{*}$ (p, Λ, γ), for some accepting state p. (Recall that $s = $ Start(M).) In this case, the computation $(s, \alpha, \Lambda) \vdash_{\overline{M}}^{*} (p, \Lambda, \gamma)$ is called an *acceptable computation*.

4.1.6 Let f be a partial function from [In-symbols(M)]* into [Out-symbols(M)]*. M is said to *compute the partial function f* provided that conditions (1), (2), and (3) hold for all input stings α.

1. $f(\alpha)$ is defined if and only if M has some valid output for α.
2. For any input α, M has at most one valid output.
3. If $f(\alpha)$ is defined, then $f(\alpha)$ is the valid output for the input α.

A partial function f which can be computed by some finite-state transducer is called a *finite-state transduction*. If it can be computed by a deterministic finite-state transducer, then it is called a *deterministic finite-state transduction*.

One can argue that moves under Λ are not natural and that a move of the transducer should always depend on the symbol scanned. We have allowed moves under Λ because it is mathematically convenient and because it is consistent with the other literature on the subject. However, this is just a convention of convenience; our definition is equivalent to one in which the move depends on the symbol scanned and allows the possibility of not advancing the input.

4.2 Examples

4.2.1 M, defined as follows, is a deterministic finite-state transducer that performs binary addition. States$(M) = \{<$carry$>, <$no carry$>\}$. The input symbols of M consist of the symbol ¢, together with all pairs of 0's and 1's. That is, In-symbols$(M) = \{\phi\} \cup [\{0, 1\} \times \{0, 1\}]$. The output symbols of M are 0 and 1. The start state is $<$no carry$>$. The state $<$no carry$>$ is also the only accepting state. The transition function δ is defined by Table 4.1. If $\delta(q, x) = \{(p, y)\}$, then q, x, p and y are in the first, second, third, and fourth columns respectively. For any input of the form

$$(a_1, b_1) \ (a_2, b_2) \ ... \ (a_n, b_n)\phi$$

M has a valid output consisting of the binary numeral obtained by adding the two binary numerals $a_n a_{n-1}...a_1$ and $b_n b_{n-1}...b_1$. The output and input are written backwards. That is, the low-order bit is on the left end.

Table 4.1

q State	x Input	p Next state	y Output
$<$no carry$>$	$<0, 0>$	$<$no carry$>$	0
$<$no carry$>$	$<1, 0>$	$<$no carry$>$	1
$<$no carry$>$	$<0, 1>$	$<$no carry$>$	1
$<$no carry$>$	$<1, 1>$	$<$carry$>$	0
$<$no carry$>$	ϕ	$<$no carry$>$	Λ
$<$carry$>$	$<0, 0>$	$<$no carry$>$	1
$<$carry$>$	$<1, 0>$	$<$carry$>$	0
$<$carry$>$	$<0, 1>$	$<$carry$>$	0
$<$carry$>$	$<1, 1>$	$<$carry$>$	1
$<$carry$>$	ϕ	$<$no carry$>$	1

4.2.2 Next we give an example of a nondeterministic finite-state transducer that computes the partial function f defined by the equations: $f(a^i b^j) = b^i a^j$, $f(a^i c^j) = c^i a^j$ for all positive integers i and j. The function f is undefined for all other arguments. Let M be defined by State$(M) = \{0, <1b>, <1c>, <2b>, <2c>\}$, In-symbols$(M)$ = Out-symbols(M) = $\{a, b, c\}$, the start state is 0, the accepting states are $<2b>$, $<2c>$, and the

Table 4.2

State	Input	Next state	Output
0	a	$<1c>$	c
0	a	$<1b>$	b
$<1c>$	a	$<1c>$	c
$<1b>$	a	$<1b>$	b
$<1c>$	c	$<2c>$	a
$<1b>$	b	$<2b>$	a
$<2c>$	c	$<2c>$	a
$<2b>$	b	$<2b>$	a

transition function δ is defined in Table 4.2.

The value of the transition function, $\delta(p, x)$, is empty for all pairs p and x which do not occur in Table 4.2. The transducer is nondeterministic because $\delta(0, a)$ contains two instructions, $(<1c>, c)$ and $(<1b>, b)$. Below are two computations of M on the input a^2b. The first has a valid output; the other does not.

$$(0, a^2b, \Lambda) \mid\!- (<1b>, ab, b) \mid\!- (<1b>, b, b^2) \mid\!- (<2b>, \Lambda, b^2a)$$
$$(0, a^2b, \Lambda) \mid\!- (<1c>, ab, c) \mid\!- (<1c>, b, c^2)$$

The second computation ends without processing the entire input string.

*THE PUMPING LEMMA FOR FINITE-STATE TRANSDUCERS

The remainder of this chapter is devoted to showing that there are many common functions which cannot be computed by finite-state transducers. The techniques used are the same as those we used to show that certain languages are not finite-state languages. The fundamental result is again a pumping lemma.

4.3 Theorem (The Pumping Lemma for Transducers) Suppose M is a nondeterministic finite-state transducer with k states, ξ is a string over the output alphabet of M, length$(\xi) \geqslant k$, and both p and q are states of M. If $(p, \Lambda, \Lambda) \mid\!\frac{*}{M} (q, \Lambda, \xi)$, then ξ can be written in the form $\xi = \alpha\beta\gamma$, where β is nonempty and $(p, \Lambda, \Lambda) \mid\!\frac{*}{M} (q, \Lambda, \alpha\beta^i\gamma)$, for all integers $i \geqslant 0$.

PROOF The idea is the same as that for 3.10, the pumping lemma for finite-state acceptors. If $\text{length}(\xi) \geq k$, then M must make at least k moves in which it outputs a symbol and so M must pass through at least $k+1$ states. But M has only k states. So there must be some state such that, on at least two occasions in the computation, M enters this state. Thus ξ can be written $\xi = \alpha\beta\gamma$ where β is nonempty and

$$(p, \Lambda, \Lambda) \mid_{\overline{M}}^* (p_2, \Lambda, \alpha) \mid_{\overline{M}}^* (p_2, \Lambda, \alpha\beta) \mid_{\overline{M}}^* (q, \Lambda, \alpha\beta\gamma) = (q, \Lambda, \xi)$$

for some state p_2. Since M can go from state p_2 back to state p_2 and output β in the process, it follows that, for any $i \geq 0$, M can go from state p_2 back to state p_2 i times and output β^i in the process. So

$$(p, \Lambda, \Lambda) \mid_{\overline{M}}^* (p_2, \Lambda, \alpha) \mid_{\overline{M}}^* (p_2, \Lambda, \alpha\beta^i) \mid_{\overline{M}}^* (q, \Lambda, \alpha\beta^i\gamma) \quad \square$$

The pumping lemma for transducers actually applies in a slightly more general setting than that given in the statement of the theorem. Let M, p, q, and ξ be as in the statement of the theorem. Let ν and μ be any strings over the input alphabet and output alphabet of M respectively. Now suppose $(p, \nu, \mu) \mid_{\overline{M}}^* (q, \nu, \mu\xi)$. Since the computation does not depend on ν and μ, we can conclude that $(p, \Lambda, \Lambda) \mid_{\overline{M}}^* (q, \Lambda, \xi)$ and so, by Theorem 4.3, we can conclude that $\xi = \alpha\beta\gamma$, where β is nonempty and $(p, \Lambda, \Lambda) \mid_{\overline{M}}^* (q, \Lambda, \alpha\beta^i\gamma)$ for all $i \geq 0$. But, if $(p, \Lambda, \Lambda) \mid_{\overline{M}}^* (q, \Lambda, \alpha\beta^i\gamma)$, then $(p, \nu, \mu) \mid_{\overline{M}}^* (q, \nu, \mu\alpha\beta^i\gamma)$, since the computation does not depend on ν and μ. Hence, if we know that $(p, \nu, \mu) \mid_{\overline{M}}^* (q, \nu, \mu\xi)$, then we can conclude that $(p, \nu, \mu) \mid_{\overline{M}}^* (q, \nu, \mu\alpha\beta^i\gamma)$ for all i. In fact, the only reason for setting $\mu = \nu = \Lambda$ in the theorem and proof was to simplify notation. The proof given would work fine if we just carried ν and μ along throughout. We will frequently use the pumping lemma for transducers in just this sort of situation, where ν or μ are not empty.

4.4 Theorem There are functions f such that f is computed by a nondeterministic finite-state transducer but f is not computed by any deterministic finite-state transducer.

PROOF The transducer given in Example 4.2.2 is a nondeterministic finite-state transducer which computes the partial function f defined by the equations:

$$f(a^i b^j) = b^i a^j, \quad f(a^i c^j) = c^i a^j \quad \text{for all positive } i \text{ and } j$$

The function f is undefined for other arguments.

We will use 4.3, the pumping lemma, to show that f is not computed by any deterministic finite-state transducer. Assume M is a deterministic finite-state transducer and M computes f. We will derive a contradiction. Consider the input $a^{k+1}b$, where k is the number of states in M. We first establish a preliminary result.

Claim: M will not output any symbols until it reads the b in the input $a^{k+1}b$.

The first symbol outputted on this input is b. M is deterministic. Hence, if M outputs a symbol before reading the b, then the first symbol outputted on any input which begins with a^{k+1} is a b. But this is impossible, since it implies that the first symbol of the valid output string for the input string $a^{k+1}c$ is b; the first symbol of the valid output for $a^{k+1}c$ is a c, since M computes $f(a^{k+1}c) = c^{k+1}a$. So the claim is established.

M can output at most one symbol when it reads the last b in $a^{k+1}b$. Thus, by the Claim, M must output $b^k a$ after it reads the entire input $a^{k+1}b$. (It may, in fact, output all of $b^{k+1}a$ after reading the entire input. The point is that at least the last $k+1$ symbols of output are outputted after all the input is read.) So $(s, a^{k+1}b, \Lambda) \mid^*_M (p, \Lambda, b) \mid^*_M (q, \Lambda, bb^k a)$ is a valid computation, where s is the start state of M, q is some accepting state of M, and p is some intermediate state in the computation. Setting $b^k a = \xi$ in the pumping lemma for transducers, we conclude that $b^k a = \alpha\beta\gamma$ when β is nonempty and $(s, a^{k+1}b, \Lambda) \mid^*_M (q, \Lambda, b\alpha\beta^i\gamma)$ is valid for all $i \geq 0$. But q is an accepting state. So M has infinitely many valid outputs for the input $a^{k+1}b$. This contradicts the fact that M computes f, and thus has only one valid output for $a^{k+1}b$. We have derived a contradiction. Hence, the assumption that some deterministic transducer computes f is false, and the proof of the theorem is completed. $\square$

Before leaving Theorem 4.4, we should note that we could find a total function which is computed by a nondeterministic finite-state transducer but is not computed by any deterministic finite-state transducer . If we extend f such that $f(\alpha) = \Lambda$, for all α which previously were undefined, then the above proof still shows that f is not computed by any deterministic finite-state transducer. It is an easy exercise to modify Example 4.2.2 to get a nondeterministic transducer that computes this total function.

*THE MULTIPLICATION FUNCTION

The next result shows that one of the most fundamental arithmetic functions cannot be computed by a finite-state transducer.

4.5 Theorem No finite-state transducer can do multiplication. More precisely, there does not exist any deterministic or nondeterministic finite-state transducer which computes a function f with the following properties.

1. f is a function from $(\{0,1\} \times \{0, 1\})^*$ into $\{0, 1\}^*$
2. $f(<a_1, b_1> <a_2, b_2>...<a_n, b_n>) = c_1 c_2...c_m$ where $c_m c_{m-1}...c_1$ is the binary numeral (without leading zeros) obtained by multiplying the two binary numerals $a_n a_{n-1}...a_1$ and $b_n b_{n-1}...b_1$.

A number of points should be emphasized about this result. In order to prove that finite-state transducers cannot do multiplication, we must have a precise way to state the problem. The result, though, does not depend on our choice of how to formalize the problem. It would remain true for any reasonable way of formalizing the phrase "no finite-state transducer can multiply numbers written in the ordinary way." For example, it does not help to give the transducer end markers. Also, if the transducer reads the input in high-order bit first instead of low-order bit first, it still could not multiply the numerals. We have also insisted that the two numerals to be multiplied are of the same length. This is just a technical point. By using leading zeros, we can get any two numbers as input. Finally, the choice of base two is purely a notational convenience. The theorem is true for any base.

In order to prove Theorem 4.5, we will need a lemma.

4.6 Lemma Suppose M is a finite-state transducer with k states and suppose that M computes some partial function f. Then, in every acceptable computation, M never outputs more than k symbols without reading an input symbol. That is, if $(p_0, \rho\eta, \Lambda) \overset{*}{\mid-} (p_1, \eta, \nu) \overset{*}{\mid-} (p_2, \eta, \nu\xi) \overset{*}{\mid-} (p_3, \Lambda, \nu\xi\mu)$ is an acceptable computation, then length$(\xi) < k$.

PROOF The proof is by contradiction. We will assume that the lemma is false for some finite-state transducer M which computes some partial function f and will go on to derive a contradiction. With this in mind, suppose there is an acceptable computation as described in the lemma, except that length$(\xi) \geqslant k$. Then, applying the Pumping Lemma 4.3 to the partial computation,

$$(p_1, \eta, \nu) \overset{*}{\mid-} (p_2, \eta, \nu\xi)$$

it follows that $\xi = \alpha\beta\gamma$, where β is nonempty and

$$(p_1, \eta, \nu) \overset{*}{\mid-} (p_2, \eta, \nu\alpha\beta^i\gamma)$$

for all i. So, for all i,

$$(p_0, \rho\eta, \Lambda) \overset{*}{\mid-} (p_3, \Lambda, \nu\alpha\beta^i\gamma\mu)$$

is an acceptable computation. So M has infinitely many valid outputs for the input $\rho\eta$. This is a contradiction, since M computes f and so has only one valid output, namely $f(\rho\eta)$, for the input $\rho\eta$. $\square$

Proof of Theorem 4.5

Suppose there is a finite-state transducer M that computes the function f described in the statement of Theorem 4.5. We will derive a contradiction and therefore show that there can be no such M. We will look at what M does on inputs of the form:

3. $<0, 1> <a_1, 0> <a_2, 0> \ldots <a_{n-1}, 0> <a_n, 0> <1, 1>$

That is, we will see what happens when M tries to multiply the two binary numerals $1a_n a_{n-1} \ldots a_1 0$ and $10^n 1$, for suitability chosen binary digits a_i. Since the product of these two numerals is $1a_n a_{n-1} \ldots a_1 1 a_n a_{n-1} \ldots a_1 0$, the only valid output should be $0a_1 a_2 \ldots a_n 1 a_1 a_2 \ldots a_n 1$.

Let k be the number of states for M. Choose $n > k$ and consider a computation that produces such a valid output. We focus our attention on what happens after the substring $0a_1a_2...a_n1$ has been outputted. Using Lemma 4.6 we can make some observations about how much of the input has been read at this point in the computation. Since $n > k$, M must have read at least the first symbol $<0, 1>$. Since there are still $n + 1$ symbols left to be outputted and $n > k$, M must not yet have read the last symbol $<1, 1>$. Hence we can decompose the computation as follows:

4. $(s, <0, 1> <a_1, 0> <a_2, 0> ... <a_{n-1}, 0> <a_n, 0> <1, 1>, \Lambda) \vdash^*$
    $(q, <a_t, 0> <a_{t+1}, 0>...<a_{n-1}, 0> <a_n, 0> <1, 1>, 0a_1a_2...a_n1) \vdash^*$
    $(p, \Lambda, 0a_1a_2...a_n 1a_1a_2...a_n1)$

where s is the start state, p is an accepting state, q is some state, and $t \leqslant n$.

There are 2^n such strings $a_1a_2...a_n$ of binary digits and only $k < n < 2^n$ states. So, two distinct such input strings must leave M in the same state q at this point in the computation. That is, there are two distinct strings $a_1a_2...a_n$ and $a'_1a'_2...a'_n$ such that (4) above and (5) below hold.

5. $(s, <0, 1> <a'_1, 0> <a'_2, 0>...<a'_{n-1}, 0> <a'_n, 0> <1, 1>, \Lambda) \vdash^*$
    $(q, <a'_{t'}, 0> <a'_{t'+1}, 0>...<a'_{n-1}, 0> <a'_n, 0> <1, 1>,$
    $\qquad 0a'_1a'_2...a'_n1) \vdash^* (p', \Lambda, 0a'_1a'_2...a'_n 1a'_1a'_2...a'_n1)$

where s is again the start state, p' is an accepting state, q is the same state as in (4) and $t' \leqslant n$. Combining (4) and (5), we see that the following computation produces a valid output.

6. $(s, <0, 1> <a_1, 0> <a_2, 0>...<a_{t-1}, 0> <a'_{t'}, 0> <a'_{t'+1}, 0>...$
    $...<a'_{n-1}, 0><a'_n, 0> <1, 1>, \Lambda) \vdash^* (q, <a'_{t'}, 0> <a'_{t'+1}, 0>...$
    $...<a'_{n-1}, 0><a'_n, 0> <1, 1>, 0a_1a_2...a_n1) \vdash^*$
    $(p', \Lambda, 0a_1a_2...a_n 1a'_1a'_2...a'_n1)$

From (6) it follows that:

7. The product of the two binary numerals
    $1a'_na'_{n-1}...a'_{t'}a_{t-1}a_{t-2}...a_10$ and 10^m1 is
    $1a'_na'_{n-1}...a'_11a_na_{n-1}...a_10$

The value of m is the number of digits written as a_i or a_j', for some i or j. (It will turn out that $m = n$ but we are not yet justified in concluding this, since we have not yet determined that $t = t'$.) If we perform the multiplication mentioned in (7) by the usual multiplication algorithm, we get another expression for the product. Equating these two expressions for the product, we conclude that

8. $1a'_na'_{n-1}...a'_11a_na_{n-1}...a_10 =$
    $\qquad\qquad 1a'_na'_{n-1}...a'_{t'}a_{t-1}a_{t-2}...a_11a'_na'_{n-1}...a'_{t'}a_{t-1}a_{t-2}...a_10$
    From (8) it follows that

$\qquad t = t'$ and $a'_na'_{n-1}...a'_1 = a'_na'_{n-1}...a'_{t'}a_{t-1}a_{t-2}...a_1 = a_na_{n-1}...a_1$

So $a'_1a'_2...a'_n = a_1a_2...a_n$. But this is a contradiction, since $a_1a_2...a_n$ and $a'_1a'_2...a'_n$ were chosen to be distinct. Since we derived a contradiction, no such M can exist. □

EXERCISES

1. Define a deterministic finite-state transducer to do binary subtraction.

2. Define a deterministic finite-state transducer that converts base-two numerals into base-eight numerals.

3. Prove that the following functions are not finite-state transductions: $f(\alpha) = \alpha\alpha$, for all $\alpha \in \{a, b\}^*$; $g(\alpha) = \alpha\alpha^R$, for all $\alpha \in \{a, b\}^*$. Recall that α^R denotes α written backwards.

4. Prove that no finite-state transducer can convert base-two numerals into base-ten numerals.

5. Prove: If f is any partial function and n is any integer, then we can find a deterministic finite-state transducer "with end markers" which computes a function h such that h and f agree for all input strings of length at most n, that is, for all α of length at most n:
    a. $h(\alpha\mathcal{c})$ is defined if and only if $f(\alpha)$ is defined and
    b. if $f(\alpha)$ is defined, then $f(\alpha) = h(\alpha\mathcal{c})$, where $\mathcal{c}$ is a new symbol.

6. Prove: If f is a finite-state transduction, then there is an integer m such that the following holds for all arguments α for which $\alpha \neq \Lambda$ and for which $f(\alpha)$ is defined: $\text{length}(f(\alpha)) \leqslant m \text{ length}(\alpha)$.

7. Formalize and prove the following statement: The exponentiation functions cannot be computed by any finite-state transducers.

8. Prove that the logarithm functions are not finite-state transductions.

9. Formalize and prove the following statement: No finite-state transducer can do division.

10. Let M be a deterministic two-way finite-state acceptor. The states of M may be any well-defined mathematical entities. Suppose it turns out that the states of M just happen to be symbols over some alphabet which is disjoint from the input alphabet of M. Let f be the function on "coded id's" of M which is defined as follows:

    $f(\alpha p\beta) = \alpha'p'\beta'$, provided p, p' are states of M, provided α, β, α' and β' are strings of M and provided $(p, \alpha \triangleright \beta) \mid_{\overline{M}} (p', \alpha' \triangleright \beta')$. So f is really just $\mid_{\overline{M}}$ with some notational changes which allow id's to be represented as strings of symbols rather than ordered pairs. Design a deterministic finite-state transducer which computes f.

11. Prove: L is a finite-state language if and only if $L = f^{-1}$ (*yes*) for some finite-state transduction f. By definition, f^{-1} (*yes*) $= \{\alpha \mid f(\alpha) = yes\}$. By *yes* we mean the string with the three letters $y-e-s$.

12. Prove: If f is a finite-state transduction and L is a finite-state language, then $f^{-1}(L)$ is a finite-state language. By definition, $f^{-1}(L) = \{\alpha \mid f(\alpha)$ is in $L\}$.

13. Prove: If L is a finite-state language and f is a finite-state transduction, then $f(L)$ is a finite-state language. By definition, $f(L) = \{\gamma \mid \gamma = f(\alpha)$ for some α in $L\}$. (*Hint*: There is a lot of detail in this one.)

14. Prove: The *composition* of finite-state transductions yields another finite-state transduction. In other words: Let Σ, Γ and Δ be three alphabets. Let g, respectively f, be a finite-state transduction from Σ^* to Γ^*, respectively from Γ^* to Δ^*. Define the partial function h from Σ^* to Δ^* by $h(\alpha) = f(g(\alpha))$ provided both $g(\alpha)$ and $f(g(\alpha))$ are defined; $h(\alpha)$ is undefined otherwise. It then follows that h is a finite-state transduction. (*Hint*: This is not too hard but there can be a lot of detail to worry about.)

15. Define a *finite-state transducer of type 2* to be the same as a finite-state transducer (4.1.1), except that δ is a partial function from $S \times \Sigma$ into finite subsets of $S \times (\Gamma \cup \{\Lambda\}) \times \{\rightarrow, \downarrow\}$. Interpret $(q, b, \rightarrow) \in \delta(p, a)$ to mean that, in state p scanning input symbol a, the transducer can go to state q, output b and advance to the next symbol. Interpret $(q, b, \downarrow) \in \delta(p, a)$ in the same way except that the transducer does not advance to the next symbol. Define what it means for a finite-state transducer of type 2 to compute a function in the same way as for ordinary finite-state transducers. Prove that for any partial function $f : f$ is computed by a finite-state transducer of type 2 if and only if it is computed by an ordinary finite-state transducer.

16. Let Σ and Γ be two finite alphabets. A *homomorphism* from Σ^* to Γ^* is a mapping h such that $h(a_1 a_2 ... a_n) = h(a_1) h(a_2) ... h(a_n)$ whenever $a_1, a_2, ..., a_n$ are letters in Σ. A homomorphism is completely determined by its value on individual letters in Σ.
    Assume that h is a homomorphism from Σ^* to Γ^* and prove that
    a. h is a finite-state transduction and
    b. if $L \subseteq \Sigma^*$ is a cfl, then $h(L) = \{h(w) \mid w \in L\}$ is also a cfl.

Chapter
Five

Turing Machines
and Computable
Functions

In this chapter we introduce a formal mathematical construct that captures the intuitive notion of an effective procedure. The model is called a Turing machine and is named after its originator, Alan M. Turing. The model is very simple. This is very convenient for developing a mathematical theory. However, its simplicity may lead you to question whether such a simple construct can really accomplish all the tasks that can, in an intuitive sense, be done by an effective procedure. To help demonstrate that Turing machines can model any effective procedure, we will develop a programming language with strong expressive power and then prove that any program written in this programming language can be translated into a Turing machine that accomplishes the same task. If you believe that any effective procedure can be expressed in this programming language, then it will follow that any effective procedure can be expressed with the Turing machine model. The intuitive notion of an effective procedure is somewhat vague, and certainly not a formal mathematical construct. So we will not be able to prove mathematically that any effective procedure can be expressed in this programming language. However, this programming language is powerful enough and enough like some common general-purpose programming languages that it should be intuitively clear that any effective procedure can be written in this programming language. We will actually define three programming languages, each one successively more sophisticated. The last of the three will look very much like the programming language PASCAL, and it will have the expressive power we promised. Before giving any formal definitions, we will give an informal description of the Turing machine model.

THE TURING MACHINE MODEL

A Turing machine is similar to a two-way finite-state acceptor. It differs from a two-way finite-state acceptor in that it is allowed to write as well as read on the tape containing the input. In order to allow the Turing machine to write an arbitrarily long string, the tape containing the input extends infinitely far in both directions. At the start of a computation, the tape contains the input string and all of the tape except for the portion containing the input is blank. This should not sound like a totally unreasonable definition for a machine that is designed to capture the notion of an effective procedure. When discussing finite-state acceptors, we said that such acceptors could not model effective procedures because they did not have access to an unbounded storage facility for storing intermediate results. To get the Turing machine model from the finite-state acceptor model, we have merely added such a storage facility in the simplest way possible. In the next few paragraphs we make this definition a little bit more precise. We then go on to give a formal mathematical definition of the Turing machine model.

A Turing machine is a finite-state machine attached to a storage tape that is infinitely long in both directions. The finite-state machine may be any device so long as it is finite, discrete, and communicates with the tape in the appropriate manner. The finite-state machine is usually referred to as the *finite-state control*. The tape is divided into squares. Each square of the tape is capable of holding any one symbol from a fixed specified finite tape alphabet. One element of the tape alphabet is distinguished to serve as the blank symbol. The finite-state control communicates with the tape by means of a device called the *tape head*. The tape head may be positioned at any one square of the tape. Using the tape head, the finite-state control can read the single symbol at the tape head location and may change this symbol to any symbol in the tape alphabet. Figure 5.1 is a diagrammatic representation of a Turing machine. The Turing machine, like the previously discussed machine models, operates in discrete time. In one time unit, the finite-state control can move the tape head a maximum of one square left or right. As with two-way finite-state acceptors, we think of the tape as being stationary and the tape head as moving. Despite our intuitive view of a stationary tape and a moving head, it is still true that the tape mechanism is similar to an ordinary magnetic tape drive as used on many common computers. The only difference is that a Turing machine must move its head only one square per unit time. There are no fast rewind facilities.

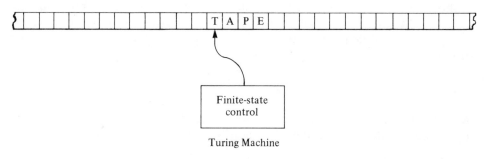

Turing Machine

Figure 5.1

At any point in time, the finite-state control will be in one state and the tape head will be scanning one symbol on the tape. On the basis of this state and this symbol, the machine will change the symbol scanned to some, possibly different, symbol, will shift the tape head a maximum of one square left or right, and will change the state of the finite-state control to some, possibly different, state. All this constitutes a single move of the Turing machine. For now we will assume that there is always at most one move possible. So, for the present, we are only considering deterministic machines.

One state is designated as the start state and a subset of all the states is designated as the set of accepting states. We will always insist that the machine halt when the finite-state control enters an accepting state. A computation of a Turing machine proceeds in much the same way as that of a two-way finite-state acceptor, except that the tape may be written on and that there is a way to get arbitrary strings as output. The input is a string of nonblank symbols from the tape alphabet. Initially, the input string is written on the tape, preceded and followed by an infinite string of blanks, the tape head is positioned at the first symbol of the input string, and the finite-state control is placed in the start state. The computation proceeds in discrete steps as described above. There will be an output only if the machine halts in a particular configuration. If the machine halts with the tape head scanning the first symbol of a blank-free string β, with the rest of the tape blank, and with the finite-state control in an accepting state, then β is the output. In any other situation, there is no output. In particular, there is no output if the machine halts with the finite-state con-trol in some nonaccepting state or if the machine halts with the tape head posi-tioned any place other than at the first symbol of a unique blank-free string on the tape. There will be a convention to allow the empty string as output, but that need not concern us in this informal description. The convention on where the tape head must be is purely for mathematical convenience. Any other reasonable convention would give similar results. We now give a formal mathematical definition of these concepts.

5.1 Definitions

5.1.1 A (*simple*) *Turing machine* is a six-tuple $M = (S, \Sigma, \delta, s, B, Y)$ where S is a finite set of *states*, Σ is a finite set of symbols referred to as the *tape alphabet*, s is an element of S called the *start state*, B is an element of Σ called the *blank symbol*, and Y is a subset of S called the *accepting states*. The third element, δ, may be any partial function from $S \times \Sigma$ into $S \times \Sigma \times \{\leftarrow, \rightarrow, \downarrow\}$ provided that $\delta(q, a)$ is undefined whenever q is in Y. The function δ is called the *transition function*. If $\delta(p_1, a_1) = (p_2, a_2, \rightarrow)$, then this is to be interpreted to mean the following. If the finite control of M is in state p_1 and the tape head is scanning symbol a_1, then M will do all of the following in one move: replace a_1 by a_2, change the state of its finite control to p_2, and shift its tape head one square to the right. If we replace $\rightarrow$ by $\leftarrow$ or $\downarrow$ respectively, then the tape head instructions would be changed to shift left or to remain stationary respectively. We will employ the following notation: States(M) denotes S, Symbols(M) denotes Σ, Instructions(M) denotes δ, Start(M) denotes s, Blank(M) denotes B, and Accepting-states(M) denotes Y.

5.1.2 An *id* of M is a pair $(p, \alpha{\triangleright}\beta)$, where p is in S, $\alpha\beta$ is a string in Σ^*, and $\triangleright$ is a symbol which is not in Σ. The intuitive meaning of $(p, \alpha{\triangleright}\beta)$ is pretty much the same as that for a two-way finite-state acceptor: The storage tape contains $\alpha\beta$, preceded and followed by an infinite string of blanks. The finite-state control is in state p and the tape head is scanning the first symbol of the string β.

The id $(p, \alpha{\triangleright}\beta)$ denotes, among other things, a tape containing $\alpha\beta$ preceded and followed by an infinite string of blanks. Hence, if $\alpha{\triangleright}\beta$ is replaced by $\alpha{\triangleright}\beta B$ or $B\alpha{\triangleright}\beta$ or, indeed $\alpha{\triangleright}\beta$ concatenated with any number of preceding or trailing blanks, then the meaning of the id is unchanged. We will therefore identify any two id's which differ only by leading or trailing blanks in the second coordinate.

If $(p, \alpha{\triangleright}\beta)$ is an id, then the *tape configuration* of this id is $\alpha{\triangleright}\beta$, provided that α does not begin with the blank symbol and β does not end with the blank symbol. If α begins with the blank symbol or β ends with the blank symbol, then the tape configuration of $(p, \alpha{\triangleright}\beta)$ is $\nu{\triangleright}\mu$, where $\nu{\triangleright}\mu$ is $\alpha{\triangleright}\beta$ with all leading and trailing blanks removed. Note that by our identification convention $(p, \alpha{\triangleright}\beta) = (p, \nu{\triangleright}\mu)$, where $\nu{\triangleright}\mu$ is the tape configuration of $(p, \alpha{\triangleright}\beta)$.

5.1.3 We will define a partial function Next$(\ )$ from id's of M to id's of M which has the intuitive interpretation that if Next$((p_1, \alpha_1{\triangleright}\beta_1)) = (p_2, \alpha_2{\triangleright}\beta_2)$, then M will go from id $(p_1, \alpha_1{\triangleright}\beta_1)$ to id $(p_2, \alpha_2{\triangleright}\beta_2)$ in one step. The function is defined by clauses (1), (2), and (3). The p and q range over States(M); a, b and c range over Symbols(M); α and β range over [Symbols(M)]*

1. If $\delta(p, a) = (q, b, \downarrow)$, then
    Next$((p, \alpha{\triangleright}a\beta)) = (q, \alpha{\triangleright}b\beta)$ for all α and β.
2. If $\delta(p, a) = (q, b, \rightarrow)$, then
    Next$((p, \alpha{\triangleright}a\beta)) = (q, \alpha b{\triangleright}\beta)$ for all α and β.
3. If $\delta(p, a) = (q, b, \leftarrow)$, then
    Next$((p, \alpha c{\triangleright}a\beta)) = (q, \alpha{\triangleright}cb\beta)$ for all α, β and c.

Notice that by our convention $B{\triangleright}a\beta = {\triangleright}a\beta$, where $B = $ Blank(M). So, by taking $c = B$ and $\alpha = \Lambda$, clause (3) defines Next$((p, {\triangleright}a\beta))$ whenever $\delta(p, a) = (q, b, \leftarrow)$. Also, since $\alpha{\triangleright}B = \alpha{\triangleright}$, Next$((p, \alpha{\triangleright}))$ is defined by some clause whenever $\delta(p, B)$ is defined.

To be consistent with other notations and to make the notation more compact, we will write

$$(p_1, \alpha_1{\triangleright}\beta_1) \,|{\overline{}}_M\, (p_2, \alpha_2{\triangleright}\beta_2)$$

as an abbreviation for $\text{Next}((p_1, \alpha_1 \triangleright \beta_1)) = (p_2, \alpha_2 \triangleright \beta_2)$.

If M can change from id $(p_1, \alpha_1 \triangleright \beta_1)$ to id $(p_2, \alpha_2 \triangleright \beta_2)$ in some finite, possibly zero, number of steps then, as usual, we write

$$(p_1, \alpha_1 \triangleright \beta_1) \mid_{\overline{M}}^{*} (p_2, \alpha_2 \triangleright \beta_2)$$

The formal definition of $\mid_{\overline{M}}^{*}$ is the same as it is for finite-state acceptors. When no confusion can result, we will omit the subscript M.

5.1.4 An id $(q, \nu \triangleright a\xi)$ is called a *halting id* if $\delta(q, a)$ is undefined. In other words, an id is a halting id if the transition function yields no instruction and so there is no next id.

5.1.5 Let ξ be a string in $[\text{Symbols}(M) - \{B\}]^*$. The *computation* of M on input ξ is the finite or infinite sequence of id's $(q_0, \alpha_0 \triangleright \beta_0)$, $(q_1, \alpha_1 \triangleright \beta_1)$, $(q_2, \alpha_2 \triangleright \beta_2)$ ... such that the first id $(q_0, \alpha_0 \triangleright \beta_0) = (s, \triangleright \xi)$, where $s = \text{Start}(M)$; $(q_{i-1}, \alpha_{i-1} \triangleright \beta_{i-1}) \mid_{\overline{M}} (q_i, \alpha_i \triangleright \beta_i)$ for all $i \geqslant 1$ in the sequence and, if the sequence is finite, then the last id is a halting id. In the latter case, we say that M halts on input ξ.

5.1.6 Next we consider how a simple Turing machine can be used as a device to compute functions. To do this we need a notion of output. Let β be a string in $(\Sigma - \{B\})^*$, where $\Sigma = \text{Symbols}(M)$ and $B = \text{Blank}(M)$. Let $s = \text{Start}(M)$. The Turing machine M is said to have *output* β for input ξ provided $(s, \triangleright \xi) \mid_{\overline{M}}^{*} (q, \triangleright \beta)$ for some accepting state q. In other words, M has output β for the input ξ provided that the computation of M, with input ξ, eventually halts and, when it does halt,

1. The finite-state control is in an accepting state,
2. The only thing written on the tape is β, and
3. The tape head is scanning the first symbol of β, or is scanning a blank if β is the empty string.

Notice that for any input string ξ a simple Turing machine M has at most one valid output.

5.1.7 Let f be a partial function from $(\Sigma - \{B\})^*$ into $(\Sigma - \{B\})^*$. The Turing machine M is said to *compute the function* f provided the following conditions hold for all strings ξ in $(\Sigma - \{B\})^*$.

1. $f(\xi)$ is defined if and only if M has some output for the input ξ.
2. If $f(\xi)$ is defined, then M has output $f(\xi)$ for the input ξ.

According to Definition 5.1.7, every simple Turing machine computes a unique partial function. Of course, it could turn out to be the trivial partial function which is undefined for all input strings.

If f is a partial function and f is computed by some simple Turing machine, then f is said to be a *computable function*. Computable functions are sometimes also called *partial recursive functions*. If a function is both a total function and a computable function, it is frequently referred to as a *total recursive function.* The word "recursive" was derived from one of the earliest definitions of computable functions. Since this definition made heavy use of mathematical recursion, the functions were called recursive. In the present context, the term "recursive" carries little intuitive information, but it is standard terminology.

There are a number of more complicated variations of this basic Turing machine model. That is why this version is called simple. The only variation that we will deal with at any length is the nondeterministic Turing machine. Other texts discuss machines with many tapes, but the simple Turing machine, with its one tape, is quite adequate for our purposes.

Formal definitions of deterministic and nondeterministic Turing machines will not be given until a later chapter. However, the intuitive idea of these notions should be clear, since we have already discussed them in the context of finite-state machines. Using these intuitive notions, notice that a simple Turing machine is deterministic. That is, in any configuration, there is at most one possible next configuration. Our discussion of Turing machines will be concerned primarily with these simple, and hence deterministic, Turing machines. When discussing Turing machines on any but the most formal level, we will, for this reason, use the unmodified term *Turing machine* to mean a simple, and hence deterministic, Turing machine. This convention is convenient but is in conflict with the convention we used for finite-state machines. To help alleviate any confusion, we will always use the term *simple Turing machine* in the statement of theorems. By definition, a simple Turing machine is deterministic. Therefore, there should be no question as to whether the machine in question is deterministic or nondeterministic.

5.2 Example of a Simple Turing Machine

M, defined as follows, is a simple Turing machine. M computes the function f which maps each binary numeral into the binary numeral obtained by adding one to it. States(M) contains four states: $<$start$>$, n, c, and $<$accept$>$. The start state is $<$start$>$ and Accepting-states$(M) = \{<$accept$>\}$. Symbols$(M) = \{0, 1, B\}$, Blank$(M) = B$, and $\delta =$ Instructions(M) is defined by:

Find the right-hand end of input:

$\delta(<$start $>$, 0$) = (<$start $>$, 0, $\rightarrow$)

$\delta(<$start $>$, 1$) = (<$start $>$, 1, $\rightarrow$)

$\delta(<$start $>$, B) $= (c, B, \leftarrow$)

Add (n and c are no carry and carry states respectively):

$$\delta(n, 0) = (n, 0, \leftarrow) \qquad \delta(c, 0) = (n, 1, \leftarrow)$$
$$\delta(n, 1) = (n, 1, \leftarrow) \qquad \delta(c, 1) = (c, 0, \leftarrow)$$
$$\delta(n, B) = (<\text{accept}>, B, \rightarrow) \qquad \delta(c, B) = (n, 1, \leftarrow)$$

In this case, $f(\Lambda) = 1$, but it is easy to redefine the machine so that $f(\Lambda)$ is undefined.

*TL*Δ, A PROGRAMMING LANGUAGE FOR TURING MACHINES

Turing machines are not programmable computers. At an intuitive level you can think of the transition function as being the program but if you change the transition function, you change the machine. So when we talk of a programming language for Turing machines, what we really mean is a programming language that is, in some sense, equivalent to Turing machines. Each program in the language will ultimately describe a different Turing machine. Our first programming language for Turing machines is called *TL*Δ. This language is very simple and, in fact, is little more than a notional variant of the Turing machine model. Later on we will use *TL*Δ to define more complicated programming languages. The definition is divided into two parts, the syntax and the semantics of the language. The syntax of the language describes those strings of symbols which are allowed as programs. The semantics tells how these strings of symbols are to be interpreted.

5.3 Syntax of *TL*Δ

Let Δ be an arbitrary finite alphabet. We will describe a language *TL*Δ. The elements of *TL*Δ will be programs describing simple Turing machines whose nonblank tape symbols are the symbols in Δ. *TL*Δ stands for "Turing language with alphabet Δ." Technically speaking, we are defining a whole family of languages, one for each alphabet Δ. However, they are all essentially the same and so there is really only one language construct being defined.

5.3.1 A *Boolean expression* of *TL*Δ is a string of form **SCAN** $= a$, where a is either a single symbol in Δ or is the string *BLANK*.

5.3.2 A *TL*Δ *label* is any nonempty string of symbols that does not contain any of the fourteen symbols, **IF, THEN, BEGIN, END, SCAN, POINTER, GOTO, ACCEPT**, $\downarrow$, $\rightarrow$, $\leftarrow$, $=$, :, ;.

5.3.3 The *pointer instructions* of *TL*Δ are the three strings **POINTER**$\rightarrow$, **POINTER**$\leftarrow$, and **POINTER**$\downarrow$. Pointer instructions, like **POINTER**$\rightarrow$, are two symbols long. **POINTER** is one symbol and $\rightarrow$ is another symbol.

5.3.4 A *usual TL*Δ statement is a string of the form shown in Procedure 5.1, where <Boolean> is a Boolean expression, <label 1> and <label 2> are any *TL*Δ labels, <pointer move> is a pointer instruction, and a is either a symbol in Δ or the string *BLANK*. <label 1> is called the label of this statement. Formally, this is a string of symbols all run together with no blanks. However, we will usually write it in some way such as is shown in Procedure 5.1. This is just to make it easier to read and is not part of the formal definition.

Procedure 5.1
A usual *TL*Δ statement

<label 1> : **IF** <Boolean> **THEN**
           BEGIN
                SCAN := a;
                <pointer move>;
                GOTO <label 2>
           END

The intuitive meaning of a usual *TL*Δ statement should be clear. The labels correspond to states, the symbol **SCAN** is essentially a variable containing the symbol currently under the tape head, and the pointer instruction tells how the tape head is moved. For example, consider the usual *TL*Δ statement shown in Procedure 5.2 It has the following intuitive meaning. If the finite state control is in state $L1$ and a is the symbol currently scanned by the tape head, then a is replaced by b, the tape head is shifted right one square, and the finite-state control changes to state $L2$.

Procedure 5.2
Example of a usual *TL*Δ statement

$L1$: **IF SCAN** = a **THEN**
         BEGIN
            SCAN := b;
            POINTER→;
            GOTO $L2$
         END

5.3.5 An *accepting TL*Δ *statement* is a string of the form <label> : **ACCEPT**, where <label> is any *TL*Δ label. As you might guess, the string <label> is called the label of this statement.

5.3.6 A *statement of TL*Δ is either a usual statement or an accepting statement.

5.3.7 A *TL*Δ *program* is a string of the form BEGIN σ_1; σ_2; ...; σ_n END where σ_1; σ_2; ...; σ_n is any finite list of *TL*Δ statements such that no two of these statements have the same label.

5.4 Example of a *TL*Δ Program

Procedure 5.3 is a *TL*Δ program that reads in a string of 0's and 1's, replaces all 0's by 1's, and then repositions the tape head at the beginning of the string of 1's. Although we have not yet formally defined the semantics of *TL*Δ, we can tell what this program does by giving the statements their intuitive meaning. In this case, $\Delta = \{0, 1\}$.

5.5 Semantics of *TL*Δ

5.5.1 We will define a way of obtaining a Turing machine M from a given *TL*Δ program P. M is called the *Turing machine realization* of P and will serve as the semantics of P. In an intuitive sense, the program P "compiles" or "interprets" or "translates" to the machine code M. The definition is as follows:

States(M) = the set of all labels of the statements of P.
Symbols(M) = $\Delta \cup \{B\}$, where B is any symbol which does not occur in Δ.
Blank(M) = B.
Start(M) = the label of the first statement of P.
Accepting-states(M) = the set of all labels of accepting statements.
Instructions(M) = δ, where δ is defined below.

Consider a state <label 1> and a symbol c. The state labels some *TL*Δ statement in P. If this statement is an accepting statement, then $\delta($<label 1>, $c)$ is undefined. If this statement is a usual *TL*Δ statement, then it is of the form shown in Procedure 5.4, where <arrow> is one of the three symbols $\rightarrow$, $\leftarrow$, and $\downarrow$, and where <label 2> is a *TL*Δ label. The definition of $\delta($<label 1>, $c)$, where <label 1> labels the usual *TL*Δ statement in Procedure 5.4 and where c is an arbitrary symbol of M, is given by cases:

Case 1 : $c = a$ and <label 2> labels some statement of P.
Case 1B: $c = B$, $a = BLANK$, and <label 2> labels some statement of P. In both cases 1 and 1B, $\delta($<label 1>, $c)$ = (<label 2>, b, <arrow>) provided $b \neq BLANK$. If $b = BLANK$, then $\delta($<label 1>, $c)$ = (<label 2>, B, <arrow>).

Procedure 5.3

Example of a $TL\Delta$ program

```
BEGIN
        L0:   IF SCAN = 0 THEN
                    BEGIN
                            SCAN := 1;
                            POINTER→;
                            GOTO L0
                    END;
        L1:   IF SCAN = 1 THEN
                    BEGIN
                            SCAN := 1;
                            POINTER→;
                            GOTO L0
                    END;
        L2:   IF SCAN = BLANK THEN
                    BEGIN
                            SCAN := BLANK;
                            POINTER←;
                            GOTO REWIND
                    END;
    REWIND:  IF SCAN = 1 THEN
                    BEGIN
                            SCAN := 1;
                            POINTER←;
                            GOTO REWIND
                    END;
        L3:   IF SCAN = BLANK THEN
                    BEGIN
                            SCAN := BLANK;
                            POINTER→;
                            GOTO FINISH
                    END;
    FINISH:   ACCEPT
END
```

Case 2 : $c = a$ but <label 2> does not label any statement of P.

Case 2B: $c = B$, $a = BLANK$ but <label 2> does not label any statement of P.

In both cases 2 and 2B, $\delta(<\text{label } 1>, c)$ is undefined.

Procedure 5.4
A Usual *TL*Δ Statement

```
<label 1> : IF SCAN = a THEN
              BEGIN
                 SCAN := b;
                 POINTER <arrow>;
                 GOTO <label 2>
              END
```

Case 3 :   Cases 1, 1B, 2, and 2B do not apply. This is, if a is a usual symbol, then c is not a and if $a = BLANK$, then c is not B. In this case, set $\delta(<\text{label 1}>, c) = (<\text{next-label}>, c, \downarrow)$, where $<\text{next-label}>$ is the label of the next statement in P. If there is no next statement, then $\delta(<\text{label 1}>, c)$ is undefined.

5.5.2 If f is a partial function from Δ^* to Δ^*, then P is said to *compute f* provided the Turing machine realization of P computes f. For any string ξ in Δ^*, P is said to *halt* on ξ provided the computation of the Turing machine realization of P halts on ξ. In general, any reference to a computation of P is to be interpreted to mean the appropriate computation of the Turing machine realization of P.

5.6 Example of a *TL*Δ Realization

The machine M described below is the Turing machine realization of the program shown in Procedure 5.3.

$$\text{State}(M) = \{L0, L1, L2, REWIND, L3, FINISH\}$$
$$\text{Symbols}(M) = \{0, 1, B\}$$
$$\text{Blank}(M) = B$$
$$\text{Start}(M) = L0$$
$$\text{Accepting-states}(M) = \{FINISH\}$$
$$\text{Instructions}(M) = \delta, \text{where}$$
$$\delta(L0, 0) = (L0, 1, \rightarrow)$$
$$\delta(L0, 1) = (L1, 1, \downarrow)$$
$$\delta(L0, B) = (L1, B, \downarrow)$$
$$*\delta(L1, 0) = (L2, 0, \downarrow)$$
$$\delta(L1, B) = (L2, B, \downarrow)$$
$$\delta(L1, 1) = (L0, 1, \rightarrow)$$

$$*\delta(L2, 0) = (REWIND, 0, \downarrow)$$
$$*\delta(L2, 1) = (REWIND, 1, \downarrow)$$
$$\delta(L2, B) = (REWIND, B, \leftarrow)$$
$$*\delta(REWIND, 0) = (L3, 0, \downarrow)$$
$$\delta(REWIND, 1) = (REWIND, 1, \leftarrow)$$
$$\delta(REWIND, B) = (L3, B, \downarrow)$$
$$*\delta(L3, 0) = (FINISH, 0, \downarrow)$$
$$*\delta(L3, 1) = (FINISH, 1, \downarrow)$$
$$\delta(L3, B) = (FINISH, B, \rightarrow)$$

Those values of δ which are marked by a star are never used in any computation on an input string of 0's and 1's. They are in some sense unintended useless instructions. They are an unfortunate side effect of the Turing machine realization process. However, although in some sense they make δ bigger than it need be, they cause no harm for they produce no bad computations.

$TL\Delta$ ABBREVIATIONS

In order to make $TL\Delta$ programs more readable, we will use a number of abbreviations which we will describe in this section. All of these new programming constructs are just abbreviations for certain $TL\Delta$ statements as already described and are not new types of statements. One abbreviation will be to always omit the string **POINTER**$\downarrow$, since it says "do nothing". We will also omit **GOTO** <label>, where <label> is the label of the next instruction. We will also usually omit all labels L such that, in the abbreviated program, there are no statements of the form **GOTO** L. Another abbreviation will be to omit **SCAN** $:= a$ when such a statement does not change the value of **SCAN**. We will also omit the pair **BEGIN-END** when they enclose only one of the three normal parts. When doing this, we will add or delete semicolons so as to get maximum readability. For example, the piece of program shown in Procedure 5.5a can be abbreviated to the piece of program shown in Procedure 5.5b, provided the rest of the program does not contain any occurrences of **GOTO** $L2$.

The meaning of these and other abbreviations should be clear from context. If this discussion is a bit unclear, just go on. As long as you can read the abbreviations you are all set. One important point to remember, though, is that these are abbreviations. A $TL\Delta$ program has no such statements. They are just a shorthand for use in communicating between people. To get a valid $TL\Delta$ program, you must replace the abbreviations by regular $TL\Delta$ statements as formally defined in 5.3.

The next theorem is so obvious it almost needs no proof. But since the result is fundamental to much of what we will be doing, we will devote some space to it. We would like to say that every simple Turing machine is the realization of some $TL\Delta$ program. This is not quite literally true. However, the spirit of this situation is true and is expressed by the next theorem. In order to

Procedure 5.5a
Piece of a *TL*Δ Program

$L1$: IF SCAN $= a$ THEN
    BEGIN
        SCAN := a;
        POINTER→;
        GOTO $L2$
    END;
$L2$: IF SCAN $= BLANK$ THEN
    BEGIN
        SCAN := a;
        POINTER↓;
        GOTO $L7$
    END

Procedure 5.5b
Abbreviation of Procedure 5.5a

$L1$: IF SCAN $= a$ THEN POINTER→;
    IF SCAN $= BLANK$ THEN
        BEGIN
            SCAN := a;
            GOTO $L7$
        END

---

prove the theorem, we need one lemma.

5.7 Lemma Let M be a simple Turing machine, let Δ be the set of nonblank symbols of M, and let f be the partial function from Δ^* to Δ^* computed by M. We can find another simple Turing machine M' such that M' also computes f and such that every state of M' is a $TL\Delta$ label.

PROOF Let a be any symbol that is allowed in $TL\Delta$ labels. Let $p_1, p_2, ..., p_m$ be an enumeration without repetition of all the states of M. M' is defined in terms of M and a. Symbols$(M') = $ Symbols(M), Blank$(M') = $ Blank(M), States$(M') = \{a, a^2, a^3, ..., a^m\}$, the start state of M' is a^i, where p_i is the start state of M, Accepting-states$(M') = \{a^i \mid p_i \in$ Accepting-states $(M)\}$, and

Instructions(M') = δ' where δ' is defined as follows:

$\delta'(a^i, b)$ = $(a^j, c, <\text{arrow}>)$ provided $\delta(p_i, b)$ is defined and $\delta(p_i, b)$ = $(p_j, c, <\text{arrow}>)$. Here δ = Instructions(M).

M' is just M with the states renamed. Therefore, M' computes the same function f that M does. $\square$

5.8 Theorem Let M be any simple Turing machine, let Δ be the set of nonblank symbols of M, and let f be the partial function from Δ^* to Δ^* computed by M. We can always find a $TL\Delta$ program P such that P also computes f.

PROOF By Lemma 5.7, we may assume that the states of M are $TL\Delta$ labels. Adopt the notation that B = Blank(M) and δ = Instructions(M). Let $a_1, a_2, ..., a_n$ be an enumeration of $\Delta \cup \{B\}$. For each p in States(M) and each a_i, let Symbol(p, a_i), Arrow(p, a_i), and State(p, a_i) be defined by the equation

$$\delta(p, a_i) = (\text{State}(p, a_i), \text{Symbol}(p, a_i), \text{Arrow}(p, a_i))$$

For each nonaccepting state p, define a block of $TL\Delta$ code as follows. The code is $p : \sigma_1; \sigma_2; ...\sigma_n;$ where each σ_i is as shown in Procedure 5.6. If $\delta(p, a_i)$ is undefined, then set State(p, a_i) equal to $<\text{abort}>$, where $<\text{abort}>$ is any label not in States(M); in this case, Symbol(p, a_i) and Arrow(p, a_i) are irrelevant and may be anything. Take the concatenation of all these blocks in any order, as long as the block for the start state comes first. Follow this by all statements of the form $p :$ **ACCEPT** where p is an accepting state of M. Place the symbols **BEGIN** and **END** at the beginning and end. Finally, replace all strings of the form **SCAN** = B by **SCAN** = *BLANK* and all strings of the form **SCAN** := B by **SCAN** := *BLANK*. The resulting program is the desired program P. The program P, as just described, does have some abbreviations, namely, some usual $TL\Delta$ statements do not have labels. However, it is a trivial matter to add some appropriate labels. In fact, any labels at all, as long as they are new and distinct, will do. $\square$

By Theorem 5.8 we know that a partial function is computed by some simple Turing machine if and only if it is computed by some $TL\Delta$ program. In and of itself, that is neither surprising nor very important. It is a stepping stone in our development of more sophisticated programming languages. We will develop two more programming languages, each of them equivalent to simple Turing machines. The first of these two is called $TL\Delta S$. While it is much richer than $TL\Delta$, it is also a stepping stone — hopefully, a little larger and more interesting, but, in any event, a useful stepping stone.

$TL\Delta S$, $TL\Delta$ WITH SUBPROCEDURES

The language $TL\Delta S$ can be thought of as the language $TL\Delta$ augmented to allow subprocedures. $TL\Delta$ has no variables in the traditional sense, although

Procedure 5.6
σ_i **Code**

IF SCAN $= a_i$ **THEN**
    BEGIN
        SCAN := Symbol(p, a_i);
        POINTER Arrow(p, a_i);
        GOTO State(p, a_i)
    END

the symbol **SCAN** is a kind of variable. $TL\Delta S$ has one variable **STRING**, where **STRING** is a special symbol like **SCAN**, **POINTER**, and the other special symbols of $TL\Delta$. This variable ranges over strings of symbols from Δ. The structures of the two languages $TL\Delta$ and $TL\Delta S$ are essentially the same. The only real differences are in the Boolean expressions and in what we might naturally call the basic executable statements. In $TL\Delta$, the Boolean expressions are of the form **SCAN** $= a$; the basic executable statements are of the forms **SCAN** := a, **POINTER**←, **POINTER**↓, and **POINTER**→. In $TL\Delta S$, the Boolean expressions are of the form

STRING $\in$ A

where A is the name of a finite-state language. The Boolean expression is true provided that the string stored in the variable **STRING** is a member of the language named by A. The basic executable statements of $TL\Delta S$ are of the form

STRING := f(**STRING**)

where f is the name for a computable partial function f from Δ^* to Δ^*. The intuitive meaning of such a statement is simple. If **STRING** contains the string α, then after executing this statement it will contain the string $f(\alpha)$; if $f(\alpha)$ is undefined, then this statement aborts the computation. Such symbols as f and A are in effect names for subprocedures. When we write a $TL\Delta S$ program, we are assuming that we already have programs for computing the functions named by such symbols f and that we already have programs for deciding membership in the languages named by such symbols A. These programs or subprocedures are either $TL\Delta$ programs or finite-state acceptors. With these intuitive remarks in mind, we now proceed with the definition of $TL\Delta S$. Since the syntax of $TL\Delta S$ is so much like that of $TL\Delta$, we will only define it informally.

5.9 Syntax of $TL\Delta S$

A *Boolean expression of* $TL\Delta S$ is a string of the form **STRING** $\in A$, where A may be any symbol. The symbol A is called a *subprocedure name for a language*. A $TL\Delta S$ *label* is the same thing as a $TL\Delta$ label. An *accepting statement* of $TL\Delta S$ is the same as an accepting statement of $TL\Delta$. So, in particular, accepting statements have labels. A *usual* $TL\Delta S$ *statement* is a string of the form shown in Procedure 5.7, where $<$Boolean$>$ is a $TL\Delta S$ Boolean expression, $<$label 1$>$ and $<$label 2$>$ are any $TL\Delta S$ labels, and f is any symbol. The symbol f is called a *subprocedure name for a function*. $<$label 1$>$ is called the label of the statement. A $TL\Delta S$ *schema* is a string of the form

$$\textbf{BEGIN}\ \sigma_1;\ \sigma_2;\ ...;\ \sigma_n\ \textbf{END}$$

where each σ_i is a $TL\Delta S$ statement, either accepting or usual, and where no two σ_i have the same label.

A careful reading of the above definition will show that the definition of a $TL\Delta S$ schema does not depend on Δ. However, the semantics does depend on Δ. Technically speaking, we are again defining a whole family of languages, one for each alphabet Δ.

Procedure 5.7
A Usual $TL\Delta S$ Statement

```
<label 1>  :  IF <Boolean> THEN
           BEGIN
               STRING := f (STRING);
               GOTO <label 2>
           END
```

5.10 Semantics of $TL\Delta S$

A $TL\Delta S$ schema has no meaning until some meaning is assigned to each subprocedure name in the schema. If we assign a finite-state language to each subprocedure name for a language and assign a computable partial function to each subprocedure name for a function, then there is a natural meaning to the schema. A schema, together with such assignments, is called a $TL\Delta S$ program. In the following, let P be a $TL\Delta S$ schema.

5.10.1 An *assignment of language subprocedures* to P is a function G which maps each subprocedure name for a language onto a finite-state language consisting of strings from Δ^*. So, if A is a subprocedure name for a language, then $G(A)$ is a finite-state language consisting of strings over Δ.

5.10.2 An *assignment of function subprocedures* to P is a function F which maps each subprocedure name for a function onto a partial function that is computed by some $TL\Delta$ program. So, if f is a subprocedure name for a function, then $F(f)$ is a computable partial function from Δ^* to Δ^*.

5.10.3 A $TL\Delta S$ *program* is a triple (P, G, F) where P is a $TL\Delta S$ schema, G is an assignment of language subprocedures to P, and F is an assignment of function subprocedures to P.

   If G and F are obvious from context, we will sometimes leave them as understood and speak loosely of P as the program. Also, when the meaning is clear from context, we will write A for $G(A)$ and f for $F(f)$, where A and f are subprocedure names. The distinctions between A and $G(A)$ and between f and $F(f)$ are, in fact, hard to see in practice and can present some confusion. That is because they are examples of a distinction we usually do not make, or at least do not make much of. Specifically, they are examples of the distinction between a thing and its name. The symbol f is the name. $F(f)$ is the thing named by the symbol f. Since we usually name $F(f)$ by the symbol f, some of the following parts of this definition can seem bewildering. F is a function from symbols to functions and, in this definition, f is a symbol. So, since $F(f)$ is a function, $F(f)(\beta)$ can make sense. It is a function applied to β. Usually, we would just write "$f(\beta)$" for $F(f)(\beta)$, but here we wish to distinguish the function from its name. It requires patience to understand the rest of this definition.

5.10.4 An *id* of a $TL\Delta S$ program (P, G, F) is a pair (α, β) where α is a $TL\Delta S$ label and β is in Δ^*. Intuitively, α is the label of the $TL\Delta S$ statement to be executed next, and β is the string currently stored in the variable **STRING**. If α is the label of an accepting statement, then (α, β) is called an *accepting id*.

5.10.5 Let (P, G, F) be a $TL\Delta S$ program. We will define a partial function Next( ) from id's of this program to id's of this program. The intuitive interpretation is that if Next$(\alpha_1, \beta_1) = (\alpha_2, \beta_2)$, then (P, G, F) will go from id (α_1, β_1) to id (α_2, β_2) in one step. It may turn out to be a big step but still we choose to call it a step. The formal definition of Next(α, β) is by cases:

Case 1: α is not the label of any statement of P. In this case, Next(α, β) is undefined.

Case 2: α is the label of an accepting statement of P. In this case, Next(α, β) is undefined.

Case 3: α is the label of a usual statement of P. In this case, let the statement labeled by α be as shown in Procedure 5.8.

Procedure 5.8
Statement Labeled by α

α : **IF STRING** $\in A$ **THEN**
     BEGIN
          STRING := f (**STRING**);
          GOTO <label 2>
     END

In this case, we distinguish four subcases:

Subcase 3a: β is in $G(A)$ and $F(f)(\beta)$ is defined. In this case, Next$(\alpha, \beta) = $ (<label 2>, $F(f)(\beta)$). Recall that $F(f)$ is the function named by f and in most situations would be written in the sloppy notation $f(\beta)$.

Subcase 3b: β is in $G(A)$ and $F(f)(\beta)$ is undefined. In this case, Next(α, β) is undefined.

Subcase 3c: β is not in $G(A)$ and this is not the last statement in P. In this case, Next$(\alpha, \beta) = $ (<next-label>, β) where <next-label> is the label of the next statement in P.

Subcase 3d: β is not in $G(A)$ and this is the last statement in P. In this case, Next(α, β) is undefined.

To be consistent with the literature and with our other notations, we will write $(\alpha_1, \beta_1) \vdash (\alpha_2, \beta_2)$ instead of Next$(\alpha_1, \beta_1) = (\alpha_2, \beta_2)$. When it is not clear which program we are discussing, we will add subscripts to $\vdash$, either $\vdash_P$ or $\vdash_{(P,G,F)}$. As usual, $\vdash^*$ denotes any finite number, possibly zero, of applications of $\vdash$.

5.10.6 If (α, β) is an id of a $TL\Delta S$ program and Next(α, β) is undefined, then (α, β) is called a *halting id*. If, in addition, α is the label of an accepting statement, then (α, β) is called an *accepting id.*

The definition of a halting id for a $TL\Delta S$ program does not exactly correspond to our intuitive notion of a halting id. Consider an id (α, β) and adopt the notation of Definition 5.10.5. If Next(α, β) is undefined because $F(f)(\beta)$ is undefined (Subcase 3b above) and if $F(f)(\beta)$ is undefined because the program we are using to compute $F(f)$ does not halt on β, then, by our definition, (α, β) is a halting id. But, in this case, our intuitive notion of what is happening is that the entire computing process does not halt. This discrepancy between intuition and the formal definition is in part due to the fact that our definition of a $TL\Delta S$ program does not specify which $TL\Delta$ programs we should use to compute the functions named by the subprocedure names for functions. The functions are specified by the assignment of function subprocedures (the F of Definition 5.10.2) but, for any given computable function, there are many different $TL\Delta$ programs that compute that function. These different $TL\Delta$ programs may have different halting properties even though they compute the same function. Our definition fixes a convention that is independent of which $TL\Delta$ programs are used. However, the main reason for using this definition of a halting id is that it is convenient for the formal mathematical development of the notion of a $TL\Delta S$ program computing a function. Specifically, it makes it easy to define when a computation of a $TL\Delta$ program has a valid output and this definition of valid output, which we will give shortly, does correspond to our intuitive notion of a program halting in a configuration that produces a valid output.

5.10.7 A *computation* of (P, G, F) on input ξ is a finite or infinite list (α_0, β_0), (α_1, β_1) (α_2, β_2)... of id's such that:

1. $(\alpha_0, \beta_0) = (<\text{first}>, \xi)$ where $<\text{first}>$ is the label of the first statement in P.
2. $(\alpha_{i-1}, \beta_{i-1}) \vdash (\alpha_i, \beta_i)$ for all $i \geqslant 1$ in the sequence.
3. If the list is finite, then the last id is a halting id, and the program is said to *halt on input ξ*.

5.10.8 (P, G, F) is said to have *valid output* β for input ξ provided $(<\text{first}>, \xi) \vdash^* (<\text{accept}>, \beta)$, where $<\text{first}>$ is the label of the first statement in P and $<\text{accept}>$ is the label of some accepting statement in P. In other words, β is the valid output for input ξ provided that the computation on input ξ halts after executing an accepting statement and at the end of the computation the variable **STRING** contains β. Every input ξ has at most one valid output. Some input strings may, of course, produce no valid output.

5.10.9 Let f be a partial function from Δ^* to Δ^*. (Here f stands for a function rather than a symbol and therefore $f(\xi)$ has the usual meaning.) The $TL\Delta S$ program (P, G, F) is said to *compute f* provided that the following hold for all ξ in Δ^*.

1. $f(\xi)$ is defined if and only if (P, G, F) has valid output for the input ξ.
2. If $f(\xi)$ is defined, then $f(\xi)$ is the valid output for the input ξ.

As with simple Turing machines and $TL\Delta$ programs, every $TL\Delta S$ program computes a unique partial function. Again, this partial function may sometimes turn out to be trivial, but still it is a partial function.

5.11 Example of a $TL\Delta S$ Program

We will describe a $TL\Delta S$ program (P, G, F) which computes the partial function f defined so that $f(a^i b^j) = a^{i-j}$ for $i > j$, $f(a^i b^j) = b^{j-i}$ for $i \leqslant j$ and f is undefined for all other arguments. Set $\Delta = \{a, b\}$. The schema P is shown in Procedure 5.9. There are two subprocedure names for languages A and C. $G(A) = \{a^i b^j \mid i \geqslant 1$ and $j \geqslant 1\}$. $G(C) = \Delta^* - \{a^i b^j \mid i \geqslant 0$ and $j \geqslant 0\}$. There are two subprocedure names for functions I and g. $F(I)$ is the identity function which maps each string in Δ^* to itself. $F(g)$ is a function which deletes one a and one b from a string provided that string contains at least one a and one b. $F(g)$ is undefined for all other arguments.

Procedure 5.9
TLΔS **Schema** P

BEGIN
    START: **IF STRING** $\in$ C **THEN**
        BEGIN
            STRING := I(**STRING**);
            GOTO *UNDEFINED*
        END;
    LOOP: **IF STRING** $\in$ A **THEN**
        BEGIN
            STRING := g(**STRING**);
            GOTO *LOOP*
        END;
    FINISH: **ACCEPT**
END

In order show that (P, G, F) is a *TLΔS* program, we must show that $G(A)$ and $G(C)$ are finite-state languages and that $F(I)$ and $F(g)$ are computable by *TLΔ* programs. However, it is a routine exercise to show these facts.

The first usual *TLΔS* statement of schema P may deserve a short explanation. There is no statement in P which is labeled *UNDEFINED*. So the substatement

GOTO *UNDEFINED*

simply aborts the computation. Hence, if an input string ξ is in $G(C)$, then the program has no valid output for the input ξ. Hence, if f is the function computed by the program, then $f(\xi)$ is undefined for all ξ in $G(C)$, which is what we wanted. The substatement

STRING := I(**STRING**)

in the first usual $TL\Delta S$ statement of schema P accomplishes nothing. Since $F(I)$ is the identify function, it produces no change. We had to include some such statement, though. Otherwise, we would violate the definition of $TL\Delta S$ syntax. In less formal contexts, we could abbreviate the schema P by omitting that substatement. Below we discuss a few other handy $TL\Delta S$ abbreviations.

5.12 $TL\Delta S$ Abbreviations

Suppose L_1 and L_2 are finite-state languages over Δ^*. By Theorem 3.5, $L_1 \cup L_2$ and $L_1 \cap L_2$ are also finite-state languages. By Theorem 3.8, $\Delta^* - L_1$ is also a finite-state language. If we wish to write a $TL\Delta S$ program (P, G, F), where we have a Boolean expressing **STRING** $\in A$ and $G(A) = L_1 \cup L_2$, then we will sometimes write

$$(\textbf{STRING} \in A_1 \ \ \textbf{OR} \ \ \textbf{STRING} \in A_2)$$

in place of **STRING** $\in A$. In this case, we set $G(A_1) = L_1$ and $G(A_2) = L_2$. Similarly, if $G(B) = L_1 \cap L_2$, we will sometimes write

$$(\textbf{STRING} \in A_1 \ \ \textbf{AND STRING} \in A_2)$$

in place of **STRING** $\in B$, again setting $G(A_1) = L_1$ and $G(A_2) = L_2$. Similarly, if $G(C) = \Delta^* - L_1$, then we will sometimes write

$$(\textbf{NOT STRING} \ \in A_1)$$

in place of **STRING** $\in C$. In this case we again set $G(A_1) = L_1$. For example, in 5.11, we could write (**NOT STRING** $\in D$) in place of **STRING** $\in C$ and set $G(D) = \{a^i b^j \mid i \geqslant 0$ and $j \geqslant 0\}$. This is all just a kind of sloppy shorthand, and is not a formally valid way of writing $TL\Delta S$ programs, but since it does help us see some programs more clearly we will use it.

A COMPILER FOR $TL\Delta S$

We now proceed to show that anything that can be done by a $TL\Delta S$ program can be done by a $TL\Delta$ program. The proof is in two steps. First, we show that anything that can be done by a $TL\Delta S$ program can be done by a $TL\Gamma$ program, for some larger alphabet $\Gamma \supseteq \Delta$. This is the heart of the proof. Later on we will show that this $TL\Gamma$ program can be converted to an equivalent $TL\Delta$ program. If we put together all the algorithms given in the proof of this result, we get a "compiler" that takes $TL\Delta S$ programs as input and gives equivalent $TL\Delta$ programs as output. The output $TL\Delta$ program will compute the same partial function as the $TL\Delta S$ program. The formal result is more easily stated with the help of a preliminary definition.

5.13   Definition

Two programs are said to be *input / output equivalent* provided that they both compute the same partial function. We will apply this definition to two $TL\Delta$ programs, two $TL\Delta S$ programs, or a $TL\Delta$ program and a $TL\Delta S$ program, and also to other types of programs and machines.

5.14 Theorem If Δ is any alphabet with at least two elements and if (P, G, F) is any $TL\Delta S$ program, then we can find an alphabet $\Gamma \supseteq \Delta$ and a $TL\Gamma$ program P' such that P' is input/output equivalent to the $TL\Delta S$ program (P, G, F).

Before proving Theorem 5.14, we will first prove two lemmas. Both lemmas are of a rather technical nature and are only needed to cope with some technical details in the proof of Theorem 5.14. The first lemma is, nonetheless, quite intuitive. It says the following: If A is a finite-state language, then there is a computable function h_A which, for inputs ξ, answers the question: "Is ξ in A?" When we use this lemma, we will be writing a $TL\Gamma S$ program which will include a substatement of the form

$$\text{STRING} := h_A \text{ (STRING)}$$

Since, in this case, ξ will be stored in **STRING** and we do not wish to lose ξ, h_A will return $<\text{yes}>\xi$ or $<\text{no}>\xi$ instead of just $<\text{yes}>$ or $<\text{no}>$.

5.15 Lemma Let Δ be an alphabet with at least two elements. Let $<\text{yes}>$ and $<\text{no}>$ be two distinct elements of Δ. If A is any finite-state language over Δ, then the total function h_A, defined as follows, is a computable function. For each ξ in A, $h_A(\xi) = <\text{yes}>\xi$; for each ξ in $\Delta^* - A$, $h_A(\xi) = <\text{no}>\xi$.

PROOF Let M be a deterministic finite-state acceptor which accepts the language A. The states of M may be any mathematically well-defined object. We would like the states of M to be $TL\Delta$ labels. Clearly, if we just rename the states of M with $TL\Delta$ labels, then M still accepts the language A. Therefore we can, and will, assume that the states of M are $TL\Delta$ labels. (A formal proof that M can always be chosen so that its states are $TL\Delta$ labels would be similar to the proof of Lemma 5.7.) Let δ be the transition function of M. Let $p_0, p_1, ..., p_m$ be a list without repetition of all the states of M and let p_0 be the start state. Let $a_0, a_1, ..., a_n$ be a list without repetition of all the symbols of M. By Lemma 3.4, we know that we can choose M so that $\delta(p_i, a_j)$ is defined for all p_i and a_j. Let $q_{ij} = \delta(p_i, a_j)$, $i = 0, 1, ..., m$ and $j = 0, 1, 2, ..., n$. We will describe a $TL\Delta$ program that computes h_A. The program has a few abbreviations in it, but it is easy to convert it to a formally correct $TL\Delta$ program. We will describe this program by a context-free grammar. The grammar has start symbol $<\text{program}>$, and the language generated contains exactly one string. That string is the $TL\Delta$ program for h_A. The grammar is given in Table 5.1.

To see that this program computes h_A, note that all computations on an input ξ proceed as follows. The block of code $<M \text{ code}>$ is executed first. This code simulates M step by step with one embellishment: Whenever a nonaccepting state is reached, the block $<\text{end no?}>$ is executed and whenever an accepting state is reached, the block $<\text{end yes?}>$ is executed. These blocks check to see if all of ξ is read. They do this by checking for a blank. If all of ξ is read and an accepting state is reached, then the **GOTO** *INA* is executed and control passes to the block <yes rewind>. If all of ξ is read and the last p_i was not an accepting state, then control goes from the block <M code> to the block <no rewind>. So after <M code> is executed, all of ξ is read, and control passes to either <yes rewind> or <no rewind> depending on whether or not ξ is in A. Both of these rewind blocks move the pointer to the front of ξ; <yes rewind> puts <yes> in front of ξ; <no rewind> puts <ro> in front of ξ. Finally, whichever rewind block is executed, the program ends by a **GOTO** *EXITA*. The flowchart in Figure 5.2 may be of some help in understanding the program. $\square$

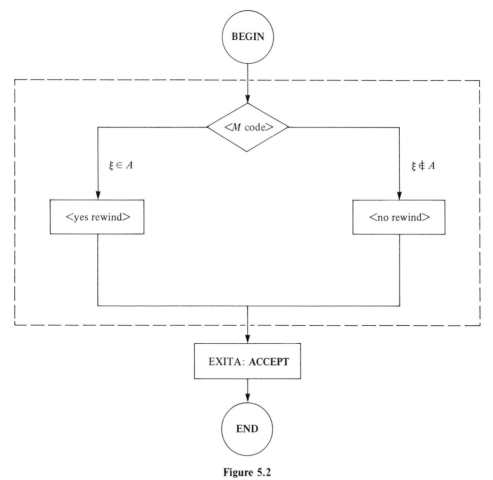

Figure 5.2

The next lemma is another technical detail but with at least a little intuitive content. In proving Theorem 5.14, we will want a simple check to see if a $TL\Delta$ program P has a valid output for a given input α. The test we will use is to check to see if the program reaches an accepting statement in the computation on input α. For an arbitrary $TL\Delta$ program P, this test unfortunately does not quite work; there may be inputs α such that, on input α, P reaches an accepting statement and yet P has no valid output for the input α. (The format conditions of Definition 5.1.6 might not hold.) The lemma says we can always rewrite the program P to get an equivalent program P'' for which this simple $TL\Delta$ program P has a valid output for a given input α. The test we will use is to check to see if the program reaches an accepting statement in the computation on input α. For an arbitrary $TL\Delta$ program P, this test unfortunately does not quite work; there may be inputs α such that, on input α, P reaches an accepting statement and yet P has no valid output for the input α. (The format conditions of Definition 5.1.6 might not hold.) The lemma says we can always rewrite the program P to get an equivalent program P'' for which this simple test does work. One cost of the rewriting is that we may have to enlarge the alphabet used by P''.

Table 5.1 Context-free Grammar for h_A Program

<program> → **BEGIN** <A code>; *EXITA* : **ACCEPT END**

<A code> → <M code> <no rewind>; <yes rewind>

<M code> → $<p_0$ code> $<p_1$ code>...$<p_m$ code>

For all p_i which are not accepting states:

$<p_i$ code> → p_i : <end no ?>; $<p_i, a_0>$; $<p_i, a_1>$;...$<p_i, a_n>$;

For all p_i which are accepting states:

$<p_i$ code> → p_i : <end yes ?>; $<p_i, a_0>$; $<p_i, a_1>$;...$<p_i, a_n>$;

For all states p_i and all symbols a_j:

$<p_i, a_j>$ → **IF SCAN** $= a_j$ **THEN**

      BEGIN

         SCAN $:= a_j$;

         POINTER→;

         GOTO q_{ij}

     END

<end yes ?> → **IF SCAN** $=$ *BLANK* **THEN**

      BEGIN

         SCAN $:=$ *BLANK*;

         POINTER↓;

         GOTO *INA*

     END

<end no ?> is just like <end yes ?> but with *INA* replaced by *OUTA*. Notice that *INA* will label the start of <yes rewind> and *OUTA* will label the start of <no rewind>.

```
<yes rewind>  →  INA : <rewind 2>;
                    IF SCAN = BLANK THEN
                        BEGIN
                            SCAN := <yes>;
                            POINTER↓;
                            GOTO EXITA
                    END
<no rewind>  →  OUTA : <rewind 1>;
                    IF SCAN = BLANK THEN
                        BEGIN
                            SCAN := <no>;
                            POINTER↓;
                            GOTO EXITA
                    END
```

For $i = 1, 2$

```
    <rewind i>  →  POINTER←;
                    LOOPi : IF (NOT SCAN = BLANK) THEN
                        BEGIN
                            POINTER←;
                            GOTO LOOPi
                    END;
```

Note: p_0, p_1, ..., p_m, *EXITA*, *INA*, *OUTA*, *LOOP*1, and *LOOP*2 must be $m + 5$ distinct labels, but this is easy to ensure.

5.16 Lemma If f is computed by a $TL\Delta$ program P, then there is an alphabet $\Gamma \supseteq \Delta$ and a $TL\Gamma$ program P'' such that

1. P'' also computes f.
2. For any input α, if P'' reaches an accepting statement in the computation of P'' on α, then P'' has a valid output for the input α.

PROOF Since the details for the construct of P'' are long and routine, we will merely sketch the construction of P'' and leave the details as one more exercise. Let $\Gamma = \Delta \cup \{<\text{dirty blank}>\}$, where $<\text{dirty blank}>$ is a new symbol which will serve as a pseudo blank symbol. The program P'' will simulate the program P step by step with one small change. Whenever P would write a blank symbol, P'' will write the symbol $<\text{dirty blank}>$. Whenever P'' reads the symbol $<\text{dirty blank}>$, P'' will simulate P reading the true blank. In this way P'' can tell, for any input α, whether or not P would reach an accepting statement in the computation of P on input α. If P would reach an accepting statement on input α, then P has a valid output for the input α provided the tape configuration of P, at the end of the computation, satisfies the format conditions of Definition 5.1.6. So, when P'' has finished simulating P, it does the following. If P'' determines that P would end its computation with an accepting statement, then P'' does not execute an accepting statement. Instead, P'' checks to see if the format conditions for a valid output are satisfied. P'' then executes an accepting statement and produces a valid output only if these format conditions are satisfied. In order to check for these format conditions, P'' must check that $P's$ tape would contain a single string of nonblank characters and that the tape head is positioned properly. This can be done by scanning every square of tape used in the computation and checking to see that there is no instance of two symbols of Δ with one or more blanks or pseudo blanks between them and by checking the tape head position. To do this, P'' must somehow tell which symbols were scanned in the computation. This is the function of the pseudo blank symbol <dirty blank>. Every square scanned by P'' in its simulation of P will contain either a symbol of Δ or the symbol <dirty blank>. The piece of tape to be checked is marked by a true blank symbol at each end. We now give a little more detail of this construction of P''.

Let <P code> be the program P with the enclosing **BEGIN-END** deleted; that is, $P = $ **BEGIN** <P code> **END**. Define P'' to be the program shown in Procedure 5.10 where <new label>, <abort>, and <formcheck> are three new labels and <abort> does not label any P'' statement. <Δ^*test code> is a block of $TL\Gamma$ code that tests to see if the input is in Δ^*. If it is in Δ^*, then control is transferred to <new P code>; if it is not in Δ^*, then control is transferred to <abort> ending the computation in a nonaccepting mode. The block <new P code> is obtained from <P code> by the algorithm described in Procedure 5.11.

Procedure 5.10
Program P''

BEGIN
$$<\Delta^* test \text{ code}>;$$
$$<\text{new } P \text{ code}>;$$
<new label>   : **GOTO** <abort>;
<formcheck>   : <check code>
END

Note that the $TL\Gamma$ statements in 2 of Procedure 5.11 are $TL\Gamma$ abbreviations and technically need to be expanded to valid equivalent $TL\Gamma$ code. Notice that <new P code> does the same thing that <P code> does except that <new P code> has two symbols that it treats as blank: the usual one plus <dirty blank>; also any square that is ever scanned contains either a symbol of Δ or <dirty blank>; also, rather than accepting, <new P code> transfers control to <check code>.

Procedure 5.11
Algorithm to obtain <new P Code>

1. Replace each occurrence of
SCAN := *BLANK* by **SCAN** := <dirty blank>

2. Replace each statement of the form

> <label> : **IF SCAN** = *BLANK* **THEN**
>   **BEGIN**
>   <stuff>
>   **END**

by

> <label> : **IF (SCAN** = *BLANK* **OR SCAN** = <dirty blank>) **THEN**
>   **BEGIN**
>   <stuff>
>   **END**

3. Replace each occurrence of **ACCEPT** by **GOTO** <formcheck>

<check code> checks that the format conditions for valid output are satisfied and, if they are, produces the output P would produce; if they are not, it terminates the computation in a nonaccepting mode. <check code> needs to check if the tape contains a string of the form

$$<\text{dirty blank}>^m \beta <\text{dirty blank}>^n$$

surrounded by true blanks. Here $m \geqslant 0$, $n \geqslant 0$, and β is in Δ^*. It also has to check that the tape head is scanning the first symbol of β. If the tape contents are not of this form, then control is transferred to <abort>. If the tape contents are of this form, then the symbols <dirty blank> are replaced by true blanks, the tape head is positioned at the first symbol of β, and control is transferred to an accepting statement.

By the argument outlined at the beginning of this proof, it should be clear that P'' has the desired properties. $\square$

Proof of Theorem 5.14

Let $\Gamma = \Delta \cup \{<\text{dirty blank}>\}$ as in Lemma 5.16. To change a $TL\Delta S$ program (P, G, F) into an equivalent $TL\Gamma$ program P', we replace each usual statement of the $TL\Delta S$ program by a block of $TL\Gamma$ code that has the same effect as the $TL\Delta S$ statement. We now describe the $TL\Gamma$ code which replaces an

---

Procedure 5.12a
Usual $TL\Delta S$ Statement of P

<label 1> : **IF STRING** $\in A$ **THEN**
        BEGIN
                STRING := f(**STRING**);
                GOTO <label 2>
        END

Procedure 5.12b
$TL\Gamma$ Code for Usual $TL\Delta$ Statement

<label 1> : <nothing 1>;
    <new h_A code>;
<switch label> : <yes/no switch>;
<f label> : <nothing 2>;
    <new f code>

---

arbitrary usual $TL\Delta S$ statement. To get P' from P, replace every usual $TL\Delta S$ statement of P by a block of $TL\Gamma$ code obtained in this way. The accepting $TL\Delta S$ statements are not changed.

Consider a usual $TL\Delta S$ statement of P as shown in Procedure 5.12a. Let **BEGIN** <h_A code> **END** be a $TL\Delta$ program for the function h_A obtained from $G(A)$ as in Lemma 5.15. Let **BEGIN** <f code> **END** be a $TL\Gamma$ program for the partial function $F(f)$ such that this $TL\Gamma$ program has property (2) of Lemma 5.16. We replace the usual $TL\Delta S$ statement shown in Procedure 5.12a by the $TL\Gamma$ code shown in Procedure 5.12b. We first describe the pieces intuitively and then give precise descriptions. The statements <nothing 1> and <nothing 2> are statements which have no effect. If control is transferred to <label 1>, then this causes the code <new h_A code> to be executed. Similarly, if control is transferred to <f label>, then this causes the code <new f code> to be executed. <new h_A code> transforms tape configuration $\triangleright\xi$ to $\triangleright h_A(\xi)$ and transfers control to <switch label>. The code <yes/no switch> transfers control to <f label> if $h_A(\xi) = $ <yes>ξ and jumps control over <new f code> if $h_A(\xi) = $ <no>ξ; the

<yes/no switch> also erases the first symbol of <yes>ξ or <no>ξ. The block <new f code> changes $\triangleright\xi$ to $\triangleright f(\xi)$ and transfers control to <label 2>. If $f(\xi)$ is undefined, then <new f code> either does not terminate or else terminates the computation in a nonaccepting mode. All these pieces of code can be defined precisely as follows:

1. <switch label> and <f label> are new labels.
2. <nothing 1> is **GOTO** α, where α is the first label of <new h_A code>.
3. <new h_A code> is <h_A code> modified as follows: Every accepting statement

<label> : **ACCEPT**

is replaced by

<label> : **GOTO** <switch label>

4. <yes/no switch> is the code shown in Procedure 5.13. In Procedure 5.13, <correct label> is the label of the next $TL\Delta S$ statement provided there is a next $TL\Delta S$ statement. If this is the last $TL\Delta S$ statement, then <correct label> is a new label; hence, if this is the last $TL\Delta S$ statement, then **GOTO** <correct label> terminates the program in a nonaccepting configuration.

Procedure 5.13
<yes/no switch> Code

```
IF SCAN = <yes> THEN
   BEGIN
        SCAN := BLANK;
        POINTER→;
        GOTO <f label>
   END;
IF SCAN = <no> THEN
   BEGIN
        SCAN := BLANK;
        POINTER→;
        GOTO <correct label>
   END
```

---

5. <nothing 2> is **GOTO** α where α is the first label of <new f code>.
6. <new f code> is <f code> modified as follows: every accepting statement

<label> : **ACCEPT** is replaced by
<label> : **GOTO** <label 2>

Recall that <label 2> is the label after **GOTO** in the usual $TL\Delta S$ statement. A new statement **GOTO** <abort> is added to the end of this block of code, where <abort> is a label that will label no statement of the final $TL\Gamma$ program.

To get a $TL\Gamma$ program, P', which is equivalent to (P, G, F), replace each usual $TL\Delta S$ statement by the $TL\Gamma$ code derived from it by the process just described. Note that it is only the usual statements that are changed. The accepting statements are left as they are. One must ensure that all the blocks of <h_A code> and <f code> have different labels from each other and different labels from P. This is easy to do and it ensures that we do not use the same label in two different places.

To see that P' is equivalent to (P, G, F), note that P' simulates (P, G, F) step by step. It will take many P' steps to simulate one step of (P, G, F), but P' does change the string on its tape just as (P, G, F) would change the string stored in **STRING**. Statements (1), (2) and (3) below explain the simulation. In these statements we are considering how P' behaves when it is supposed to simulate an arbitrary $TL\Delta S$ statement like the one shown in Procedure 5.12a.

1. If ξ is in $G(A)$, then $(<\text{label } 1>, \triangleright \xi) \mid^{\ast} (<\text{switch label}>, \triangleright <\text{yes}>\xi) \mid^{\ast} (<f \text{ label}>, \triangleright \xi) \mid^{\ast} (<\text{label } 2>, \triangleright f(\xi))$, provided $f(\xi)$ is defined. If ξ is in $G(A)$ and $f(\xi)$ is undefined, then the computation from $(<\text{label } 1>, \triangleright \xi)$ will either halt in a nonaccepting mode or will never terminate. To see this, note that by using Lemma 5.16 we have ensured that if <f code> executes an accepting statement, it means that $f(\xi)$ is defined. So, in <new f code> a transfer to <label 2> occurs if and only if $f(\xi)$ is defined.

2. If ξ is not in $G(A)$ and the above usual $TL\Delta S$ statement is not the last statement in P, then $(<\text{label } 1>, \triangleright \xi) \mid^{\ast} (<\text{switch label}>, \triangleright <\text{no}>\xi) \mid^{\ast} (<\text{next label}>, \triangleright \xi)$, where <next label> is the label of the next $TL\Delta S$ statement.

3. If ξ is not in $G(A)$ and the above usual $TL\Delta S$ statement is the last statement in P, then $(<\text{label } 1>, \triangleright \xi) \mid^{\ast} (<\text{switch label}>, <\text{no}>\xi) \mid^{\ast} (<\text{exit label}>, \triangleright \xi)$, where <exit label> does not label any statement in P'. □

We now know that every $TL\Delta S$ program is input/output equivalent to some simple Turing machine. Conversely, it is trivially true that any simple Turing machine, with nonblank symbols Δ, is input/output equivalent to a $TL\Delta S$ program. To see this, recall that every simple Turing machine is input/output equivalent to a $TL\Delta$ program. Also, every $TL\Delta$ program is trivially input/output equivalent to a $T^L\Delta S$ program; if a $TL\Delta$ program computes a partial function f, then

BEGIN STRING $:= f(\textbf{STRING})$; **ACCEPT END**

is a $TL\Delta S$ program that also computes f. (Here we are being a bit informal because we are using the same letter f to represent both a subprocedure name in a schema and to represent the function it names.) From these facts we would like to conclude that, for any finite alphabet Δ with at least two symbols, $TL\Delta S$ programs, $TL\Delta$ programs, and simple Turing machines with nonblank symbols Δ are all equivalent in computing power. This is true. However, there is still one missing link in the proof of this equivalence. We know that every $TL\Delta S$ program is input/output equivalent to a $TL\Gamma$ program for some larger Γ but we have not yet shown that every $TL\Delta S$ program is equivalent to a $TL\Delta$ program. Our next result shows that certain well-behaved $TL\Delta S$ programs can be converted to $TL\Delta$ programs. Later on we will use this result to show that any $TL\Delta S$ program can be converted to an input/output equivalent $TL\Delta$ program.

5.17 Lemma Let Δ be an alphabet with at least two elements. Suppose (P, G, F) is a $TL\Delta S$ program such that $F(f)$ is a total function for each f which is a subprocedure name for a function occurring in P. Under these conditions, we can find a $TL\Delta$ program P' which is input/output equivalent to (P, G, F).

PROOF Notice that if f is a subprocedure name for a function occurring in P then, since $F(f)$ is total, the $TL\Delta$ program which computes $F(f)$ satisfies condition (2) of Lemma 5.16. So, if we apply the construction given in the proof of Theorem 5.14 to (P, G, F), we do not need to use Lemma 5.16 in order to obtain a $TL\Gamma$ program for $F(f)$ which satisfies condition (2) of this lemma. Instead, we can use the $TL\Delta$ program for $F(f)$. If we do this, then the entire construction in the proof of Theorem 5.14 can be done with Δ rather than Γ as the set of nonblank symbols. So we obtain a $TL\Delta$ program P' rather than a $TL\Gamma$ program. □

Using a $TL\Delta S$ program, we can now prove a result which, in addition to being of some intrinsic interest, will prove to be useful in deriving later results. Suppose we wish to construct a simple Turing machine to compute a partial function f from Δ^* to Δ^*. It might be convenient to have some additional symbols, which are not in Δ, to use in intermediate calculations. Our next result shows that, while it might be convenient, it is never necessary.

5.18 Theorem Suppose Δ and Γ are alphabets such that Δ contains at least two symbols and such that $\Delta \subseteq \Gamma$. Suppose g is a partial function computed by some simple Turing machine M with Γ as the set of nonblank symbols. If $g(\alpha)$ is undefined for all α not in Δ^*, then we can find a simple Turing machine M' such that M' also computes g and such that Δ is the set of nonblank symbols of M'.

PROOF We will describe a $TL\Delta S$ program that computes g and satisfies the hypothesis of Lemma 5.17. From this $TL\Delta S$ program we know that we can obtain a $TL\Delta$ program and ultimately a simple Turing machine M' that computes g and has Δ as its set of nonblank symbols. In order to do this, we will code symbols in Γ as strings in Δ^*. It will turn out to be convenient to also code the states of M as strings in Δ^*.

Let $a_1, a_2, ..., a_n$ be an enumeration without repetition of the symbols in Γ. Let $p_1, p_2, ..., p_m$ be an enumeration without repetition of the states of M. Let c and d be two symbols in Δ. So c and d are a_i and a_j for some i and j. However, it will be convenient to denote them by c and d. We will code each symbol in Γ and each state of M as a different string, of length $n + m$, in $\{c, d\}^*$. For each symbol a_i, define $\text{code}(a_i) = c^i d^{n+m-i}$. For each state p_i, define $\text{code}(p_i) = c^{n+i} d^{m-i}$. It does not matter what coding we use so long as each state and symbol is given a different code and as long as all codes have the same length. We extend this coding to obtain a coding of strings in Δ^* and ultimately of id's of M. If $a_{i_1} a_{i_2} ... a_{i_l}$ is in Δ^*, then

$$\text{code}(a_{i_1} a_{i_2} ... a_{i_l}) = \text{code}(a_{i_1}) \text{code}(a_{i_2}) ... \text{code}(a_{i_l})$$

If $(p_j, \alpha \triangleright \beta)$ is an id of M with tape configuration $\alpha \triangleright \beta$, then

$$\text{code}(p_j, \alpha \triangleright \beta) = \text{code}(\alpha) \text{code}(p_j) \text{code}(\beta)$$

To compute $\text{code}(p_j, \alpha \triangleright \beta)$, think of p_j as a symbol and represent the id as $\alpha p_j \beta$; then replace each symbol in the string $\alpha p_j \beta$ by its code. The result is $\text{code}(p_j, \alpha \triangleright \beta)$.

We now define some languages and functions to serve as subroutines in our $TL\Delta S$ program. $A = \{\text{code}(p, \triangleright \beta) \mid p$ is an accepting state of M and β is in $\Delta^*\}$. $B = \{\text{code}(p, \alpha \triangleright \beta) \mid (p, \alpha \triangleright \beta)$ is a halting id of $M\}$. For any string ξ in Δ^*, $<\text{initial}>(\xi) = \text{code}(s, \triangleright \xi)$, where s is the start state of M. For any id $(p, \alpha \triangleright \beta)$ of M, $<\text{next}>(\text{code}(p, \alpha \triangleright \beta)) = \text{code}(p', \alpha' \triangleright \beta')$, provided $(p, \alpha \triangleright \beta) \mid_{\overline{M}} (p', \alpha' \triangleright \beta')$. For any other string ξ in Δ^*, $<\text{next}>(\xi) = \xi$. For any string β in Δ^* and any state p, $<\text{decode}>(\text{code}(p, \triangleright \beta)) = \beta$. For any string ξ in Δ^*, which is not of the form $\text{code}(p, \triangleright \beta)$, $<\text{decode}>(\xi) = \xi$. Notice that $<\text{initial}>$, $<\text{next}>$, and $<\text{decode}>$ are all total functions. The $TL\Delta S$ program to compute g is given in Procedure 5.14. In any execution of this program, only the first parts of the definitions of $<\text{next}>$ and $<\text{decode}>$ will ever be applicable. The only reason for including the second parts of these definitions is to ensure that the functions are total, and hence, that Lemma 5.17 can be applied.

Since this program simulates M step by step, it clearly computes g. However, in order to show that this is a $TL\Delta S$ program, we must show that there are $TL\Delta$ programs to compute $<\text{initial}>$, $<\text{next}>$, and $<\text{decode}>$ and that both A and B are finite-state languages. This is rather long and detailed but not too difficult. So we leave it as an exercise. □

Theorem 5.18 provides the missing link that was needed in order to prove our assertion that $TL\Delta S$ programs, $TL\Delta$ programs, and simple Turing machines with nonblank symbols Δ are all equivalent in computing power. Our next result formalizes this equivalence.

5.19 Corollary If Δ is any alphabet with at least two symbols and f is any partial function from Δ^* to Δ^*, then the following statements are all equivalent.

1. f is computed by some $TL\Delta S$ program.
2. f is computed by some $TL\Delta$ program.
3. f is computed by some simple Turing machine with nonblank symbols Δ.

PROOF In the remarks following the proof of Theorem 5.14, we saw, among other things, that (3) implies (2) and (2) implies (1). Hence, to establish this result, we need only show that (1) implies (3). With this goal in mind, suppose (1) is true. Then by Theorem 5.14, f is computed by some $TL\Gamma$ program for some $\Gamma \supseteq \Delta$. By the definition of what it means for a $TL\Gamma$ program to compute a function, it then trivially follows that f is computed by some simple Turing machine with nonblank symbols Γ. Applying Theorem 5.18, it then follows that f is computed by some simple Turing machine with nonblank symbols Δ. So (3) is established. Having shown that (1) implies (3), we have completed the proof. $\square$

Procedure 5.14
Program to Compute g

```
BEGIN
    START : STRING := <initial> (STRING);
    LOOP  : IF STRING ∈ A THEN GOTO EXIT;
            IF STRING ∈ B THEN GOTO ABORT;
            STRING := <next> (STRING);
            GOTO LOOP;
    EXIT  : STRING := <decode> (STRING);
            ACCEPT
END
```

$PS\Delta$ — A HIGH-LEVEL LANGUAGE FOR PROCEDURES TO COMPUTE FUNCTIONS

$TL\Delta S$ is a good language in that we can easily convert any $TL\Delta S$ program to a $TL\Delta$ program which can, in turn, be implemented on a Turing machine which is our model of a computer. Also, it is a lot more versatile and easier to read than $TL\Delta$. Still, it is a very cumbersome language. We now define a language that will allow us to state algorithms much more clearly. This language is $PS\Delta$. We will then give a "compiler" to convert $PS\Delta$ programs to $TL\Delta S$

programs. $PS\Delta$ is the language we will use. $TL\Delta S$ is only used as a bridge to get from $PS\Delta$ programs to Turing machines. It is easy to go step by step from $PS\Delta$ to $TL\Delta S$ to $TL\Delta$ to Turing machines. It would be insanely complicated to go directly from $PS\Delta$ to Turing machines. Keep in mind that we are developing a theory about what things can and cannot be done by programs. To do this, it is helpful to know that every $PS\Delta$ program can be converted to a $TL\Delta S$ program. However, $TL\Delta$ and $TL\Delta S$ are just aids to developing this theory. They are not languages used by any real computers. So we will never implement our $PS\Delta$ compiler in the "real world." Therefore, there is no need for the algorithms we present to be efficient. Our goal will be to make them correct, easy to prove correct, and easy to understand. Efficiency is not important to our purpose here.

In some respects, $PS\Delta$ is like $TL\Delta S$ but has a nicer control structure and more variables. $TL\Delta S$ has one variable **STRING**. $PS\Delta$ has variables **STRING**1, **STRING**2, **STRING**3, ..., each of which is capable of holding an arbitrary string out of Δ^*. The basic Boolean statements of $PS\Delta$ are of the form **STRING**$j \in A$, where A is the name of a finite-state language. In $PS\Delta$, we also allow **AND**, **OR**, and **NOT** to build more complicated Boolean expressions. The basic executable statements of $PS\Delta$ are of the forms

$$\textbf{STRING}\,i := f(\textbf{STRING}\,j) \text{ and } \textbf{STRING}\,i := \textbf{STRING}\,j\,\textbf{STRING}\,k$$

where f is the name of a computable partial function, and where the juxtaposition denotes concatenation. If **STRING**j contains α then, after

$$\textbf{STRING}\,i := f(\textbf{STRING}\,j)$$

is executed, **STRING**i contains the string which is usually denoted by $f(\alpha)$; **STRING**j is not changed (unless $j = i$). If $f(\alpha)$ is undefined, then the computation will abort at this point. If **STRING**j contains α and **STRING**k contains β then, after

$$\textbf{STRING}\,i := \textbf{STRING}\,j\,\textbf{STRING}\,k$$

is executed, **STRING**i contains $\alpha\beta$; **STRING**j and **STRING**k are not changed (unless i equals j or k). By repeated applications of the concatenation operation we will be able to concatenate any number of strings. Also, we will be able to write code that sets some **STRING**i equal to a constant string. Putting these things together, we will be able to produce code equivalent to

$$\textbf{STRING}\,i := f(\textbf{STRING}\,j\,\#\,\textbf{STRING}\,k)$$

where $\#$ is some special symbol used as a punctuation mark. Although $PS\Delta$ only has functions of one argument, we will be able to produce code that is clearly equivalent to having functions of two, or any number, of arguments.

The symbols like f and A are in effect names for subprocedures. When we write a $PS\Delta$ program, we are assuming that we already have programs for computing the functions named by such symbols f and that we already have programs for deciding membership in the languages named by such symbols A.

The situation with regard to these subprocedure names is basically the same as it was for the language $TL\Delta S$. The only difference is that, since we now know that $TL\Delta$ and $TL\Delta S$ programs are equivalent, we will use $TL\Delta S$ programs rather than $TL\Delta$ programs as subprocedures. For $PS\Delta$, the subprocedures are either $TL\Delta S$ programs or finite-state acceptors.

The structure of $PS\Delta$ is quite different from that of $TL\Delta S$. In $PS\Delta$ simpler statements can be put together to get more complicated statements by means of the following constructs: **IF-THEN-ELSE**, **BEGIN-END** and **WHILE-DO**. These constructs may be nested. There are no **GOTO**'s and, since the **BEGIN-END** is just like any other construct, there is no distinction between a single statement and a complete schema (program). These constructs are explained in detail below.

5.20 Syntax of $PS\Delta$

Let Γ and Δ be any alphabets. Intuitively, Δ is the alphabet of our work space. $PS\Delta$ programs manipulate strings of symbols from Δ. Γ is an alphabet used to write names for subprocedures. We might as well take $\Gamma = \Delta$, but sometimes it is easier to read our programs if Γ is not the same as Δ. First, we define $PS\Delta$ schemata over Γ in an informal way and then go on to give a formal definition in terms of a context-free grammar. The definition of $PS\Delta$ schemata over Γ will depend, in a minor way, on Γ but will not depend on Δ at all. However, the semantics of $PS\Delta$ programs does depend on Δ and the semantics is the motivation of much of the syntax. For this reason we will use the term $PS\Delta$ schema, even though the schema does not depend on Δ.

5.20.1 A *name* is any string in Γ^*.

5.20.2 A *number* is any base ten numeral with no leading zeros.

5.20.3 A *variable* is any string of the form **STRING** i, where i is a number.

5.20.4 An *atomic Boolean* expression is any string of the form

$$\textbf{STRING}\, i \in A$$

where **STRING** i is a variable and A is a name. A is called a *subprocedure name for a language*.

5.20.5 A *Boolean expression* is any well-formed expression built up from atomic Boolean expressions using **AND, OR, NOT**, and parentheses.

5.20.6 An *atomic statement* is any string in one of the following two forms:

$$\textbf{STRING}\, i := f(\textbf{STRING}\, j) \text{ or } \textbf{STRING}\, i := \textbf{STRING}\, j\, \textbf{STRING}\, k$$

where **STRING** i, **STRING** j, and **STRING** k are variables and f is a name called a *subprocedure name for a function*.

5.20.7 A *statement* is either an atomic statement or a string made up from

Boolean expressions and previously madeup statements according to one of the following three patterns:

1. **IF** <Boolean> **THEN** <statement 1>
                    ELSE <statement 2>
2. **WHILE** <Boolean> **DO** <statement>
3. **BEGIN**σ_1; σ_2; ...σ_n **END**

where <Boolean> is a Boolean expression; <statement 1>, <statement 2>, <statement>, σ_1, σ_2, ..., σ_n are statements. For readability, we will punctuate these with spaces but, technically, there are no spaces. Notice that we can nest these three constructs inside each other any way we want.

5.20.8 A *PSΔ schema over* Γ is a statement. Unlike *TLΔS*, there is no distinction between schemata and statements. A string is called a *PSΔ* schema if it is a *PSΔ* schema over Γ, for some Γ.

    We now repeat the above definition in a slightly more precise way by giving a context-free grammar for *PSΔ* schemata over Γ.

5.20.9 A *CFG* for *PSΔ* schemata with names in Γ^*: A *PSΔ schema over* Γ is any string generated by the following context-free grammar. The start symbol is <statement>. The nonterminal symbols are all symbols in angular brackets < >, and the rest of the symbols are terminal symbols.

1. <statement> → **IF** <Boolean> **THEN** <statement>
                                  ELSE <statement>
    <statement> → **BEGIN** <statement list> **END**
    <statement list> → <statement>
    <statement list> → <statement list> ; <statement>
    <statement> → **WHILE** <Boolean> **DO** <statement>
    <statement> → <atomic statement>
    <atomic statement> →
        STRING <number> := <name> (**STRING** <number>)
    <atomic statement> →
        STRING <number> := **STRING** <number> **STRING** <number>
2. <number> → <nonzero digit> | <nonzero digit> <digit string>
    <nonzero digit> → 1 | 2 | ... | 9
    <digit string> → <digit> | <digit string> <digit>
    <digit> → 0 | 1 | 2 | ... | 9
    <name> → <name> <Γ letter> | <Γ letter>
    <Γ letter> → a, for each a in Γ
3. <Boolean> → (<Boolean> **AND** <Boolean>)
    <Boolean> → (<Boolean> **OR** <Boolean>)
    <Boolean> → (**NOT** <Boolean>)
    <Boolean> → <atomic Boolean>
    <atomic Boolean> → **STRING** <number> $\in$ <name>

5.21 Semantics of *PS*Δ

5.21.1 A *PS*Δ *program* is a triple (P, G, F) where P is a *PS*Δ schema, G is a function which maps subprocedure names for languages in P to finite-state languages, and F is a function which maps subprocedure names for functions in P to partial functions which are computed by *TL*Δ*S* programs. G is called an *assignment of language subprocedures* to P. F is called an *assignment of function subprocedures* to P. In what follows, (P, G, F) is a *PS*Δ program.

5.21.2 Let n be the largest number such that the variable **STRING**n occurs in P. So **STRING**1, **STRING**2, ..., **STRING**n are all the variables in P. Some variables might actually not occur in P. All that is important is that the list includes all the variables that do occur in P. A *storage configuration* of this program is an ordered n tuple $(\alpha_1, \alpha_2, ..., \alpha_n)$, where each α_i is in Δ^*. Intuitively, α_i is the string stored in the variable **STRING**i.

A *PS*Δ program gets its input in **STRING**1. Initially, all the other variables contain the empty string. The initial storage configuration has $\alpha_1 = $ the input string and $\alpha_i = \Lambda$ for $i > 1$. The *PS*Δ program changes the storage configuration as follows: An atomic statement of the form

$$\textbf{STRING}\, i := f\,(\textbf{STRING}\, j\,)$$

changes the contents of **STRING**i to $F(f)(\alpha_j)$, where α_j is the contents of **STRING**j and $F(f)$ is the partial function named by f. In less formal terms, **STRING**i gets changed to "$f(\alpha_j)$". If $F(f)(\alpha_j)$ is undefined, the computation aborts. If $j \neq i$, then **STRING**j is not changed by this atomic statement. An atomic statement of the form

$$\textbf{STRING}\, i := \textbf{STRING}\, j\, \textbf{STRING}\, k$$

changes the contents of **STRING**i to $\alpha_j \alpha_k$, where α_j is the contents of **STRING**j and α_k is the contents of **STRING**k. **STRING**j and **STRING**k are not changed by this atomic statement, unless $j = i$ or $k = i$. A statement of the form

$$\textbf{BEGIN}\ \sigma_1;\ \sigma_2;...\sigma_n\ \textbf{END}$$

has the same effect as executing $\sigma_1, \sigma_2, ..., \sigma_n$ one after the other. A statement of the form

$$\textbf{IF}\ b\ \textbf{THEN}\ \sigma_1\ \textbf{ELSE}\ \sigma_2$$

has the same effect as σ_1 if b is true and the same effect as σ_2 if b is false. A statement of the form

$$\textbf{WHILE}\ b\ \textbf{DO}\ \sigma$$

has the same effect as executing σ again and again until b is false. Every time σ is executed, the storage configuration changes. Thus b may change from true to false. In short, *PS*Δ programs assign the usual meaning to the

IF-THEN-ELSE, WHILE-DO and **BEGIN-END** constructs. All this formalizes as follows.

5.21.3 A storage configuration $(\alpha_1, \alpha_2, ..., \alpha_n)$ is said to make the atomic Boolean expression **STRING** $i \in A$ *true* if α_i is in $G(A)$. It is said to make it *false* if α_i is not in $G(A)$. In this way a storage configuration assigns true or false to each atomic Boolean expression. Once true or false is assigned to each atomic Boolean expression, true or false is then assigned to more complicated Boolean expressions in the usual way. One way to describe how a storage configuration assigns true or false to a Boolean expression is as follows: Consider the context-free grammar with start symbol <Boolean> and the rewrite rules given in (3) of 5.20.9. Using these rules, we can construct a parse tree for the Boolean expression. Replace each node labeled by <atomic Boolean> by either true or false, depending on whether the atomic Boolean expression under it is made true or false by the storage configuration. Then work your way up the tree by the following rules.

1. (**NOT** α) has the opposite value of α.
2. (α **AND** β) is true if both α and β are true, otherwise it is false.
3. (α **OR** β) is true if at least one of α and β is true, otherwise it is false.

5.21.4 Let G be a fixed but arbitrary assignment of language subprocedures and let F be a fixed but arbitrary assignment of function subprocedures. We will define a function called *Effect* which has two arguments: a schema P such that (P, G, F) is a $PS\Delta$ program and a storage configuration I of this program. Effect does depend on G and F as well as P and I. Technically speaking, we would expect Effect to have two additional arguments for G and F. However, in this definition we consider G and F to be fixed. When we use Effect, G and F will be clear from context. Intuitively, if I_1 and I_2 are storage configurations and Effect$(I_1, P) = I_2$, then (P, G, F) changes storage configuration I_1 to storage configuration I_2. Effect is defined by induction. The induction follows the pattern of the parse tree for the statement P and is given by cases.

1. If P is **STRING** $i := f(\textbf{STRING} j)$, $I = (\alpha_1, \alpha_2, ..., \alpha_m)$ and $F(f)(\alpha_j)$ is defined, then Effect$(I, P) = (\beta_1, \beta_2, ..., \beta_m)$, where $\beta_i = F(f)(\alpha_j)$ and $\beta_k = \alpha_k$ for $k \neq i$. If P and I are as just described but $F(f)(\alpha_j)$ is undefined, then Effect(I, P) is undefined.
2. If P is **STRING** $i := $ **STRING** j **STRING** k and $I = (\alpha_1, \alpha_2, ..., \alpha_m)$, then Effect$(I, P) = (\beta_1, \beta_2, ..., \beta_m)$, where $\beta_i = \alpha_j \alpha_k$ and $\beta_t = \alpha_t$ for $t \neq i$.
3. If P is **BEGIN** $\sigma_1; \sigma_2; ...; \sigma_n$ **END**, then
3a. Effect$(I, P) = $ Effect(Effect(I, σ_1), **BEGIN** $\sigma_2; \sigma_3; ...; \sigma_n$ **END**), provided $n \geqslant 2$.
3b. Effect$(I, P) = $ Effect(I, σ_1), if $n = 1$.
4. If P is **IF** b **THEN** σ_1 **ELSE** σ_2 and I makes b true, then Effect$(I, P) = $ Effect(I, σ_1). If P is **IF** b **THEN** σ_1 **ELSE** σ_2 and I makes b false then Effect$(I, P) = $ Effect(I, σ_2).

5. If P is **WHILE** b **DO** σ and I makes b true then Effect$(I, P) =$ Effect(Effect$(I, \sigma), P)$. If P is **WHILE** b **DO** σ and I makes b false, then Effect$(I, P) = I$.

Notice that in Case (5), Effect might be undefined. This would happen if executing σ again and again always produced storage configurations which make b true. In other words, there can be an infinite loop. An alternate way of stating (5) is the following:

6. If P is **WHILE** b **DO** σ, then Effect$(I, P) = J$ provided there are storage configurations $I_1, I_2, ..., I_t$ such that

   (a) $I_1 = I$,
   (b) I_i makes b true for $i < t$,
   (c) Effect$(I_i, \sigma) = I_{i+1}$ for $i < t$,
   (d) I_t makes b false, and
   (e) $I_t = J$.

Note that $t = 1$ is possible. If no such sequence of storage configurations exists, then Effect(I, P) is undefined.

There are two ways that Effect(I, P) can be undefined: one way is described in (1) and one way is described in (6). Also, since the constructs given in (1) and (6) may be nested inside a **BEGIN-END** or an **IF-THEN-ELSE**, any P that contains a **WHILE-DO** or a statement of the form **STRING** $i := f(\textbf{STRING} j)$ might possibly have Effect(I, P) undefined for some I.

5.21.5 If Effect(I, P) is defined, we say that (P, G, F) *halts* on the storage configuration I. We say that (P, G, F) *halts on input* α if it halts on the storage configuration $(\alpha, \Lambda, \Lambda, ..., \Lambda)$. If the program halts on input α, then there is always an output, namely, the string held in the variable **STRING**1 at the end of the computation. This notion of output is formalized next.

5.21.6 (P, G, F) is said to have *output* β for the input α provided Effect$((\alpha, \Lambda, \Lambda, ..., \Lambda), P) = (\beta, \gamma_2, \gamma_3, .., \gamma_n)$ for some strings $\gamma_2, \gamma_3, ..., ..., \gamma_n$.

5.21.7 (P, G, F) is said to *compute the partial function f* from Δ^* to Δ^* provided

1. (P, G, F) halts on input α if and only if $f(\alpha)$ is defined.
2. If (P, G, F) halts on input α then (P, G, F) has output $f(\alpha)$ for the input α.

Observe that, as was the case with $TL\Delta$ and $TL\Delta S$ programs, every $PS\Delta$ program defines a unique partial function.

A COMPILER FOR $PS\Delta$

$PS\Delta$ is the programming language with strong expressive powers that we referred to at the beginning of this chapter. To complete the plan we outlined there, we must show that any $PS\Delta$ program can be converted to a $TL\Delta S$ program and so ultimately can be converted to a simple Turing machine. The promised equivalence between $PS\Delta$ programs and simple Turing machines is expressed in the next theorem.

5.22 Theorem Let Δ be any alphabet with at least two elements and let (P, G, F) be a $PS\Delta$ program. Then we can find a simple Turing machine that has Δ as its nonblank symbols and that is input/output equivalent to (P, G, F).

Theorem 5.22 is proven by developing a chain of lemmas which describe how a $PS\Delta$ program can be transformed into an equivalent $TL\Gamma S$ program, for suitable Γ, and then transformed from a $TL\Gamma S$ program into a simple Turing machine. The general plan of attack is to first show that, given a $PS\Delta$ program, we can find an equivalent $PS\Gamma$ program with only one string variable. Since a $TL\Gamma S$ program has but one variable, this is a reasonable first step toward our subgoal of obtaining a $TL\Gamma S$ program. The alphabet Γ will have one more symbol than the alphabet Δ. This extra symbol will, in effect, serve as a separator symbol so that several strings from Δ^* can be coded as a single string in Γ^*. For example, α, β, and γ in Δ^* would be coded as $\#\alpha\#\beta\#\gamma\#$, where $\#$ is the extra symbol. After reducing the program to a program with only one variable, we show that this one variable $PS\Gamma$ program is equivalent to a $PS\Gamma$ program which also has only one string variable and in which all Boolean expressions are atomic Boolean expressions. This last type of $PS\Gamma$ program has essentially the same type of Boolean expressions and essentially the same type of atomic statements as a $TL\Gamma S$ program. To get an equivalent $TL\Gamma S$ program, we need do little more than translate the various $PS\Gamma$ constructs, like **WHILE-DO**, into $TL\Gamma S$ statement by judicious use of **GOTO**'s. Once we have obtained a $TL\Gamma S$ program which is equivalent to our initial $PS\Delta$ program, it is fairly easy, given our previous results, to obtain the desired equivalent simple Turing machine. We now proceed with this plan of attack.

5.23 Lemma If Δ is any alphabet, L is any finite-state language over Δ, $\#$ is any symbol not in Δ, and i, n are any fixed positive integers such that $i \leqslant n$, then $\{\#\alpha_1\#\alpha_2\#...\#\alpha_n\# \mid \alpha_i \in L$ and, for all j, $\alpha_j \in \Delta^*\}$ is a finite-state language.

PROOF The proof is left as an exercise. $\square$

5.24 Lemma Suppose f is a computable partial function from Δ^* to Δ^*; suppose $\Gamma = \Delta \cup \{\#\}$, where $\#$ is a symbol not in Δ, and suppose i, j and n are positive integers such that both i and j are at most n. Let g be the partial function from Γ^* to Γ^* defined as follows: If $\alpha_1, \alpha_2, .., \alpha_n \in \Delta^*$ and $f(\alpha_j)$ is defined, then $g(\#\alpha_1\#\alpha_2\#...\#\alpha_n\#) = \#\beta_1\#\beta_2\#...\#\beta_n\#$, where $\beta_i = f(\alpha_j)$

and $\beta_k = \alpha_k$ for all $k \neq i$. For all other arguments, g is undefined. The function g, defined in this way, is a computable function.

PROOF The proof of this result is not too difficult. However, it consists of doing a large amount of $TL\Gamma$ programming. Most of the programming is tedious and one learns little by doing it. So, rather than give the full proof, we will just outline what needs to be done. To prove this lemma, it will suffice to show that given a $TL\Delta S$ program for f, we can produce a $TL\Gamma S$ program for g. To change the $TL\Delta S$ program for f into a $TL\Gamma S$ program for g, proceed as follows:

1. At the beginning, insert a piece of code that replaces α_i by α_j, and then position the tape head in front of the string in the ith position.
2. The $TL\Delta S$ code does not expect to see any #'s; so, before each usual $TL\Delta S$ instruction, insert a piece of code that checks if **SCAN** = #. If **SCAN** = #, then the $TL\Delta S$ code for f would see a blank if it were computing f. Hence if **SCAN** = #, then the $TL\Gamma S$ program needs some code to insert a blank after which control passes back to the usual $TL\Delta S$ instruction. There is a lot of detail here. To insert a blank you need to move a whole string over one square.
3. At the end, insert some code to eliminate any extra blanks. The computation that changed α_j to $f(\alpha_j)$ may have used a lot of space which is now blank; so, instead of $\#f(\alpha_j)\#$ in the ith position, you might have $\#B^m f(\alpha_j)B^r\#$, where B is the blank symbol and $m > 0$ or $r > 0$.

There is a lot of programming involved but you need not actually do it. All you need do is be certain that it can be done. □

5.25 Lemma Suppose i, j, k and n are positive integers such that i, j, and k are all less than n; suppose Δ is an arbitrary alphabet, and suppose # is a symbol that is not in Δ. Define the partial function h from $(\Delta \cup \{\#\})^*$ to $(\Delta \cup \{\#\})^*$ by $h(\#\alpha_1\#\alpha_2\#...\#\alpha_n\#) = \#\beta_1\#\beta_2\#...\#\beta_n\#$, where $\beta_i = \alpha_j\alpha_k$ and $\beta_t = \alpha_t$ for $t \neq i$. The function h, defined in this way, is a computable function.

PROOF The proof is left as an exercise. It is long and detailed but not difficult. □

Lemmas 5.23, 5.24, and 5.25 will allow us to convert a $PS\Delta$ program into an equivalent $PS\Gamma$ program with only one variable. The details of this conversion will be given later on. We now turn to the task of taking a one variable $PS\Gamma$ program and changing it to an equivalent $PS\Gamma$ program in which all Boolean expressions are atomic.

5.26 Lemma Suppose (P, G, F) is a $PS\Gamma$ program such that P has only the one variable **STRING**1. Then we can find an input/output equivalent $PS\Gamma$ program (P', G', F') such that P' has only the one variable **STRING**1 and such that every Boolean expression in P' is an atomic Boolean expression.

PROOF P' has the same function subprocedures as P. So $F = F'$. In fact, P' is the same as P except for the Boolean expressions. To obtain P' from P, introduce a new name for each Boolean expression of P. If β is a Boolean expression, A_β will denote the name associated with the expression β. To get P' from P, replace each Boolean expression β by the atomic Boolean expression **STRING**1 $\in A_\beta$. It remains to define G'. $G'(A_\beta)$ is defined so that it is a finite-state language and so that the following holds: α is in $G'(A_\beta)$ if and only if α makes the Boolean expression β true. If we define G' in such a way that it has these properties, then we will know that (P', G', F') is equivalent to (P, G, F). G is defined by induction on how the Boolean expression β is built up.

1. If β is the atomic Boolean expression **STRING**1 $\in C$, then $G'(A_\beta) = G(C)$.
2. If β is (**NOT** γ), then $G'(A_\beta) = \Gamma^* - G'(A_\gamma)$.
3. If β is (γ **AND** ξ), then $G'(A_\beta) = G'(A_\gamma) \cap G'(A_\xi)$.
4. If β is (γ **OR** ξ), then $G'(A_\beta) = G'(A_\gamma) \cup G'(A_\xi)$.

For any β, $G'(A_\beta)$ is obtained by combining finite-state languages using union, intersection, and complement. We know that the finite-state languages are closed under these operations (Theorems 3.5 and 3.8). So $G'(A_\beta)$ is a finite-state language. It remains to show:

Claim: α is in $G'(A_\beta)$ if and only if α makes β true.

This claim is proven by induction on the number of occurrences of Boolean operations **AND, OR, NOT**, in β. Assume that A_β and $G'(A_\beta)$ are defined as above for all Boolean expressions β, including those β which do not occur in P.

Base Case — No Operations: In this case, β is an atomic Boolean expression and the claim follows immediately using (1).

Induction Step: The induction has three cases, depending on what the outside operation is.

Case 1: β is (**NOT** γ) and, by induction hypothesis, α is in $G'(A_\gamma)$ if and only if α makes γ true. In this case, $G'(A_\beta) = \Gamma^* - G'(A_\gamma)$. So the following chain of statements are all equivalent: α is in $G'(A_\beta)$; α is not in $G'(A_\gamma)$; α makes γ false; α makes β true.

Case 2: β is (γ **AND** ξ) and, by induction hypothesis, α is in $G'(A_\gamma)$ if and only if α makes γ true; also, by the induction hypothesis, α is in $G'(A_\xi)$ if and only if α makes ξ true. In this case, $G'(A_\beta) = G'(A_\gamma) \cap G'(A_\xi)$. So the following chain of statements are equivalent: α is in $G'(A_\beta)$; α is in $G'(A_\gamma)$ and α is in $G'(A_\xi)$; α makes γ true and α makes ξ true; α makes $\beta = (\gamma$ **AND** $\xi)$ true.

Case 3: β is (γ **OR** ξ) and, by induction hypothesis, α is in $G'(A_\gamma)$ if and only if α makes γ true; α is in $G'(A_\xi)$ if and only if α makes ξ true.   This case is left as an exercise.

This ends the proof.   □

5.27 Lemma If (P, G, F) is a $PS\Gamma$ program such that P has only the one variable **STRING1** and such that all Boolean expressions in P are atomic Boolean expressions, then we can find an input/output equivalent $TL\Gamma S$ program (P', G', F').

PROOF To get (P', G', F'), proceed as follows. Set $G' = G$. Let g be a new subprocedure name for a function. Define $F'(g)$ to be the function which concatenates a string with itself; that is, $F'(g)(\alpha) = \alpha\alpha$. Set $F'(f) = F(f)$, for all subprocedure names for functions which occur in P. In order to define P', we will give a recursive algorithm to obtain a schema $T(P)$ from any arbitrary $PS\Gamma$ schema P. $T(P)$ is essentially the schema P' for the desired $TL\Gamma S$ program equivalent to P. To obtain P' from $T(P)$ requires only very minor syntactic changes and we can intuitively think of $T(P)$ as essentially being P'. Procedure 5.15 is the algorithm for obtaining $T(P)$.

The recursive algorithm for $T(P)$ can also be thought of in a somewhat more intuitive and somewhat less formal way. To obtain $T(P)$ from P, eliminate all of the **BEGIN-END**'s, **IF-THEN-ELSE**'s, and **WHILE-DO**'s by the methods given in (1), (2), and (3) of Procedure 5.15. For example, suppose $P =$ **IF** β **THEN** σ_1 **ELSE** σ_2, where β is a Boolean expression and σ_1, σ_2 are statements. Eliminate the outer **IF-THEN-ELSE** to obtain the code shown in Procedure 5.16, where $L1$ and $L2$ are new labels. If σ_2 contains no **BEGIN-END**'s, **IF-THEN-ELSE**'s, or **WHILE-DO**'s, then leave it as is. If it contains at least one such construct, eliminate them one by one starting with the outermost one. Similarly, eliminate these constructs from σ_1. Finally, replace all atomic statements of the form

$$\text{\textbf{STRING1}} := \text{\textbf{STRING1 STRING1}} \text{ by}$$
$$\text{\textbf{STRING1}} := g(\text{\textbf{STRING1}})$$

The result is $T(P)$.

Let $T_2(P)$ denote the string obtained from $T(P)$ by replacing all occurrences of **STRING1** by **STRING**. P' is then defined to be the following $TL\Delta S$ schema:

> **BEGIN**
> $T_2(P)$;
> L : **ACCEPT**
> **END**

where L is a label which does not occur in $T_2(P)$.

It is now easy to see that (P', G', F') is a $TL\Gamma S$ program that is input/output equivalent to (P, G, F) . To see that the two programs are equivalent, note the $T_2(P)$ does exactly the same thing to the contents of the **STRING** as P does to the contents of **STRING1**. In particular, $T_2(P)$ halts by

Procedure 5.15
Recursive Algorithm for $T(P)$

1. If $P = \textbf{BEGIN } \sigma_1; \sigma_2;...; \sigma_n \textbf{ END}$ then $T(P)$ is
$T(\sigma_1); T(\sigma_2); ...; T(\sigma_n)$.

2. If $P = \textbf{IF } \beta \textbf{ THEN } \sigma_1 \textbf{ ELSE } \sigma_2$ then $T(P)$ is
  IF β **THEN GOTO** $L1$;
   $T(\sigma_2)$;
  GOTO $L2$
 $L1$: <nothing 1>;
   $T(\sigma_1)$;
 $L2$: <nothing 2>

where <nothing 1> and <nothing 2> are any $TL\Gamma S$ statements that have no effect on the program. For example, each might be a **GOTO** to the next statement.

3. If $P = \textbf{WHILE } \beta \textbf{ DO } \sigma$, then $T(P)$ is
 $L1$: **IF** β **THEN GOTO** $L2$;
   GOTO $L3$;
 $L2$: <nothing 1>;
   $T(\sigma)$;
   GOTO $L1$;
 $L3$: <nothing 2>

where $L1$, $L2$ and $L3$ are new labels and both <nothing 1> and <nothing 2> are $TL\Gamma S$ statements that have no effect on the program.

4. If P is **STRING1** $:= f(\textbf{STRING1})$ then
$T(P)$ is P.

5. If P is **STRING1** $:= \textbf{STRING1 STRING1}$
then $T(P)$ is **STRING1** $:= g(\textbf{STRING1})$

END OF ALGORITHM.

---

running out of statements if and only if P halts. When we say $T_2(P)$ halts by running out of statements we mean that the statement labeled by L in P' will be executed in P'. So P has output β for an input α if and only if, on input α, P' reaches an accepting id with β stored in **STRING**. That is, P has output β for an input α if and only if P' does. $\square$

Proof of Theorem 5.22

Let (P, G, F) be a $PS\Delta$ program. Let $\Gamma = \Delta \cup \{\#\}$, where $\#$ is not in Δ. We first produce a $PS\Gamma$ program (P_2, G_2, F_2) such that this program has

Procedure 5.16
Code Equivalent to IF β THEN σ_1 ELSE σ_2

IF β THEN GOTO $L1$;
   σ_2;
   GOTO $L2$;
$L1$: <nothing 1>
   σ_1;
$L2$: <nothing 2>

---

just the one variable **STRING**1 and such that this program behaves the same as the $PS\Delta$ program on inputs α in Δ^*. That is, if one has a valid output for α, then the other has the same valid output for α. Using Lemma 5.26, we then produce a $PS\Gamma$ program (P_3, G_3, F_3) which is equivalent to (P_2, G_2, F_2) and which has the additional property that all Boolean expressions in (P_3, G_3, F_3) are atomic Boolean expressions. Using Lemma 5.27, we then produce a $TL\Gamma S$ program (P_4, G_4, F_4) which is equivalent to (P_3, G_3, F_3). The desired simple Turing machine is produced from this program. We now proceed to fill in the steps.

To obtain the one variable $TL\Gamma S$ program (P_2, G_2, F_2), proceed as follows: Let **STRING**1, **STRING**2, ..., **STRING**n be a list that includes all the variables of P. P_2 will be designed so that it simulates P. The one variable of P_2 will hold a string $\#\alpha_1\#\alpha_2...\#\alpha_n\#$, where each substring α_i is the string that P would keep in **STRING**i. To get P_2 from P, first change all atomic Boolean expressions in the following way. If **STRING**$i \in A$ is an atomic Boolean expression of P, then replace it by **STRING**1 $\in A_i$, where A_i is a new symbol and set $G_2(A_i) = \{\#\alpha_1\#\alpha_2\#...\#\alpha_n\# \mid \alpha_i \in G(A)$ and, for all j, $\alpha_j \in \Delta^*\}$. By Lemma 5.23, $G_2(A_i)$ is a finite-state language. Note that, in an intuitive sense, **STRING**1 $\in A_i$ is true for P_2 if and only if **STRING**$i \in A$ is true for P. So far, things look good for the simulation. Next change all statements of the form

STRING$i := f(\text{**STRING**}j)$ to **STRING**1 $:= f_{ij}(\text{**STRING**1})$

where f_{ij} is a new symbol and $F_2(f_{ij})$ is the partial function g obtained from f as in Lemma 5.24. Next change all statements of the form

STRING$i := \text{**STRING**}j \, \text{**STRING**}k$ to **STRING**1 $:= h(\text{**STRING**1})$

where h is a new symbol and $F_2(h)$ is defined in the same way as the function h in Lemma 5.25.

By Lemmas 5.24 and 5.25, the $F_2(f_{ij})$ and $F_2(h)$ are computable partial functions. Also, $F_2(f_{ij})$ changes a string $\#\alpha_1\#\alpha_2...\#\alpha_n\#$ just as $F(f)$ would change the storage configuration $(\alpha_1, \alpha_2, ..., \alpha_n)$ and $F_2(h)$ changes the storage configuration $(\alpha_1, \alpha_2, ..., \alpha_n)$ in the correct way. So the simulation should work. The only thing left to do is some bookkeeping at the beginning and end of the simulation. Let P'_2 be the code obtained by modifying P in the way just described. P_2 is

> **BEGIN**
>   **STRING**1 := q (**STRING**1);
> P'_2;
>   **STRING**1 := p (**STRING**1)
> **END**

where q and p are new symbols and $F_2(q)$ and $F_2(p)$ are defined as follows:

$$F_2(q)(\alpha) = \#\alpha\#^n = \#\alpha\#(\Lambda\#)^{n-1} \; for \; all \; \alpha \; in \; \Delta^*$$
$$F_2(p)(\#\alpha_1\#\alpha_2\#...\alpha_n\#) = \alpha_1 \; for \; all \; \alpha_1, \alpha_2, ..., \alpha_n \; in \; \Delta^*$$

The values of $F_2(q)$ and $F_2(p)$ can be undefined for other arguments. $F_2(q)$ puts α into the simulated storage configuration. $F_2(p)$ takes α_1 out of the simulated storage configuration. It is easy to show that $F_2(q)$ and $F_2(p)$ are computable. Since P'_2 does a step-by-step simulation of P, it should be clear that (P, G, F) and (P_2, G_2, F_2) are input/output equivalent.

Applying Lemmas 5.26 and 5.27, we immediately obtain a $TL\Gamma S$ program (P_4, G_4, F_4) which is input/output equivalent to (P_2, G_2, F_2) and hence is input/output equivalent to the $PS\Delta$ program (P, G, F) .

We know by Theorems 5.14 and 5.18 that (P_4, G_4, F_4) is input/output equivalent to a simple Turing machine M with nonblank symbols Δ. Hence (P, G, F) is input/output equivalent to M and the theorem is proven. $\square$

We now know that, given a $PS\Delta$ program, we can obtain our choice of a $TL\Delta S$ program, a $TL\Delta$ program, or a simple Turing machine that is input/output equivalent to the given $PS\Delta$ program. Our next theorem says we can translate in the other direction as well. Given a simple Turing machine, we can find an input/output equivalent $PS\Delta$ program.

5.28 Theorem Given a simple Turing machine M with nonblank symbols Δ, we can find a $PS\Delta$ program that is input/output equivalent to M.

PROOF The proof is extremely simple. The desired $PS\Delta$ program is (P, G, F) where the schema P is

> **BEGIN STRING**1 := f(**STRING**1) **END**

where $F(f)$ is the unique partial function computed by M and where G is irrelevant and hence arbitrary. $\square$

For the sake of future reference, we summarize all these equivalences in one theorem. The result is immediate from Corollary 5.19 and Theorems 5.22 and 5.28.

5.29 Theorem If Δ is an alphabet with at least two symbols and f is any partial function from Δ^* to Δ^*, then the following statements are equivalent:

1. f is computed by some $PS\Delta$ program.
2. f is computed by some $TL\Delta S$ program.
3. f is computed by some $TL\Delta$ program.
4. f is computed by some simple Turing machine with nonblank symbols Δ.

We now know that $PS\Delta$ programs, $TL\Delta S$ programs, $TL\Delta$ programs, and simple Turing machines are all equivalent in computing power. So, when discussing programs, we are free to talk about either $PS\Delta$ programs or $TL\Delta S$ programs or $TL\Delta$ programs or simple Turing machines, whichever is most convenient, and we will know that our results apply to all four notions of programs. $PS\Delta$ is a clearly powerful language that is fairly easy to write programs in. Simple Turing machines and $TL\Delta$ program have a simple structure and are frequently easy to analyze. When we wish to write procedures, we will usually write them in $PS\Delta$. On the other hand, when we wish to prove theorems which require that we analyze all things that can happen in our programming language, then we will usually use $TL\Delta$ programs or simple Turing machines.

One feature that is common to many programming languages but is missing from $PS\Delta$ is arrays. We could have added arrays and facilities for handling them in $PS\Delta$. We would still have been able to show that $PS\Delta$ with arrays is equivalent to simple Turing machines. The proof would not have been essentially different but would have been longer and more complicated. Similarly, we could have added almost any other common programming language construct to $PS\Delta$ and still have obtained the same equivalence with simple Turing machines.

One thing that may seem a little unusual about $PS\Delta$ is that it is not completely self-contained. It requires subprocedures written in $TL\Delta S$. Remember that our goal was to make $PS\Delta$ expressive and powerful. This subprocedure structure can only add to the power and expressiveness of $PS\Delta$. It allows $PS\Delta$ to use any subprocedure which can be written in $TL\Delta S$ as a sort of primitive operation. In fact, by our results on the equivalence of $PS\Delta$ and $TL\Delta S$, we can build up a library of subroutines using $PS\Delta$ as well as $TL\Delta S$ programs. If we wanted to implement a particular realization of $PS\Delta$, we could fix a collection of subprocedures, but the language so obtained would be only a subset of $PS\Delta$. If we choose our collection of subprocedures with care, it will be as powerful as $PS\Delta$ but it would not be as expressive and its power would not be as obvious. In any event, we have no intentions of implementing $PS\Delta$. It is only an abstract construct designed to show the power of simple Turing machines.

THE CHURCH/TURING THESIS

$PS\Delta$ is a very versatile programming language. It should be clear that you can implement a wide variety of informally described digital procedures or programs in *PS*Δ. (We use the words "program," "effective procedure," and "digital procedure" interchangeably.) As we develop the theory of Turing machines further, you should eventually become convinced that any informally described digital procedure can be implemented on a Turing machine. What we mean by a digital procedure is not exactly clear since it is, in this context, an informal concept and not a precisely defined mathematical notion. Nonetheless, it does convey real meaning to people concerned with computers and programming. If we assume that any digital procedure can be implemented on a Turing machine, then we have a mathematically precise notion of what constitutes a digital procedure. Under this assumption, digital procedures are equivalent to Turing machines. So given this assumption, we can develop a rigorous theory of digital procedures. The assumption that any digital procedure can be implemented on a Turing machine is referred to as *Turing's thesis* and also as *Church's thesis.*

5.30 The Church/Turing Thesis Any partial function that can be computed by a well-defined digital-type procedure can be computed by some simple Turing machine.

Stated in this way, the Church/Turing thesis is very believable. *PS*Δ has all the essential features of the general-purpose programming language PASCAL. It is in fact true that, given any program written in PASCAL or any other common programming language, we can find a *PS*Δ program, and hence a simple Turing machine, which computes the same partial function as this program. Similarly, any procedure written in the instruction set of any commonly marketed digital computer can be implemented on a Turing machine. As we develop more techniques for handling Turing machines and as you become more familiar with the model, this should become clear to you. The proofs of these facts would be long, tedious, and somewhat maddening. But, given time and patience, there would be no insurmountable problems in constructing formal proofs of these facts. However, we will never use the Church/Turing thesis in a proof except as a kind of shorthand. We may sometimes give an informal algorithm for something and say "by the Church/Turing thesis this can be done on a Turing machine." However, whenever we do this, we will have in mind a particular method of implementing the task on a Turing machine. We will not bother to write it down simply because it is a routine but tedious task. So all the mathematics presented here is valid whether or not you believe the Church/Turing thesis. However, the results are not very interesting unless you believe in some close approximation to the Church/Turing thesis. This thesis is why Turing machines are worth studying. They are worth studying because programming is worth studying, and if you believe the Church/Turing thesis, then the study of what things can possibly be done by Turing machines is the same thing as the study of what things can possible be done by any sort of computer program.

This thesis or hypothesis was formulated independently by Alonzo Church and Alan M. Turing. Church's original formulation was not in terms of machines but in terms of a mathematically equivalent but very different definition of the class of formally computable functions. This definition made heavy use of the notion of mathematical recursion and so these functions were called recursive functions. This is the reason that computable functions are frequently called partial recursive functions. We will use the words "computable" and "recursive" interchangeably. Since the original work by Church and Turing in the 1930's, many other characterizations of the computable functions have been given. One commonly advanced argument for the validity of the Church/Turing thesis is that so many different definitions of the computable functions are provably equivalent.

It should be noted that the choice of Turing machines as a formal model for digital computers has, to a certain extent, been made on the basis of personal taste. We could use any one of a wide variety of formal machine models, all of which are provably equivalent. Most of these models do, however, have a striking resemblance to Turing machines and the choice of Turing machines as the model to focus on does have much to recommend it. Two conspicuous advantages of the model are that it has a very strong intuitive appeal and that it has been extensively studied. It is possibly the most frequently used model of a computer and is certainly the most completely analyzed model.

EXERCISES

1. Write a $TL\Delta$ program to compute the function f defined as follows:
   a. $f(a^i b^j) = a^{i-j}$ if $i > j$
   b. $f(\alpha) = \Lambda$ for all other arguments.
      $\Delta = \{a, b\}$

2. Write a $TL\Delta$ program to compute the function f defined as follows: $f(a^i b a^j) = a^i b^2 a^j$ for all i, j; $f(\alpha) = \alpha$ for all other arguments. $\Delta = \{a, b\}$.

3. Write a $TL\Delta S$ program to do binary addition. Use any Δ you wish. Do not forget to write $TL\Delta$ programs for all the function subprocedure names and finite-state machines for all the language subprocedure names.

4. Write a $PS\Delta$ program to do binary multiplication.

5. Prove: If f and g are computable partial functions from Δ^* to Δ^*, then the composition of f and g is a computable partial function. The *composition* of f and g is the function h defined by the equation $h(\alpha) = f(g(\alpha))$. [The equality is to be interpreted to mean that $h(\alpha)$ is only defined if $g(\alpha)$ and $f(g(\alpha))$ are both defined and, in this case, $h(\alpha) = f(g(\alpha))$.]

6. Prove Lemmas 5.23 and 5.25.

7. Complete the proof of Lemma 5.26 by doing case 3 of the induction.

8. Prove that the set of all $TL\Delta$ programs with labels in $\{0, 1\}^*$ is not a finite-state language. (In fact, it is not even a cfl but this is harder to prove.)

9. Suppose you change the definition of $TL\Delta$ syntax so that you no longer require that each statement have a unique label. (You need not worry about what such programs would mean. Just consider the syntax.) Prove that, with this change, the set of $TL\Delta$ programs with labels in $\{0, 1\}^*$ is a finite-state language.

10. Let Δ be any alphabet. Write a $PS\Gamma$ program to compute the total function syntax defined as follows: $\text{syntax}(\alpha) = 1$, provided α is a $TL\Delta$ program with labels in $\{0, 1\}^*$ and $\text{syntax}(\alpha) = 0$ otherwise. Take Γ to be any convenient alphabet that contains all the symbols needed to write $TL\Delta$ programs with labels in $\{0, 1\}^*$.

11. Let Σ be an alphabet. Let ¢ be a symbol which is not in Σ. Let f be a function from $(\Sigma \cup \{¢\})^*$ to $(\Sigma \cup \{¢\})^*$ and let w_0 be a string in Σ^*. The function h is said to be defined from f and w_0 by *recursion on notation* provided the following two equations hold:
   a. $h(\Lambda) = w_0$
   b. $h(xa) = f(h(x)¢a)$, for all $x \in \Sigma^*$ and all $a \in \Sigma$.
   Prove: If f is a computable function, w_0 is any word and h is defined from f and w_0 by recursion on notation, then h is a computable function.

12. Let $m \geqslant 2$ be a natural number. Let Γ be the alphabet consisting of the m digits 0, 1, 2, ..., $m-1$. For any natural number x, let $(x)_m$ denote the base m numeral (without leading zeros) for x. So $(x)_m$ is a string in Γ^*. Let f be a function from natural numbers to natural numbers. Let f_m be the partial function from Γ^* to Γ^* defined by: (1) $f_m((x)_m) = (f(x))_m$ for all natural numbers x and (2) f_m is undefined on all other strings. f is said to be *computable in base m* provided f_m is a computable function.
   Prove: For any n, $m \geqslant 2$ and any function f on the natural numbers, f is computable in base m if and only if f is computable in base n. [f is said to be *computable* if f is computable in base m for some, equivalently all, $m \geqslant 2$.]

13. Let f be a total function from the natural numbers to the natural numbers. Define a partial function h from the natural numbers to the natural numbers as follows: $h(x) = \min \{y \mid y \leqslant x \text{ and } f(y) = 0\}$; if no such y exists, then $h(x)$ is undefined.
   Prove: If f is a computable total function, then h is a computable function.

Chapter
Six

Universal Turing
Machines
and the
Halting Problem

A Turing machine is unlike many real computers in that it is not a programmable computer. We can think of $TL\Delta$ programs as if they were programs for Turing machines but they are not, in any sense we have seen so far, programs for one fixed Turing machine. Two different $TL\Delta$ programs yield two different simple Turing machines as their Turing machine realizations. In some of our following work it will be convenient to have Turing machines that can be programmed. These Turing machines would, in effect, receive two input strings: one a program and one the data for that program. Such Turing machines would, in some sense, execute the program on the data. In this way we would obtain a single Turing machine which could be programmed to compute any computable function.

The Turing machine model does not have a facility to accept arbitrary programs included in its definition. However, with a minimum of coding we can define a method whereby certain Turing machines can naturally be viewed as being programmable. These machines are called *universal Turing machines.* They are called universal because they can, in a very natural sense, compute any computable function. The intuitive concept of a universal Turing machine is fairly simple. A universal Turing machine is one that computes a function u of two arguments, a program P, and a data string α. The value of u on P and α will be the output of the program P on input α. Since we have defined Turing machines as computing only functions of one argument, we will need to do a small amount of coding. Rather than making u a function of two arguments P and α, we make u a function of one argument. In the cases of interest, the one argument to u will be the string $P\text{¢}\alpha$, where ¢ is a special punctuation symbol, P is the program, and α is the input or data for P. The formal definition restates these intuitive ideas more precisely.

A UNIVERSAL TURING MACHINE

6.1 Definition A simple Turing machine is said to be a *universal Turing machine* for the alphabet Δ provided that it computes a partial function u with the following properties:

1. u is a partial function from Γ^* to Γ^* where Γ is an alphabet which includes all the symbols of Δ, one symbol $\math022$ not in Δ, and possibly other symbols.
2. For each computable partial function f from Δ^* to Δ^*, there is a string P in Γ^* such that $u(P\math022\alpha) = f(\alpha)$, for all $\alpha \in \Delta^*$. (The equality $u(P\math022\alpha) = f(\alpha)$ is to be interpreted to mean that if one side is defined, then the other side is defined and they are equal.)

Intuitively, P is a program for f. Thus, intuitively, a universal Turing machine is one that can be programmed to compute any computable function.

6.2 Theorem For any alphabet Δ, we can find a universal Turing machine for the alphabet Δ.

PROOF We will write a program for a universal Turing machine for the alphabet Δ. This program will compute a partial function u such that:

> If P is a $TL\Delta$ program for a function f and all labels of P are in $\{0, 1\}^*$, then $u(P\math022\alpha) = f(\alpha)$ for all α in Δ^*.

If f is any computable function from Δ^* to Δ^*, then it is computed by a $TL\Delta$ program P. Clearly, we can fix up P so that all its labels are in $\{0, 1\}^*$. So any Turing machine that computes u will be a universal Turing machine for the alphabet Δ. So once we have a $PS\Gamma$ program to compute u, we are done. We will state the program for u in a very informal way that is similar to a $PS\Gamma$ program for some suitably large Γ. However, as stated, it is certainly not a valid $PS\Gamma$ program. It is, however, easy, though tedious, to convert it to a correct $PS\Gamma$ program. Finally, the $PS\Gamma$ program can be converted to an equivalent Turing machine. Rather than do the actual conversions, we will appeal to the Church/Turing thesis.

The program will have three variables **STRING2**, **STRING3**, and **STRING4**, in addition to **STRING1** which holds the input. (When converted to a correct $PS\Gamma$ program, it would have these variables plus a few others.) Given input $P\math022\alpha$, where P is a $TL\Delta$ program and α is in Δ^*, the program will first put P in **STRING2**, the label of the start state of P in **STRING3**, and the tape configuration $\triangleright\alpha$ in **STRING4**. So **STRING3** and **STRING4** together hold the start id of the Turing machine realization of P. The program then computes the next id and the next id after that, and so forth. Each id is stored in the two variables **STRING3** and **STRING4**, the state in **STRING3**, the tape configuration in **STRING4**. If the computation halts in an accepting state, then the string in the tape configuration is retrieved from **STRING4** and outputted. Procedure 6.1 is the program.

Procedure 6.1
Program to Compute u

BEGIN
    IF [the Input is not of the form $P\mathcal{c}\alpha$, where P is a $TL\Delta$ program
      with labels in $\{0, 1\}^*$ and α is in Δ^*]
      THEN [abort the computation]
      ELSE [continue];
    STRING2 := P;
    STRING3 := Start state of P;
    STRING4 := $\triangleright\alpha$;
    WHILE [(**STRING3, STRING4**) is not a halting id] **DO**
      BEGIN
          STRING3 := [State of next id after
            (**STRING3, STRING4**)];
          STRING4 := [Tape configuration of next id after
            (**STRING3, STRING4**)]
      END;
    IF [**STRING3** is an accepting state **AND STRING4** is of the form
      $B^n\triangleright\xi B^m$ where B is the blank symbol, $\xi \in \Delta^*$, $n \geqslant 0$ and $m \geqslant 0$]
      THEN [Output ξ]
      ELSE [abort the computation]
END

In order to convert this program to a valid $PS\Gamma$ program, we will need to know that the following partial functions from Γ^* to Γ^* are all computable. In all cases, we assume Γ contains all the symbols of Δ, plus the two special symbols $\mathcal{c}$ and $\triangleright$, plus a symbol B to serve as the blank symbol, plus all the symbols needed to write $TL\Delta$ programs with labels in $\{0, 1\}^*$ plus possibly other symbols.

1. FORM$(\xi) = 1$ if $\xi = P\mathcal{c}\alpha$ where P is a $TL\Delta$ program with labels in $\{0, 1\}^*$ and α is in Δ^*. FORM$(\xi) = 0$ otherwise,
2. $p(P\mathcal{c}\alpha) = P$ if α does not contain $\mathcal{c}$. For any other argument ξ, $p(\xi)$ is undefined.
3. $g(P\mathcal{c}\alpha) =$ the start state of P provided P is a $TL\Delta$ program. For any argument ξ which is not of the form $P\mathcal{c}\alpha$, $g(\xi)$ is undefined.
4. $k(P\mathcal{c}\alpha) = \triangleright\alpha$ if α is in Δ^*. For any argument ξ which is not of the form $P\mathcal{c}\alpha$, $k(\xi)$ is undefined.
5. $l(P\mathcal{c}q) = 1$ if P is a $TL\Delta$ program, and q is an accepting state of P. For all other arguments ξ, $l(\xi) = 0$.

6. $m(P¢q_1¢\alpha_1 \triangleright \beta_1) = q_2$ provided P is a $TL\Delta$ program, α_1, β_1 are in $(\Delta \cup \{B\})^*$, q_1 is a state of P, and q_2 is the state of the id obtained from $(q_1, \alpha_1 \triangleright \beta_1)$ by executing one step of P. If there is no next id, then m is undefined. For arguments ζ not of the above form, $m(\zeta)$ is undefined.

7. $n(P¢q_1¢\alpha_1 \triangleright \beta_1) = \alpha_2 \triangleright \beta_2$ provided P, q_1, α_1, and β_1 satisfy the conditions given in (6) and $\alpha_2 \triangleright \beta_2$ is the tape configuration of the id obtained from $(q_1, \alpha_1 \triangleright \beta_1)$ by executing one step of P. If there is no next id, then n is undefined. For arguments ζ which are not of the above form, $n(\zeta)$ is undefined.

Using Exercise 5-10 it is not difficult to show that Form is a computable function. It is easy to write informal algorithms for Turing machines to compute the remaining functions defined above. By the Church/Turing thesis, we know that these informal algorithms can be converted to precisely defined Turing machines. So all the functions defined above are computable and our program for computing u is a correct but very informal program. By the Church/Turing thesis, it can be converted to an equivalent Turing machine. It is easy to see that it can be converted to a PST program and from this to a Turing machine. Therefore, we do not need the Church/Turing thesis. We are only using it to spare ourselves the task of writing a lot of tedious and uninteresting PST code. □

In order to extract one additional result which will prove useful later on, we now reexamine the proof of Theorem 6.2. Let U be the universal Turing machine derived from the PST program in the proof of Theorem 6.2. The theorem says that, on input $P¢\alpha$, U has output equal to the output of program P on input α. The proof shows even more, namely that U, in some sense, computes this output in the same way that P would. More precisely, U on input $P¢\alpha$ performs a step-by-step simulation of P on input α. In particular, U halts on input $P¢\alpha$ if and only if P halts on input α. This observation is recorded in the next lemma.

6.3 Lemma Let Δ be an alphabet. Let U be the particular universal Turing machine, for the alphabet Δ, which was defined by the PST program in the proof of Theorem 6.2. It then follows that, for any $TL\Delta$ program P and any string α in Δ^*: U halts on the input $P¢\alpha$ if and only if P halts on the input α.

THE HALTING PROBLEM

When writing a program P, we can make a mistake and inadvertently introduce an unintended infinite loop. If we make such a mistake, it can turn out that on some input α the program never halts, even though it was our intention to have P halt on α and produce some output. The problem of testing whether or not a given program P halts on a given input α is called the *halting problem*. It would be very helpful when checking programs for correctness to have at our disposal a program which takes as input any other program P and any input string α for P and gives us as output the answer to the following question: "Does the computation of P on input α eventually halt?" In this section we will see that no such checking program can be written. We will give a proof that no such checking program exists for programs P written in the language $TL\Delta$. A similar result holds for any programming language which is general-purpose, in the sense that it can be used to write programs to compute all the computable functions. $TL\Delta$ was chosen as a convenient programming language to study. The proof for any other general-purpose programming language would be similar. In order to give the proof, we will need to first limit the types of labels we use in $TL\Delta$ programs and then consider some ways of coding $TL\Delta$ programs as strings of symbols other than in the usual way.

In the rest of this chapter, we will always assume that all labels in $TL\Delta$ programs are elements of $\{0, 1\}^*$. Since any program can trivially be rewritten so that all its labels are in $\{0, 1\}^*$, this is not a significant restriction. The only reason for restricting the labels in this way is that we want all the $TL\Delta$ programs under consideration to be strings of symbols from some fixed finite set of symbols. We would get the same results with any other alphabet in place of $\{0, 1\}$.

A $TL\Delta$ program is a string of symbols. Suppose Γ is an alphabet that includes all the symbols needed to write $TL\Delta$ programs with labels in $\{0, 1\}^*$. Since a $TL\Delta$ program is a string in Γ^*, a $TL\Delta$ program may serve as the input to a $TL\Gamma$ program. Therefore, one program may be the input to another program. We will want a $TL\Delta$ program to be a legitimate input string for itself. Unfortunately, a $TL\Delta$ program is a string over a larger alphabet than Δ and so cannot be an input to itself. In order to overcome this difficulty, we will define a way of coding any $TL\Delta$ program as a string in Δ^*. This coding will be called the *homogeneous coding* of the program. This coding is called homogeneous because we could have developed universal Turing machines using homogeneous codings instead of $TL\Delta$ programs. If we were to develop universal Turing machines in this way, then we would have homogeneity of programs and data.

6.4 Definition

Let Δ be an alphabet with at least two elements. Let b and c be two distinct symbols in Δ. Let Γ be the alphabet consisting of all symbols needed to write $TL\Delta$ programs with labels in $\{0, 1\}^*$. So Γ is, in general, a larger set of symbols than Δ. We will describe a method of coding each symbol of Γ as a distinct string of symbols in $\{b, c\}^*$. We will then use this coding to show how every string in Γ^* can be coded as a string in $\{b, c\}^*$. Since every $TL\Delta$ program with labels in $\{0, 1\}^*$ is a string in Γ^* and since $\{b, c\}$ is a subset of Δ, this will give us a method to code every such $TL\Delta$ program as a string in Δ^*

Let k be the number of symbols in Γ and let $a_1, a_2, ..., a_k$ be an enumeration, without repetition, of the symbols in Γ. So $\Gamma = \{a_1, a_2, ..., a_k\}$. (If Δ contains l symbols, then $k = 16 + l$, provided Δ does not contain any of the 16 special symbols used to write $TL\Delta$ programs with labels in $\{0, 1\}^*$. The

16 symbols are the 14 symbols listed in Definition 5.3.2 plus the two symbols 0 and 1. However, all we care about is that there is some such k.) For each symbol a_i in Γ, define $\text{hcode}(a_i) = cb^i$. Each symbol of Γ is then coded as a distinct string in $\{b, c\}^*$. For each string $a_{i_1} a_{i_2} ... a_{i_n}$ in Γ, define $\text{hcode}(a_{i_1} a_{i_2} ... a_{i_n})$ to be the string

$$\text{hcode}(a_{i_1})\text{hcode}(a_{i_2})...\text{hcode}(a_{i_n})$$

For example, $\text{hcode}(a_2 a_3 a_1 a_2) = cbbcbbbcbcbb$.

If P is a $TL\Delta$ program with labels in $\{0, 1\}^*$, then P is a string in Γ^* and $\text{hcode}(P)$ is a string in Δ^*. The string $\text{hcode}(P)$ is called the *homogeneous coding* of P. Since $\text{hcode}(P)$ is a coded version of P, $\text{hcode}(P)$ can be considered a program. Hence, we have homogeneity of program and data, because we can think of the string $\text{hcode}(P)$ as being an input for the program $\text{hcode}(P)$.

Our next result gives us an example of a function which is not computable. Hence, we will see that not all functions are computable. The function d, defined in the next theorem, was specifically designed to be a function which is not computable. It is not a function that arises naturally in very many contexts. The only thing that is interesting about this function d is that it is not computable. However, knowing that this function d is not computable will help us to show that no program exists to solve the halting problem. In other words, showing d is not computable is a technical result that will later be used to show that some interesting functions are not computable.

Functions like d are frequently called *diagonal functions*. The reason for the term "diagonal" is that d is concerned with the result of running programs on themselves. If we consider a two-dimensional array indexed by elements (α, β) consisting of programs α and inputs β, then the function d deals primarily with the diagonal elements (α, α). If we number programs by positive integers and number the possible inputs by positive integers, then every element (α, β) is associated with a pair of integers and hence a point in the cartesian plane or, less formally, a point on graph paper. The points (α, α) all lie on the main diagonal.

6.5 Theorem Let Δ be any alphabet with at least two elements. Let $<\text{yes}>$ and $<\text{no}>$ denote two distinct elements of Δ. Let d be any partial function from Δ^* to Δ^* such that the following holds for all P which are $TL\Delta$ programs with labels in $\{0, 1\}^*$.

1. If P has output $<\text{yes}>$ for the input $\text{hcode}(P)$, then $d(\text{hcode}(P)) = <\text{no}>$.
2. If P does not have output $<\text{yes}>$ for the input $\text{hcode}(P)$, then $d(\text{hcode}(P)) = <\text{yes}>$.

Under these conditions, d is not a computable function.

PROOF The proof is by contradiction. Suppose there were such a function d which was computable. Then d is computed by some $TL\Delta$ program P_d with labels in $\{0, 1\}^*$. From the description of d, the following statements are seen to be equivalent:

3. $d(\text{hcode}(P_d)) = <\text{yes}>$.
4. P_d does not have output $<\text{yes}>$ for the input $\text{hcode}(P_d)$.

To see that (3) and (4) are equivalent, substitute P_d for P in (1) and (2) above. But P_d computes d. Thus (4) is equivalent to the following:

5. $d(\text{hcode}(P_d)) \neq <\text{yes}>$.

So (3) and (5) are equivalent and we have a contradiction, as promised. □

We will use Theorem 6.5 to construct a proof that no computer program can solve the halting problem. This result about the halting problem is formalized using a function called *Check*. The function Check takes a program P and an input string α for P and then tells whether or not P halts on the input α. The formal definition of Check is given in the statement of Theorem 6.7, but we need not concern ourselves with a precise definition of Check at this point. When we formalize the assertion that the halting problem cannot be solved by any computer program, we get the formally precise statement that Check is not computable. So our task will be to prove that Check is not computable. To do this, we use a very common technique for showing that a given function is not computable. We now outline this technique.

Suppose that we wish to show that a function f is not computable. (In the case of the halting problem, f will be the function Check.) Using this particular proof technique, we assume that f is computable and derive a contradiction. More specifically, we find some other function g for which we already have a proof that g is not computable. Under the assumption that f is computable, we then show that g is computable. This is, of course, a contradiction. So we conclude that f is not computable. In more detail, the technique goes as follows.

We assume that f is computable. That means that we are assuming that we have a program to compute f. So we are free to write programs assuming that we have available a subprocedure to compute f. Using our assumed subprocedure for f, we then write a program to compute the function g. But we know that g is not computable. Hence, we have a contradiction and can conclude that our assumption about f being computable must have been incorrect. In this way, we prove that f is not computable.

In the case of the halting problem, f is the function Check and g is the function d of Theorem 6.5. So our goal, in the proof that no program can solve the halting problem, will be to write a program for d using an assumed subprocedure for Check. The function *Fix*, defined in the next lemma, is specifically designed to help us achieve this goal.

6.6 Lemma Let Δ be any finite alphabet. We can find a computable function Fix which has the following properties: If P is any $TL\Delta$ program with labels in $\{0, 1\}^*$, then $\text{Fix}(P) = P'$, where P' is a $TL\Delta$ program with labels in $\{0, 1\}^*$ and is such that on any input ξ, if P has output $<\text{yes}>$, then P' has output $<\text{yes}>$; if P does not have output $<\text{yes}>$ on input ξ, then P' does not halt on the input ξ.

PROOF We will give an informally stated algorithm to obtain $P' = \text{Fix}(P)$ from P. Let $L1$, $L2$, and $L3$ be three labels which do not occur in P. To obtain P' from P, proceed as follows:

1. Whenever there is a **GOTO** $<\text{label}>$ such that the $<\text{label}>$ does not occur in P, replace **GOTO** $<\text{label}>$ by **GOTO** $L3$.
2. Replace each occurrence of **ACCEPT** by **GOTO** $L1$.
3. Add the following code to the end of the program.
   $L3$: **GOTO** $L3$;
   $L1$: **IF** [the tape configuration is $\triangleright <\text{yes}>$]
       THEN GOTO $L2$;
       ELSE GOTO $L3$;
   $L2$: **ACCEPT**

Statement $L1$ is not a $TL\Delta$ statement. It is more like a $PS\Delta$ statement. By the same techniques we used to compile $PS\Delta$ programs to $TL\Delta$ programs, we can convert $L1$ to equivalent $TL\Delta$ statements.

    P' clearly has the desired properties. By the Church/Turing thesis we know that the above informal algorithm to obtain P' from P can be converted to a Turing machine program to compute Fix. So Fix is a computable function. $\square$

    We are now ready to prove that there can be no program to solve the halting problem.

6.7 Theorem (Unsolvability of the halting problem) Let Δ be any alphabet with at least two elements. Let $<\text{ok}>$ and $<\infty \text{ loop}>$ be any two distinct symbols in Δ. Let Check be any partial function with the following properties:

1. If P is any $TL\Delta$ program with labels in $\{0, 1\}^*$ and α is in Δ^*, then $\text{Check}(P\math00a2\alpha) = <\text{ok}>$ provided that the computation on P on input α halts.
2. If the computation of P on input α does not halt, then $\text{Check}(P\math00a2\alpha) = <\infty \text{ loop}>$.

Under these conditions Check is not a computable function.

PROOF Suppose Check is such a function and suppose Check is computable. We will derive a contradiction. Specifically, we will use Check as a subprocedure to write a program to compute a function d as in Theorem 6.5. Since any such d is not computable, this will be a contradiction.

Procedure 6.2
Program to Compute d
(The input is in **STRING**1)

IF [**STRING**1 is not of the form hcode(P) for some $TL\Delta$ program P]
  THEN [abort the computation]
  ELSE
    BEGIN
      STRING2 := Decode(**STRING**1);
      STRING2 := Fix(**STRING**2);
      STRING1 := Check(**STRING**2¢**STRING**1);
      IF STRING1 = <ok>
        THEN [Output <no>]
        ELSE [Output <yes>]
    END

The program to compute d uses four subprocedures for functions: one subprocedure for Check plus three other subprocedures for functions called *Fix*, *Syntax*, and *Decode*. We are assuming that we have a subprocedure for Check. However, the other three functions must be defined and shown to be computable. Fix is the function defined and shown to be computable in Lemma 6.6. The function Syntax takes strings of symbols from the alphabet used to write $TL\Delta$ programs and maps each such string onto 0 or 1. For any string α, Syntax$(\alpha) = 1$ if α is a syntactically correct $TL\Delta$ program with labels in $\{0, 1\}^*$ and Syntax$(\alpha) = 0$ otherwise. By Exercise 5-10 we know that Syntax is a computable function. For the definition of Decode, let b and c be the two symbols in Δ which we used to express the homogeneous coding of $TL\Delta$ programs in Definition 6.4. Decode is the inverse of hcode. That is, for any string β in $\{b, c\}^*$, Decode$(\beta) = \gamma$ provided γ is the unique string such that hcode$(\gamma) = \beta$. The string γ need not be a $TL\Delta$ program. All we require is that hcode$(\gamma) = \beta$. If there is no string γ such that hcode$(\gamma) = \beta$, then Decode(β) is undefined. We leave it as an easy exercise to show that Decode is computable. That takes care of the subprocedures for functions. The program also has one subprocedure for a language called *HCODES*. HCODES is a subprocedure name for the language consisting of all strings β in $\{b, c\}^*$ such that $\beta = $ hcode(γ), for some string γ. It is another easy exercise to see that this language is a finite-state language.

We are now ready to give the program to compute the function d. Let <yes> and <no> denote two distinct symbols in Δ. The function d maps strings in Δ^* to strings in Δ^*, in fact, to one of the two symbols in Δ which we are denoting <yes> and <no>. It will be convenient to use more symbols than Δ in the program for d. Hence, the program for d will be a $PS\Gamma$ program, where Γ is a larger alphabet than Δ. Γ will be the set of symbols needed to write $TL\Delta$ programs with labels in $\{0, 1\}^*$. This is a minor point and in any event we know by Theorems 5.18 and 5.29 that if there is such a $PS\Gamma$ program to compute d, then there is also a $PS\Delta$ program to compute d. Procedure 6.2 is the program.

The first Boolean condition in Procedure 6.2 is equivalent to

[**STRING** 1 is not in HCODES] **OR** [Syntax (Decode (**STRING** 1)) = 0]

With this observation in mind, it is not difficult to convert Procedure 6.2 into an equivalent and syntactically correct $PS\Gamma$ program. One can either carry out the details of the translation, which do involve a little more than just rewriting the first Boolean expression, or else one can appeal to the Church/Turing thesis.

It remains to show that the function d computed by this program has the properties described in Theorem 6.5. To see this, let P be an arbitrary $TL\Delta$ program with labels in $\{0, 1\}^*$. The following string of statements are equivalent.

1. P has output <yes> for input hcode(P).
2. Fix(P) has output <yes> for input hcode(P).
3. Fix(P) halts on input hcode(P).
4. Check(Fix(P)¢hcode(P)) = <ok>.
5. d(hcode(P)) = <no>.

By the equivalences of (1) and (5) we see that d has property (1) of Theorem 6.5. To see that d has property (2) of Theorem 6.5, note the following chain of equivalences:

6. P does not have output <yes> for the input hcode(P).
7. Fix(P) does not halt on input hcode(P).
8. Check(Fix(P)¢hcode(P)) = <∞ loop>.
9. Check(Fix(P)¢hcode(P)) ≠ <ok>.
10. d(hcode(P)) = <yes>.

Since (6) and (10) are equivalent, property (2) of Theorem 6.5 is established. □

The previous theorem says that there is no algorithm to test for a program P and an input α, whether or not P halts on α. Since you cannot do that test, you might suspect that there is no algorithm to test for a program P whether or not P halts on all inputs. This suspicion is well founded. The next theorem says that no algorithm exists to test if a program halts on all inputs.

6.8 Theorem Let Δ be any alphabet with at least two elements. Let <ok> and <∞ loop> be two distinct symbols in Δ. Let Checkall be a partial function with the following properties:

1. If P is a $TL\Delta$ program with labels in $\{0, 1\}^*$ and for all α in Δ^* P halts on α, then Checkall$(P) = \,<$ok$>$.
2. If P is a $TL\Delta$ program with labels in $\{0, 1\}^*$ and for at least one α in Δ^*, P does not halt on α, then Checkall$(P) = \,<\infty$ loop$>$.

Under these assumptions, Checkall is not a computable function.

Before giving the proof of Theorem 6.8, we will present one lemma that will be used in that proof.

6.9 Lemma If Δ is any finite alphabet and $¢$ is any symbol which is not in Δ, then there is a computable partial function, denoted *Specialize*, such that the following is true for any P which is a $TL\Delta$ program with labels in $\{0, 1\}^*$ and any α in Δ^*.

1. $P_\alpha = $ Specialize$(P¢\alpha)$ is a $TL\Delta$ program with labels in $\{0, 1\}^*$.
2. P halts on input α if and only if P_α halts on all inputs.

PROOF We will first give an informal procedure to obtain a $TL\Delta$ program P_α from $P¢\alpha$. Later we will make this procedure precise. The function Specialize is defined by setting Specialize$(P¢\alpha)$ equal to this P_α, for all appropriate $TL\Delta$ programs P and all strings α in Δ^*. For any input ξ which is not of the form $P¢\alpha$ as just described, the value of Specialize(ξ) is irrelevant and we do not care what, if any, output the procedure produces on these other inputs. By definition, P_α is the output of the procedure we will give below. Since Specialize is defined by a procedure, it is, by the Church/Turing thesis, a computable function. We now present the procedure for P_α.

Informally, P_α can be described as operating in the following way: First P_α erases its input. Then it writes α on its tape. After that, it behaves just like P on input α.

Clearly, any such P_α will have the property that, on any input β from Δ^*, P_α halts on β if and only if P halts on input α. Since P_α essentially ignores its input, P_α halts on one input from Δ^* if and only if it halts on all input strings from Δ^*. So P_α halts on all inputs if and only if P halts on the particular input α. So property (2) holds.

In order to complete the proof, all we need to do is make the procedure for obtaining P_α from $P¢\alpha$ precise. For some readers it may already be precise enough. Those readers can appeal to the Church/Turing thesis to conclude that Specialize is computable and end the proof here. Those who wish more detail should read the rest of this proof.

Let **BEGIN** $<P$ code$>$ **END** be the $TL\Delta$ program P. Let $\alpha = a_1a_2...a_n$, where the a_i are individual symbols. Procedure 6.3 is a description of the $TL\Delta$ program P_α in terms of the $TL\Delta$ program P and the string α. The program contains a few abbreviations but it can easily be made into a syntactically correct $TL\Delta$ program. The labels $<$erase$>$ and $<$rewind$>$ are any two labels, from $\{0, 1\}^*$, which do not occur in $<P$ code$>$.

Procedure 6.3
Program P_α

BEGIN
$<$erase$>$: **IF SCAN** $\neq$ **BLANK THEN**
    BEGIN
        SCAN := **BLANK**;
        POINTER$\rightarrow$;
        GOTO $<$erase$>$
    END;
    SCAN := a_1:
    POINTER$\rightarrow$;
    SCAN := a_2;
    POINTER$\rightarrow$;
        $\vdots$
    POINTER$\rightarrow$;
    SCAN := a_n;
$<$rewind$>$: **IF SCAN** $\neq$ *BLANK* **THEN**
    BEGIN
        POINTER$\leftarrow$;
        GOTO $<$rewind$>$
    END;
    POINTER$\rightarrow$;
    $<P$ code$>$
END

The program for Specialize would take an input of the form $P\text{¢}\alpha$, where P is a $TL\Delta$ program with labels in $\{0, 1\}^*$ and where α is in Δ^*. It would then produce the $TL\Delta$ program just described. This $TL\Delta$ program is the desired output P_α. We have now given the procedure to compute Specialize in enough detail so that you should be convinced that, with enough time and patience, the procedure can be converted to a program for a simple Turing machine to compute Specialize. So Specialize is certainly computable and the proof of this lemma is completed. $\square$

Proof of Theorem 6.8

The proof uses the same general strategy used to prove Theorem 6.7 (unsolvability of the halting problem). We assume that Checkall is computable and then use Checkall as a subprocedure in a program which computes a function known to be not computable. Since this is, of course, a contradiction, we conclude that Checkall is itself not computable. In this proof we use the function Check from Theorem 6.7 rather than the function d from Theorem 6.5 as the known noncomputable function.

With the above general goal in mind, let us assume that there is a computable function Checkall as described in the theorem. We will derive a contradiction; namely, we will show that there is a computable function Check as in Theorem 6.7. The program for Check is simple. Given input $P\text{¢}\alpha$, where P is a $TL\Delta$ program with labels in $\{0, 1\}^*$ and where α is in Δ^*, the program for Check outputs the value Checkall(Specialize($P\text{¢}\alpha$)). So Check($P\text{¢}\alpha$) = Checkall(Specialize($P\text{¢}\alpha$)).

If P halts on α, then P_α = Specialize($P\text{¢}\alpha$) halts on all inputs and so Check($P\text{¢}\alpha$) = Checkall(P_α) = <ok>. By a similar argument, it follows that if P does not halt on α, then Check($P\text{¢}\alpha$) = Checkall(Specialize($P\text{¢}\alpha$)) = <∞ loop>. Therefore, this function Check is indeed the type of function referred to by Theorem 6.7. Also, since Specialize is known to be computable and since Checkall is assumed to be computable, it follows that Check is a computable function. This contradicts Theorem 6.7 and so the proof is complete. □

The unsolvability of the halting problem, Theorem 6.7, says that there is no program which can test all program/input pairs to see whether or not the given program halts on the given input. However, there are programs which can sometimes tell us if some programs halt on some inputs. These programs are not guaranteed to halt on all program/input pairs and so do not always give an answer. The next theorem describes the function computed by one of these programs.

6.10 Theorem Let Δ be any finite alphabet and let ¢ be a symbol which is not in Δ. It then follows that there is a computable partial function *Weakcheck* which has the following properties for all P which are $TL\Delta$ programs with labels in $\{0, 1\}^*$ and all strings α in Δ^*.

1. Weakcheck($P\text{¢}\alpha$) = <ok>, provided that the computation of P on input α halts.
2. Weakcheck($P\text{¢}\alpha$) ≠ <ok>, provided the computation of P on input α does not halt. (In this case Weakcheck($P\text{¢}\alpha$) might be anything, including being undefined, so long as it is not <ok>.)

PROOF The idea of the proof is quite simple. The program Weakcheck simulates the program P on the input α. If the simulation halts, then the program outputs <ok>. If the simulation does not halt, then there is no output. It will turn out that, if Weakcheck($P\text{¢}\alpha$) ≠ <ok>, then it will be undefined.

It is easy to formalize this idea using a universal Turing machine. Let U be the universal Turing machine of Lemma 6.3 and let u be the function computed by U. The following is a $TL\Gamma S$ program for Weakcheck, where Γ denotes the alphabet of U and <ok> is some symbol in Γ.

```
BEGIN
    STRING := u(STRING);
    STRING := <ok>;
    ACCEPT
END
```

If a $TL\Gamma$ program for U is used to compute u, then the above $TL\Gamma S$ program clearly computes a function Weakcheck with the desired properties. To see this, assume that the input is $P\mathcal{c}\alpha$, where P is a $TL\Delta$ program with labels in $\{0, 1\}^*$ and α is a string in Δ^*. The computation starts with $P\mathcal{c}\alpha$ in **STRING**. So, by Lemma 6.3, the computation of U terminates and $u(\textbf{STRING})$ is defined if and only if P halts on input α. Hence, the $TL\Gamma S$ program executes the two remaining statements if and only if P halts on input α. In particular, the $TL\Gamma S$ program executes the accepting statement if and only if P halts on input α. Therefore, the $TL\Gamma S$ program has an output if and only if P halts on input α. If this $TL\Gamma S$ program does have an output, then the output is the contents of **STRING**. Hence, this $TL\Gamma S$ program outputs $<ok>$ if and only if P halts on α. $\square$

EXERCISES

1. Prove that the function Decode, defined in the proof of Theorem 6.7, is a deterministic finite-state transduction and hence a computable function.

2. Prove that the language HCODES, defined in the proof of Theorem 6.7, is a finite-state language.

3. Let Δ be any alphabet. Let f be a function with the following properties: (1) $f(P) = <\infty \text{ loop}>$ if P is a $TL\Delta$ program with labels in $\{0, 1\}^*$ such that P does not halt on input Λ. (2) $f(P) = <ok>$ if P is a $TL\Delta$ program with labels in $\{0, 1\}^*$ such that P halts on input Λ. Prove that f is not a computable function.

4. Let Δ be a finite alphabet. Every $TL\Delta$ program computes a partial function. Prove that there is no algorithm which, given a $TL\Delta$ program as input, will decide whether or not that $TL\Delta$ program computes a total function. (This is only a slight variation of Theorem 6.8.)

5. Prove that the partial computable function Weakcheck of Theorem 6.10 cannot be extended to a total computable function. That is, show that there is no total computable function f such that, on any input ξ, $f(\xi) = <ok>$ if and only if Weakcheck$(\xi) = <ok>$. (This is only a minor variant of Theorem 6.7.)

6. Let Δ be a fixed alphabet, let a be a symbol in Δ, and let $\mathcal{c}$ be a symbol which is not in Δ. Prove that there is no computable partial function f such that the following holds for all $TL\Delta$ programs P with labels in $\{0, 1\}^*$ and all strings α in Δ^*: (1) $f(P\mathcal{c}\alpha) = <yes>$, provided that, in the computation on input α, the Turing machine realization of P at

sometime writes the symbol a on its tape. (2) $f(P\text{¢}\alpha) = $ <no>, provided that, in the computation on input α, the Turing machine realization of P never writes the symbol a on its tape.

7. Let Δ be a finite alphabet with at least two elements. Let f be any partial function with the following property: If P is a $TL\Delta$ program with labels in $\{0, 1\}^*$, then (1) $f(P)$ is a $TL\Delta$ program with labels in $\{0, 1\}^*$, (2) For every string $\alpha \in \Delta^*$, P halts on α if and only if $f(P)$ does not halt on α. Prove that f is not computable.

Chapter Seven

Turing Machines as Accepting Devices

Accepting devices, such as finite-state acceptors, are procedures which classify their possible input strings into two classes, those accepted and those not accepted. One can think of these procedures as answering the yes/no question: "Is the input acceptable?" In the case of finite-state acceptors, the procedures to answer such yes/no questions were defined to be what are called *partial procedures* or *partial algorithms*. They are said to be partial because they need not always supply an answer. In this particular case, if the answer is yes, then the procedure must output the correct answer. If the answer is no, the procedure need not output anything. Turing machines can be used as accepting devices in a similar way. The languages defined by the Turing machine partial procedures, which need only supply the yes answers, are called *recursively enumerable languages*. The languages defined by Turing machine total procedures or algorithms are called *recognizable languages*. In the case of recognizable languages, the Turing machine program must supply the no answers as well as the yes answers. In other words, every input string must be either accepted or rejected by such a Turing machine. By the Church/Turing thesis, Turing machines are powerful enough to accomplish the equivalent of any programming construct. Thus, recursively enumerable languages are really those languages which can be defined by partial effective procedures of any sort — as long as the procedure always provides the correct yes answers. Recognizable languages are languages that can be defined by some sort of total effective procedure or algorithm. In this chapter we explore some of the differences between and some of the relationships between these partial and total procedures.

RECURSIVELY ENUMERABLE LANGUAGES

Thus far we have used Turing machines to compute functions. They are also frequently used as accepting devices. A Turing machine M is said to accept an input string w provided that if M is started in the usual start configuration with input w, then M will eventually reach a configuration which has the finite-state control of M in an accepting state. As usual, the language accepted by M is the set of all input strings accepted by M. This is stated formally in the following definition.

7.1 Definition

7.1.1 If M is a simple Turing machine and s is the start state for M, then the *language accepted by* M is defined and denoted as follows: $A(M) = \{w \mid (s, \triangleright w) \mathrel{\vdash^*} (q, \alpha \triangleright \beta)$ for some accepting state q and some strings α and $\beta\}$.

7.1.2 A language L is said to be *recursively enumerable* (*re*) provided $L = A(M)$ for some simple Turing machine M.

The word "recursively" in the term "recursively enumerable" carries no intuitive meaning when the theory of computation is developed in the way that we have done it in this text. It is there for the same historical reason as the modifier "recursive" in the term "recursive function." Although the modifier "recursively" carries no intuitive content, the term "recursively enumerable" is a standard term and we shall use it. The word "enumerable," on the other hand, does have important intuitive content. It can be shown that a language L is a recursively enumerable language if and only if there is a program to "enumerate" all the strings in L. We could formally define what it means for a program to enumerate a language. However, since we will not be using the concept, we will merely give an informal definition.

As we have already noted, a program need not halt. If a program has the facility to repeatedly output strings and if the program does not halt, then it can output an infinite number of strings. Of course, there will not be a time when it is through outputting. Still, such a program defines a possibly infinite list $\alpha_1, \alpha_2, \alpha_3, \ldots$ of the outputted strings. A program P is said to *enumerate the language* L provided that P outputs a list in the manner just described and L is exactly equal to the set of strings which appear on this list. It is perfectly acceptable if a string appears more than once on this list. All we require is that each string in L appears at least once on the list and that all strings on the list are in L. The most interesting cases have infinite lists, but finite lists are also allowed. We have said nothing about the input to P and indeed there is no need for P to have any input at all. When discussing programs that enumerate languages, we assume that the program has no input. This is all rather informal, but hopefully, clear. For example, it is fairly trivial to write a procedure which enumerates all base ten numerals, without leading zeros, in the usual order: 1, 2, 3, 4, ... It is slightly harder, but still not too difficult, to write a procedure to enumerate all strings over a fixed alphabet, say $\{a, b\}$, to have a concrete case. One way to enumerate all the strings in $\{a, b\}^*$ is to first enumerate all the strings of length zero (there is only one), then all the strings of length one, then length two, and so forth. This requires a subprocedure which, given a natural number n, will output all strings of a's and b's which are of length exactly n. Clearly, such a subprocedure can be written.

We will now give an informal proof of the fact that a language L is accepted by a simple Turing machine if and only if there is a program to enumerate L.

First assume that we have program P_E which enumerates L. A program P_A to accept L could work as follows: Given input ξ, P_A simulates P_E and produces a list of strings $\alpha_1, \alpha_2, \alpha_3, \ldots$ that P_E would output. So $\alpha_1, \alpha_2, \alpha_3, \ldots$ is a list of all the strings in L. However, P_A will not actually output these strings. Instead, P_A will compare each of these strings α_i to the input ξ. If $\alpha_i = \xi$, then P_A accepts ξ. If $\alpha_i \neq \xi$, then P_A continues with its simulation of P_E, produces α_{i+1}, and compares α_{i+1} to ξ. The process is repeated with each of the α_i. P_A accepts exactly those strings which P_E would output on its list. That is, P_A accepts the language L enumerated by P_E. By the Church/Turing thesis, the program P_A can be converted to a program for a simple Turing machine which accepts L. Hence, we have seen that, if there is a program to enumerate a language L, then there is a simple Turing machine that accepts L. The converse is not as easy to see but still can be demonstrated. A proof outline is given in the next two paragraphs.

Assume we have a program P_A for a simple Turing machine that accepts a language L. We wish to describe a program P_E which enumerates L. First consider the special case where P_A is a total algorithm. That is, consider the case where P_A halts on all inputs. In this special case, the description of P_E is fairly easy. Let Σ be an alphabet such that all strings in L are in Σ^*. By Exercise 7-1, we know that there is a program to enumerate Σ^*. The program P_E will simulate this program to produce the infinite list of all the strings in Σ^*. The list is not actually outputted but is used by P_E in an intermediate computation. Let $\beta_1, \beta_2, \beta_3, \ldots$ denote the list of all strings in Σ^*. After adding each β_i to the list, P_E simulates P_A to see if P_A would accept β_i. If P_A would accept β_i, then P_E outputs β_i. If P_A would not accept β_i, then P_E does not output β_i. In either case, P_A goes on to add β_{i+1} to the list and to check β_{i+1}. This list $\beta_1, \beta_2, \beta_3, \ldots$ need not actually be retained. After each β_i is checked, it can be discarded. In this way, P_E outputs a list of exactly those elements of Σ^* which P_A would accept, and that is a list of exactly the elements in L. Hence, P_E enumerates L. Therefore, we have displayed a program to enumerate L, at least in the special case where P_A halts on all inputs.

If P_A does not halt on some input, then the above program P_E does not quite work. The problem is that if P_A does not halt on some string β_i, then P_E never gets to consider β_{i+1}. Thus, if β_{i+1} is in L, then it should be outputted but actually it is never outputted. To overcome this problem, modify P_E as follows: Provide P_E with a counter N, which can be incremented through the positive integers. P_E initializes N to one and then repeatedly does the following: It produces $\beta_1, \beta_2, \ldots, \beta_N$; it simulates N steps of P_A on each of $\beta_1, \beta_2, \ldots, \beta_N$; if any of these β_i would be accepted by P_A, it outputs those β_i that would be accepted; it then increments N by one. This routine is repeated again and again as N is stepped through 1, 2, 3, and so forth. Since, for each value of N, only N steps of P_A are simulated on each β_i, the individual simulations of P_A always end. Thus every β_i is eventually considered. Of course, if β_i is accepted by P_A in k steps, then the program P_E will not output β_i until the value of N is at least k, but this is no problem. All we require is that if P_A accepts a string β_i, then β_i is eventually outputted by P_E. With this modification, P_E enumerates the language L accepted by P_A, even if P_A does not halt on all inputs. Hence, in every case, if L is accepted by some simple Turing machine, then there is some program to enumerate L.

The above is all rather informal. Also, we will never use this equivalence between enumerating programs and accepting programs. Still, the ideas in this discussion are worth digesting.

In defining the language accepted by a Turing machine, we placed no constraints on what the machine did on an input which is not accepted. If the input is not accepted, the machine may either halt in a nonaccepting state or it might not halt at all. Thus recursively enumerable languages are defined by partial algorithms that need not always halt. This point is made more explicit by the next theorem.

7.2 Theorem Let Σ be an alphabet, let L be a subset of Σ^*, and let $<yes>$ be an element of Σ. L is recursively enumerable if and only if there is a computable partial function f such that

1. If α is in L, then $f(\alpha) = <yes>$ and
2. If α is in $\Sigma^* - L$, then $f(\alpha) \neq <yes>$. (When we say that $f(\alpha) \neq <yes>$, we allow the possibility that $f(\alpha)$ is undefined. That is, $f(\alpha) \neq <yes>$ means that either $f(\alpha)$ is undefined or $f(\alpha) = \beta$ and $\beta \neq <yes>$.)

PROOF First suppose that there is a computable partial function f with properties (1) and (2). It is trivial to write a $TL\Sigma S$ program to accept L. On input α, the program computes $f(\alpha)$; if $f(\alpha) = <yes>$, it accepts. Since we know there is a $TL\Sigma S$ program to accept L, we then know that there is a simple Turing machine to accept L and, hence by definition, L is an re language.

Conversely, suppose L is an re language. It then follows that there is a $TL\Sigma$ program P for a simple Turing machine that accepts L. We wish to show that there is a computable partial function f which satisfies properties (1) and (2). We will do this by describing a $TL\Gamma$ program P_f to compute such a function f, where Γ is some convenient alphabet. The intuitive idea of how P_f operates is quite simple. P_f behaves just like P except that, when P would enter an accepting state, P_f instead erases its tape, writes $<yes>$ on the tape, and only then executes an accepting statement. Such a program P_f would output $<yes>$ on exactly those inputs which P would have accepted, and hence would compute a function f which satisfies properties (1) and (2). All that remains to be done is to describe P_f precisely. It would not be improper to appeal to the Church/Turing thesis and avoid describing P_f precisely. However, since the notion of a Turing machine as an accepting device is a new notion, we will sketch the formal details.

The $TL\Gamma$ program P_f is obtained by modifying the $TL\Sigma$ program P as follows: Let $\Gamma = \Sigma \cup \{<\text{dirty blank}>\}$, where $<\text{dirty blank}>$ is a new symbol which will serve as a pseudo blank symbol. First modify P so that it never writes a blank symbol. This will serve to ensure that every tape square that is ever scanned will contain a nonblank symbol and this property will, in turn, make it easy to locate and erase all nonblank symbols. The necessary modification is to have the program behave like P, but whenever P would write a true blank, the modified program will instead write the nonblank symbol $<\text{dirty blank}>$. When scanning the symbol $<\text{dirty blank}>$, the modified program acts the same as it would when scanning a true blank. These modifications ensure that every square that is ever scanned contains some symbol other than the true blank. The program is then modified further by replacing each occurrence of **ACCEPT** by **GOTO** $<\text{output yes}>$, where $<\text{output yes}>$ is a new label. Finally, some new code, labeled by $<\text{output yes}>$, is added. This new code consists of instructions to erase all nonblank symbols from the tape, write $<\text{yes}>$ on the tape, and then execute an accepting statement. Our previous modification makes the task of locating and erasing nonblank symbols an easy one. Some care must also be taken to ensure that the block labeled $<\text{output yes}>$ is not reachable except by one of the statements **GOTO** $<\text{output yes}>$. However, this is easy to do. The details are very similar to those used in the proof of Lemma 5.16. $\square$

RECOGNIZABLE LANGUAGES (RECURSIVE LANGUAGES)

Recursively enumerable languages are those languages defined by partial algorithms. Those languages defined by total algorithms will be called recognizable languages. Recognizable languages are also frequently called *recursive languages* or *recursive sets*. The term "recursive" is used here for historical reasons and again carries little intuitive information. However, it is standard terminology.

7.3 Definition

Let Σ be an alphabet with at least two elements. Let $<\text{yes}>$ and $<\text{no}>$ be two distinct elements in Σ. Let L be a subset of Σ^*. The language L is said to be *recognizable* provided there is some computable function f such that the following hold:

1. $f(\xi) = <\text{yes}>$ for all ξ in L and
2. $f(\xi) = <\text{no}>$ for all ξ in $\Sigma^* - L$.

The relationship between recursively enumerable languages and recognizable languages is given by the following theorem.

7.4 Theorem
Let L be a language and let Σ be an alphabet such that L is a subset of Σ^*. L is a recognizable language if and only if both L and $\Sigma^* - L$ are recursively enumerable.

Procedure 7.1

Program P to Compute f
Input Is ξ

BEGIN
    STATEg := the start state of P_g;
    STATEh := the start state of P_h;
    TAPEg := $\triangleright \xi$;
    TAPEh := $\triangleright \xi$;
    WHILE [**STATE**g is not an accepting state and
        STATEh is not an accepting state] **DO**
        BEGIN
            STATEg := NEXTSg(**STATE**g¢**TAPE**g);
            TAPEg := NEXTTg(**STATE**g¢**TAPE**g);
            STATEh := NEXTSh(**STATE**h¢**TAPE**h);
            TAPEh := NEXTTh(**STATE**h¢**TAPE**h)
        END;
    IF [**STATE**g is an accepting state and
        TAPEg contains a string of the form $B^n \triangleright <\text{yes}> B^m$,
        where B is the blank symbol]
        THEN [OUTPUT $<\text{yes}>$];
    IF [**STATE**h is an accepting state and
        TAPEh contains a string of the form $B^n \triangleright <\text{yes}> B^m$,
        where B is the blank symbol]
        THEN [OUTPUT $<\text{no}>$]
    END.

PROOF Suppose L is a recognizable language and let f be a computable function as in Definition 7.3. By Theorem 7.2, it follows that L is recursively enumerable. Let g be a function such that $g(<\text{yes}>) = <\text{no}>$ and $g(<\text{no}>) = <\text{yes}>$. It is easy to see that g is computable. By Exercise 5-5 the function h, defined by $h(\alpha) = g(f(\alpha))$, is computable. Also, $h(\alpha) = <\text{yes}>$ for α in $\Sigma^* - L$ and $h(\alpha) \neq <\text{yes}>$ for α in L. Therefore, by Theorem 7.2, it follows that $\Sigma^* - L$ is recursively enumerable. Hence, if L is recognizable, then both L and $\Sigma^* - L$ are recursively enumerable.

Conversely, suppose that both L and $\Sigma^* - L$ are recursively enumerable. We will show that L is a recognizable language. By Theorem 7.2, we know that there are computable partial functions g and h such that if α is in L, then $g(\alpha) = <\text{yes}>$ and $h(\alpha) \neq <\text{yes}>$; if α is in $\Sigma^* - L$, then $h(\alpha) = <\text{yes}>$ and $g(\alpha) \neq <\text{yes}>$. Let P_g and P_h be $TL\Gamma$ programs such that P_g computes

g, P_h computes h, and both P_g and P_h satisfy condition (2) of Lemma 5.16. Γ is the alphabet mentioned in Lemma 5.16. We will describe a program P such that, on input ξ, P simulates both P_g on input ξ and P_h on input ξ "in parallel" and thereby checks to see if either P_g would output $<$yes$>$ or P_h would output $<$yes$>$. If P_g would output $<$yes$>$, then P outputs $<$yes$>$. If P_h would output $<$yes$>$, then P outputs $<$no$>$. Any P which operates in this intuitive way will compute a function f such that $f(\xi) = <$yes$>$ for ξ in L and $f(\xi) = <$no$>$ for ξ in $\Sigma^* - L$. Hence it will follow that L is a recognizable language. Notice that P cannot first simulate one of P_g and P_h and then simulate the other and still compute the desired function f. Since g and h are only partial functions, the first simulation might never terminate. That is the reason for doing the simulations "in parallel." We know that on any input string ξ in Σ^*, at least one, but not necessarily both, of P_g and P_h will halt and give us the desired information.

All that really remains to be done is to describe how P can simulate P_g and P_h "in parallel." P will do this by first simulating one step of P_h, then one step of P_g, then one step of P_h, and so forth. So the simulations are interleaved and not strictly parallel, but this is good enough. We will give an informal program P that accomplishes this and that can easily be converted to a $PS\Gamma$ program. The program has variables named by mnemonics like **STATE**g, **STATE**h, and so forth. To get a valid $PS\Gamma$ program you would, among other things, change these to **STRING**2, **STRING**3, and so forth. Also, the program uses a number of additional special symbols. The alphabet Γ will have to be expanded to include these symbols.

We next define the functions used in the program and show that they are computable. If $(p, \alpha \triangleright \beta)$ is an id of P_g and, in one step P_g will change this id to $(p_2, \alpha_2 \triangleright \beta_2)$, then NEXTS$g$ $(p\mathcal{c}\alpha \triangleright \beta) = p_2$ and NEXTTg $(p\mathcal{c}\alpha \triangleright \beta) = \alpha_2 \triangleright \beta_2$. If $(p, \alpha \triangleright \beta)$ is a halting id, then NEXTSg $(p\mathcal{c}\alpha \triangleright \beta) = p$ and NEXTTg $(p\mathcal{c}\alpha \triangleright \beta) = \alpha \triangleright \beta$. These definitions for halting id's are technicalities to ensure that the program to compute f does not halt before finding an answer. The functions NEXTSh and NEXTTh are defined analogously for the program P_h. It is easy to give informal programs for all these functions and, by the Church/Turing thesis, we know that these informal programs have equivalent $TL\Gamma$ programs. So all the functions in the program P are computable. It is easy to see that the program P, displayed in Procedure 7.1, computes a function f such that $f(\xi) = <$yes$>$ for ξ in L and $f(\xi) = <$no$>$ for ξ in $\Sigma^* - L$. This means that L is a recognizable language. $\square$

7.5 Theorem Let Δ be a finite alphabet and let $\mathcal{c}$ be a symbol not in Δ. Let $C = \{P\mathcal{c}\alpha \mid P$ is a $TL\Delta$ program with labels in $\{0, 1\}^*$, $\alpha \in \Delta^*$ and P halts on $\alpha\}$. Then C is a recursively enumerable language but not a recognizable language.

PROOF By Theorems 6.10 and 7.2, C is a recursively enumerable language. By Theorem 6.7 (unsolvability of the halting problem), C is not a recognizable language. $\square$

SUMMARY OF THE RELATIONSHIP BETWEEN VARIOUS CLASSES OF LANGUAGES

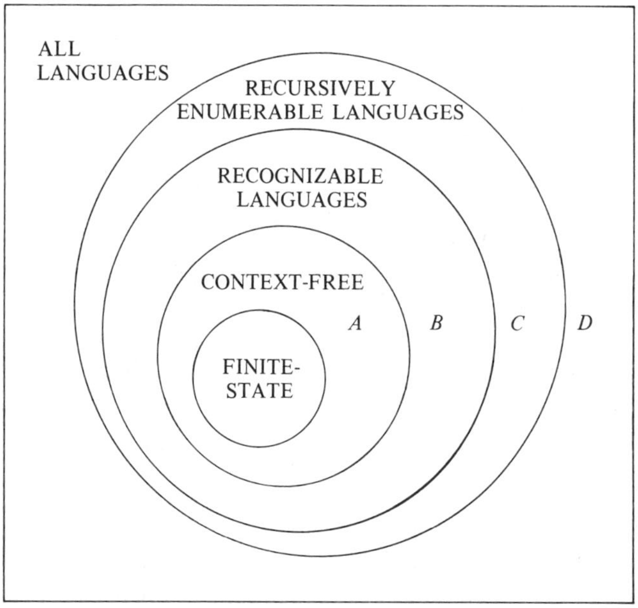

$A = \{a^n b^n \mid n \geqslant 0\}$

$B = \{a^n b^n c^n \mid n \geqslant 0\}$

$C = \{P\mathbb{c}\alpha \mid P$ is a TLΔ program with labels in $\{0, 1\}^{\star}$, α is in $\Delta^{\star}$, and P halts on input $\alpha\}$.

$D = \{P\mathbb{c}\alpha \mid P$ is a TLΔ program with labels in $\{0, 1\}^{\star}$, α is in $\Delta^{\star}$, and P does not halt on input $\alpha\}$.

Figure 7.1

Once we know that there are languages that are recursively enumerable but are not recognizable, it immediately follows that there are languages which are not even recursively enumerable. To see this, suppose that L is a subset of Σ^* and that L is recursively enumerable but not recognizable. Then $\Sigma^* - L$ is not even recursively enumerable. To see that $\Sigma^* - L$ is not recursively enumerable, note that, by Theorem 7.4, if $\Sigma^* - L$ were recursively enumerable, then L would be recognizable, which would be a contradiction. In particular, it follows that $\Sigma^* - C$ is not recursively enumerable, where C is defined in Theorem 7.5 and Σ is such that C is a subset of Σ^*. By doing a little more work with $\Sigma^* - C$ we obtain the following.

7.6 Theorem Let Δ be a finite alphabet, and let $\mathbb{c}$ be a symbol not in Δ. Let $D = \{P\mathbb{c}\alpha \mid P$ is a $TL\Delta$ program with labels in $\{0, 1\}^*$, α is in Δ^* and P does not halt on α}. Then D is not a recursively enumerable language.

PROOF Let C be as in Theorem 7.5, let Σ be an alphabet such that C is a subset of Σ^*, and let $S = \{P¢\alpha \mid P$ is a $TL\Delta$ program with labels in $\{0, 1\}^*$ and α is in $\Delta^*\}$. Using Exercise 5-10, it is easy to see that S is a recognizable language. Suppose that D were recursively enumerable. We will derive a contradiction. Observe that $\Sigma^* - C = D \cup (\Sigma^* - S)$. Now since S is a recognizable language we know, by Theorem 7.4, that $\Sigma^* - S$ is a recursively enumerable language. D is assumed to be recursively enumerable and, by Exercise 7-2, the union of two recursively enumerable languages is again recursively enumerable. Hence $\Sigma^* - C$ is recursively enumerable. But, by the remarks which preceded this theorem, we know that $\Sigma^* - C$ is not recursively enumerable. Hence we have a contradiction, as promised. $\square$

The next two results show that all context-free languages as well as the specific programming languages we have been studying are recognizable languages.

7.7 Theorem If L is a context-free language, then L is a recognizable language.

PROOF Let L be a context-free language. By Theorem 2.16, we know that there is an algorithm which can tell for any string w, whether or not w is in L. This algorithm can easily be converted to an algorithm to compute a function defined from L as in Definition 7.3. By the Church/Turing thesis, this algorithm can be converted to a $TL\Delta$ program to compute this function. $\square$

The next theorem is a rephrasing of Exercise 5-10. A similar result could be proven for $TL\Delta S$ schemas. The corresponding result for $PS\Delta$ schemas is a special case of Theorem 7.7.

7.8 Theorem Let Δ be any finite alphabet. Let T be the set of all $TL\Delta$ programs with labels in $\{0, 1\}^*$. Then T is a recognizable language.

Figure 7.1 describes the relationship between the various language classes we have studied and shows some languages which separate the classes.

EXERCISES

1. Give a procedure to enumerate all strings in $\{a, b\}^*$. Prove that, for any alphabet Σ, there is a procedure to enumerate all strings in Σ^*.

2. Prove: If L_1 and L_2 are recursively enumerable, then so are $L_1 \cup L_2$, $L_1 \cap L_2$, and L_1^*.

3. Prove: L is recursively enumerable if and only if there is a computable partial function f such that $L = \{\alpha \mid f(\alpha)$ is defined$\}$.

4. Prove: If L_1 and L_2 are recognizable languages and Σ is an alphabet such that L_1 is a subset of Σ^*, then $L_1 \cup L_2$, $L_1 \cap L_2$, and $\Sigma - L_1$ are all recognizable languages.

5. Let f be a computable partial function from Δ^* to Δ^*, where Δ is some alphabet. Let $<$default$>$ be a string not in Δ^*. Define $\hat{f}$ by $\hat{f}(\alpha) = f(\alpha)$ provided $f(\alpha)$ is defined and $\hat{f}(\alpha) = <$default$>$ for all other α in Δ^*. Prove that there is a computable partial function f such that $\hat{f}$ is not computable.

6. Let Δ be an alphabet. Let $E = \{P \mid P$ is a $TL\Delta$ program with labels in $\{0, 1\}^*$ and P halts on input $\Lambda\}$. Prove that E is a recursively enumerable language.

7. Let Δ be an alphabet. Let $F = \{P \mid P$ is a $TL\Delta$ program with labels in $\{0, 1\}^*$ and P does not halt on input $\Lambda\}$. Prove that F is not a recursively enumerable language. Use that result to prove that E, as in Exercise 6, is not a recognizable language.

Chapter Eight

*Nondeterministic Turing Machines

Thus far we have considered only deterministic Turing machines. Just like finite-state acceptors and transducers, Turing machines have a nondeterministic version as well as a deterministic version. The nondeterministic Turing machine model differs from the deterministic version in only one way. A nondeterministic Turing machine may have more than one possible action it can take in some situations. This is expressed formally by making the transition function multiple-valued. That is, it maps each state/symbol pair into a finite set of possible actions. Each action is of the same form as that of the deterministic version: a next state, a symbol to replace the currently scanned symbol, and a head movement instruction. In a way analogous to the other nondeterministic models we have studied, a nondeterministic Turing machine may have many computations associated with the same input. The intuition for the nondeterminism in Turing machines is basically the same as it was for nondeterministic finite-state acceptors.

One way to think of these nondeterministic Turing machine computations is as a type of parallel process. Whenever a state/symbol pair is mapped into a single action, then the computation proceeds just as it does for deterministic machines. Whenever a state/symbol pair is mapped onto some number $m \geqslant 2$ of actions, then m copies of the machine are created; each of the m copies follows a different one of the m possible actions. These m machines proceed to compute in parallel. If any of these parallel computations reaches a situation where more than one action is possible, then that computation branches into a set of machines running in parallel. This sort of parallel computing can be viewed as a tree of computations. At the start there is only one machine. At each instant of time, the computation yields some number of next machine configurations. If that number is greater than one, then the tree branches. Each path through the tree from root to a leaf, or infinite path if the tree is not finite, is considered a possible computation. The total process is considered successful if at least one of these possible computations is successful. To be more specific, suppose we are viewing the Turing machine as an acceptor. The

150

Turing machine is said to accept the input provided that at least one computation reaches a configuration which includes an accepting state. That is, the input is accepted provided that at least one of the parallel machines reaches an accepting state.

Viewing nondeterministic computations as parallel computations is a completely valid intuition. An alternative and equally valid intuition is to think of nondeterministic computations as computations that can guess. When the computation reaches a situation where more than one action is possible, the Turing machine guesses which action to take. When taking this guessing point of view, we always take the most optimistic point of view. We consider the process to be successful if there is at least one possible sequence of guesses which leads to a successful outcome. More specifically, if we are viewing the Turing machine as an acceptor, we say that the input is accepted provided that there is some sequence of guesses which will cause the machine to reach an accepting state. The two intuitive points of view, parallel computations and guessing computations, are of course equivalent. Each sequence of guesses corresponds to a path through the tree. One can think of the guessing computation as guessing which branches of the tree to follow.

Some care must be exercised when using this guessing intuition. For example, suppose we wish to design a nondeterministic Turing machine to accept a particular set L and suppose that L is not the trivial case $L = \Sigma^*$, where Σ is the input alphabet. Given an arbitrary input w, the Turing machine cannot simply guess that w is in L and enter an accepting state. If it did that and w were in L, then the machine would have correctly accepted w. If it did that but w were not in L, then it would have incorrectly guessed that w is in L and so it would accept some input which is not in L. Hence it would not be a Turing machine to accept L. When we say a Turing machine accepts the language L, we mean it accepts exactly those inputs which are in L. A nondeterministic Turing machine is allowed to guess, but it is not allowed to make any mistakes which would cause it to accept some input that it should not accept or to otherwise output incorrect information. An incorrect guess may cause a computation to be useless, but it cannot cause the machine to give incorrect information such as incorrectly accepting an input or giving an incorrect output string.

AN INFORMAL EXAMPLE

Having digested the above caution, one may wonder whether nondeterminism is of any value at all to a Turing machine. The situation is similar to that of finite-state acceptors. As we shall see, anything that can be done by a nondeterministic Turing machine can also be done by a deterministic Turing machine. However, it is frequently much easier to write a nondeterministic rather than a deterministic program for certain tasks. Also, the nondeterministic program may be much more efficient than any known deterministic program.

We will not have time to discuss this efficiency question in any detail, but it is a major topic of discussion in other more advanced texts.

An informal example may help to illustrate the efficiency of nondeterministic programs. Recall that a positive integer is called *composite* if it is not a prime (and it is not one). That is, it is composite if it is equal to the product of two numbers each greater than one. Suppose that we want to design a Turing machine program to accept all strings of zeros and ones which are binary numerals for composite numbers. It is quite easy to design a nondeterministic machine to do this. Given an input numeral w, the machine guesses two numerals x and y of the appropriate type. It then executes the usual multiplication algorithm to compute the product of x and y. If this product equals w, then w is composite and so the machine enters an accepting state. This is a rather vague description of the machine and there are many details to implement. For example, in order to guess the numerals x and y, the machine would guess the numerals one digit at a time. Still, it is routine to convert this informal procedure into a mathematically precise description of a nondeterministic Turing machine.

In order to see the advantage of nondeterminism in the above procedure, let us contrast it with the obvious deterministic procedure to accept the composite numbers. The deterministic procedure would check all possible factors x and y in order to see if the input w is the product of x and y. For arbitrary w, x and y range between two and w. Hence there are about w possible choices for x and about w possible choices for y. So, the deterministic procedure performs about w^2 multiplications while the nondeterministic procedure performs only one. Also, the nondeterministic program is easier to write and will be easier to read. (One can easily improve this deterministic program so that it performs only about the square root of w divisions and no multiplications. Still, this is much less efficient than the one multiplication of the nondeterministic program. Also, such improvements in efficiency are likely to make the program significantly more complicated.)

As was true of the other nondeterministic models we have seen, nondeterministic Turing machines do not correspond to any physical machines nor do they correspond very directly to any physical computing process. Even the parallel processing realization is only theoretically possible due to the extremely large number of processors needed. Nondeterministic Turing machines are a purely theoretical construct. The fact that they may be very efficient is probably not of any direct practical importance. However, we will see that, at a decrease in efficiency, nondeterministic Turing machines can be routinely converted to equivalent deterministic Turing machines. So they do provide a method to easily see that certain problems are solvable by computers. If we can find a nondeterministic program for a task, then we know that a deterministic program for that task can be found. Also, since we can routinely convert nondeterministic programs to deterministic programs, it is possible to design programming languages which use nondeterminism and which can be compiled into code for real machines. Unfortunately, this code will not closely mirror the intuition of the nondeterministic program and, furthermore, may be very inefficient. Still it is possible and may be a useful approach to the task of generating certain types of programs.

DEFINITIONS AND EXAMPLES

We now go on to define nondeterministic Turing machines formally and to prove that they are equivalent to deterministic Turing machines. The definitions are very similar to those for the deterministic case.

8.1 Definition

8.1.1 A *nondeterministic Turing machine* is a six-tuple $M = (S, \Sigma, \delta, s, B, Y)$ where all elements, except the transition function δ, are the same as for a (deterministic) simple Turing machine; that is, S is a finite set of *states*, Σ is a finite *tape alphabet*, s is an element of S called the *start state*, B is an element of Σ called the *blank*, and Y is a subset of S called the set of *accepting states*. The *transition function* δ is a mapping from $S \times \Sigma$ into subsets of $S \times \Sigma \times \{\leftarrow, \rightarrow, \downarrow\}$ such that $\delta(p, a)$ is the empty set whenever p is an accepting state. If p is a state of M and a is a tape symbol of M, then $\delta(p, a)$ is to be interpreted as the set of possible actions M may take when its finite control is in state p and its tape head is scanning a. The individual action instructions in $\delta(p, a)$ are of the same form as those for (deterministic) simple Turing machines and have the same interpretation as they did for the deterministic machines. As with simple Turing machines, we use the notation States(M), Symbols(M), Instructions(M), Start(M), Blank(M), and Accepting-states(M) to denote S, Σ, δ, s, B, and Y respectively.

8.1.2 An *id* of M is defined in the same way that id's for (deterministic) simple Turing machines were defined; that is, it is a pair $(p, \alpha \triangleright \beta)$ where p is in States(M), α, β are in [Symbols(M)]* and $\triangleright$ is a symbol which is not in Symbols(M). As with simple Turing machines, we identify any two id's which differ only by leading or trailing blanks in the second coordinate.

8.1.3 The next step relation $|_{\overline{M}}$ is a binary relation on id's of M and is defined by clauses (1), (2), and (3) below. The p and q range over States(M); $a, b,$ and c range over Symbols(M); α, β range over [Symbols(M)]*.

1. If $(q, b, \downarrow) \in \delta(p, a)$, then
   $(p, \alpha \triangleright a\beta) |_{\overline{M}} (q, \alpha \triangleright b\beta)$ for all α and β.
2. If $(q, b, \rightarrow) \in \delta(p, a)$, then
   $(p, \alpha \triangleright a\beta) |_{\overline{M}} (q, \alpha b \triangleright \beta)$ for all α and β.
3. If $(q, b, \leftarrow) \in \delta(p, a)$, then
   $(p, \alpha c \triangleright a\beta) |_{\overline{M}} (q, \alpha \triangleright cb\beta)$ for all α, β, and c.

Notice that, unlike (deterministic) simple Turing machines, an id $(p_1, \alpha_1 \triangleright \beta_1)$ of a nondeterministic Turing machine M can have more than one id

$(p_2, \alpha_2 \triangleright \beta_2)$ such that $(p_1, \alpha_1 \triangleright \beta_1) \mathrel{\vert_{\overline{M}}} (p_2, \alpha_2 \triangleright \beta_2)$.

As usual, $\mathrel{\vert_{\overline{M}}^{*}}$ denotes any finite number (possibly zero) of applications of $\mathrel{\vert_{\overline{M}}}$. Also, when no confusion results, we may drop the subscript M from $\mathrel{\vert_{\overline{M}}}$ and $\mathrel{\vert_{\overline{M}}^{*}}$.

8.1.4 An id $(p, \alpha \triangleright a\beta)$ is called a *halting id* if $\delta(p, a)$ is the empty set. In other words, an id is a halting id if the transition function yields no instruction and so there is no possible next id.

8.1.5 Let ξ be a string in $[\text{Symbols}(M) - \{B\}]^*$. A *computation* of M on input ξ is any finite or infinite sequence of id's $(q_0, \alpha_0 \triangleright \beta_0)$, $(q_1, \alpha_1 \triangleright \beta_1)$, $(q_2, \alpha_2 \triangleright \beta_2)$, ... such that: the first id $(q_0, \alpha_0 \triangleright \beta_0) = (s, \triangleright \xi)$, where $s = \text{Start}(M)$; $(q_{i-1}, \alpha_{i-1} \triangleright \beta_{i-1}) \mathrel{\vert_{\overline{M}}} (q_i, \alpha_i \triangleright \beta_i)$ for all $i \geqslant 1$ in the sequence and, if the sequence is finite, then the last id is a halting id.

8.1.6 Let ξ and β be strings in $[\text{Symbols}(M) - \{B\}]^*$ and let $s = \text{Start}(M)$. The nondeterministic Turing machine M is said to have *output β* for input ξ provided $(s, \triangleright \xi) \mathrel{\vert_{\overline{M}}^{*}} (q, \triangleright \beta)$ for some accepting state q. The formal statement of this definition is the same as in the deterministic case. However, because the relation $\mathrel{\vert_{\overline{M}}}$ may now yield more computations, it is possible for a single input to have more than one output.

8.1.7 Let f be a partial function from $[\text{Symbols}(M) - \{B\}]^*$ into itself. M is said to *compute the partial function f* provided that conditions (1), (2), and (3) hold for all input strings ξ in $[\text{Symbols}(M) - \{B\}]^*$

1. $f(\xi)$ is defined if and only if M has some output for the input ξ.
2. For any input ξ, M has at most one output.
3. If $f(\xi)$ is defined, then $f(\xi)$ is the output for the input ξ.

8.1.8 The *language accepted* by M is defined and denoted by $A(M) = \{\xi \mid (s, \triangleright \xi) \mathrel{\vert_{\overline{M}}^{*}} (q, \alpha \triangleright \beta)$ for some accepting state q and some strings α and $\beta\}$.

8.2 Example

In order to keep this example simple, we will consider a task which could be done easily by even a deterministic finite-state acceptor. Still the example will use nondeterminism in a natural way and will illustrate the technicalities of the definitions. Specifically, we will now describe a nondeterministic Turing machine M which accepts the language $L = \{a^i \mid i = 2m$ for some $m \geqslant 1$ or $i = 3m$ for some $m \geqslant 1\}$. M will nondeterministically guess that the length of the input is either a multiple of two or a multiple of three. It will then check its guess. To make things easier for us to follow, we will have M mark off its count by replacing the last a in a block of two or three a's by the blank symbol. If M checks that its guess is correct, then it accepts the input. The formal definition of M is given in the next paragraph.

States(M) = $\{<$start$>, q_0, q_1, p_0, p_1, p_2, <$accept$>\}$. The q's will count multiples of two and the p's will count multiples of three. Symbols(M) = $\{a, B\}$, Blank(M) = B, Start(M) = $<$start$>$, Accepting-states(M) = $\{<$accept$>\}$, and the transition function δ of M is defined as follows:

$$\delta(<\text{start}>, a) = \{(q_1, a, \rightarrow), (p_1, a, \rightarrow)\}$$

$$\delta(q_0, a) = \{(q_1, a, \rightarrow)\} \qquad \delta(p_0, a) = \{(p_1, a, \rightarrow)\}$$

$$\delta(q_1, a) = \{(q_0, B, \rightarrow)\} \qquad \delta(p_1, a) = \{(p_2, a, \rightarrow)\}$$

$$\delta(q_0, B) = \{(<\text{accept}>, B, \downarrow)\} \qquad \delta(p_2, a) = \{(p_0, B, \rightarrow)\}$$

$$\delta(p_0, B) = \{(<\text{accept}>, B, \downarrow)\}$$

For all other arguments, the value of δ at that argument is defined to be the empty set. Below are the two computations of M on input a^4.

$(<$start$>, \triangleright a^4) \vdash (q_1, a \triangleright a^3) \vdash (q_0, aB \triangleright a^2) \vdash$
$(q_1, aBa \triangleright a) \vdash (q_0, aBaB \triangleright B) \vdash (<$accept$>, aBaB \triangleright B)$

and

$(<$start$>, \triangleright a^4) \vdash (p_1, a \triangleright a^3) \vdash (p_2, aa \triangleright a^2) \vdash$
$(p_0, aaB \triangleright a) \vdash (p_1, aaBa \triangleright B)$

and the computation halts in a non-accepting state.

The input a^4 is accepted since there is at least one accepting computation of M on that input.

EQUIVALENCE OF NONDETERMINISTIC AND DETERMINISTIC TURING MACHINES

Deterministic Turing machines (what we called simple Turing machines) are really a special case of nondeterministic Turing machines. If M is any such deterministic Turing machine with transition function δ, then, in order to convert M to a nondeterministic Turing machine M' which satisfies the technicalities of Definition 8.1.1, we need only replace δ by the function δ' defined as follows: $\delta'(p, a) = \{\delta(p, a)\}$ if $\delta(p, a)$ is defined and $\delta'(p, a)$ is the empty set otherwise. M' then satisfies the Definition 8.1.1 of a nondeterministic Turing machine and M' is just a slight notational variation of M. In particular, M and M' have exactly the same computations and accept the same language; furthermore, if one computes a partial function then the other computes the same partial function. Hence it is trivially true that anything which can be done by such a deterministic Turing machine can also be done by some nondeterministic Turing machine. The converse is not so trivial to demonstrate but is nevertheless true.

8.3 Theorem

1. If M is any nondeterministic Turing machine, then we can find a (deterministic) simple Turing machine M_D such that $A(M_D) = A(M)$.
2. If M is any nondeterministic Turing machine and f is a partial function computed by M, then we can find a (deterministic) simple Turing machine M_D such that M_D also computes f.

PROOF The proof of (2) is similar to that of (1). We will, therefore, only prove (1) and leave the proof of (2) as an exercise.

Suppose M is a nondeterministic Turing machine. We will describe a deterministic procedure to determine if an input string ξ for M is in $A(M)$. By the Church/Turing thesis, it will then follow that we can convert this procedure to a deterministic Turing machine M_D such that $A(M_D) = A(M)$.

The procedure to determine if an input string ξ for M is in $A(M)$ essentially tries all possible computations of M on input ξ. It does this by implementing something like the parallel processing view of nondeterministic machines. The procedure keeps a list of id's of M. Initially, only the start id $(s, \triangleright\xi)$, where $s = \text{Start}(M)$, is on the list. The procedure then proceeds as follows:

1. Test to see whether or not there is some id on the list which has an accepting state as its first coordinate. If such an id is on the list, then accept the input ξ; otherwise, continue.
2. Replace each id $(p, \alpha\triangleright\beta)$ on the list by all id's $(q, \mu\triangleright\nu)$ such that $(p, \alpha\triangleright\beta) \mid_{\overline{M}} (q, \mu\triangleright\nu)$.
3. GOTO 1.

Clearly, the procedure works and accepts exactly those strings which are in $A(M)$. To implement this procedure on a Turing machine, or almost any other computing device, we must code id's as strings of symbols so that they can be entered on the list. However, this is easy. For example, $(p, \alpha\triangleright\beta)$ might be coded as $\alpha p \beta$ provided p is a symbol. Since we can always replace an arbitrary Turing machine by one whose states are symbols, this method will always work. Converting the above procedure to a Turing machine program is now routine, even if it is rather involved. $\square$

EXERCISES

1. Describe nondeterministic Turing machines to accept each of the following languages:
   a. $\{a^i \mid i = n^2 \text{ for some integer } n\}$.
   b. $\{a^i \mid i \neq n^2 \text{ for any integer } n\}$.
   c. $\{u \mathbb{¢} \mathbb{¢} v_1 \mathbb{¢} v_2 \mathbb{¢} ... \mathbb{¢} v_n \mid n \geq 1 \text{ and } u = v_i, \text{ for some } i\}$.

2. Describe nondeterministic Turing machines to compute each of the following partial functions.

    a. $f(n_1 \cent n_2) = n_3$ provided n_1, n_2, and n_3 are binary numerals and n_3 is equal to the quotient obtained when n_2 is divided by n_1.

    b. $f(m) = p_1 \cent p_2 \cent ... \cent p_n$ provided m, p_1, p_2, ..., p_n are binary numerals, $n \geqslant 0$ and p_1, p_2, ..., p_n is a list of all primes which divide (are factors of) m.

3. Prove part (2) of Theorem 8.3.

4. Let Δ be an arbitrary alphabet. Define an $NTL\Delta$ program to be the same as a $TL\Delta$ program except that in an $NTL\Delta$ program statements need not have unique labels. Describe how $NTL\Delta$ programs may be viewed as programs for nondeterministic Turing machines. That is, define a reasonable notion of the nondeterministic Turing machine realization of an $NTL\Delta$ program.

5. Define $NTL\Delta$ programs as in Exercise 4. Prove that the set of all $NTL\Delta$ programs with labels in $\{0, 1\}^*$ is finite-state language. (This is just a restatement of Exercise 9 in Chapter 5.)

6. The transition function of a nondeterministic Turing machine is, generally speaking, multiple-valued. However, it need not be multiple-valued for all arguments. Generally speaking, there will be some arguments for which it yields exactly one instruction. Hence, it may act deterministically on some inputs, in the sense that the computation happens to only use those arguments of the transition function which yield a single instruction. Prove that there is no algorithm to decide the following: Given a nondeterministic Turing machine M and an input ξ for M, decide whether or not M ever uses nondeterminism in the computation on input ξ, that is, whether or not M ever reaches a configuration in which the transition function of M yields two or more instructions.

Chapter Nine

Pushdown Automata

Context-free languages are an important class of languages because many common high-level programming languages are either context-free languages or at least have important parts of their syntax described by context-free grammars. In practice, these languages are implemented on a computer by designing a program called a compiler. A compiler takes as input a string which is a program in a high-level language and produces as output a program in a language which the machine can execute. One common method used by such compilers is to first construct a context-free parse tree for the input program and then to use this parse tree to help construct the output program. We will now consider a highly idealized model of a machine to implement the parsing phase of such compiler programs. The model is a very highly idealized picture of such a compiler process and will certainly not serve as a complete introduction to the theory of compiling. It is, however, an important model of a compiler and will serve as a good base for more advanced studies of the subject.

The model of a compiler which we will study is called a *pushdown automaton* (*pda*). In this chapter we will simplify the study by only considering the problem of constructing a program to see if an input string is a syntactically correct program, that is, to see if it can be generated by the given context-free grammar. Hence, a pda will either accept an input or not. There will be no output information other than acceptance. This is a reasonable first step for a compiler program but only a first step. We will give only an informal indication of how a pda can produce a parse tree for an input program. We will not go on to discuss how such parse trees can be used to generate the output program of the compiler. That topic is outside the scope of this book. You can, however, easily get a feel for how the parse tree can be used to produce the output program by reviewing the method for translating $PS\Delta$ programs to $TL\Delta$ programs. That method made extensive use of the context-free grammar description of $PS\Delta$.

158

The pda model makes use of a storage device called a *pushdown store*. A pushdown store is a kind of first-in/last-out list. That is, it is a list of symbols, say written right to left. The program can add or delete symbols on the left-hand end of the list. It can read the leftmost symbol but cannot read any other symbols. For example, in order to read C in the list $ABCD$, it must first delete the symbols A and B. A and B are then lost. Intuitively, one can think of a pushdown store as a stack of dinner plates; each plate has one symbol written on it. In this case, the symbols are stored bottom-to-top rather than right-to-left. The rules for manipulating this stack of symbols are that only the symbol on the top plate can be read, but plates may be removed and either smashed or washed so the symbol on it is lost. Also, a symbol may be written on a plate and added to the top of the stack. In this way information (symbols) can be put in the stack and later retrieved. A possible origin for the term "pushdown store" is that just such a method for storing plates is often used in cafeterias. A stack of plates is stored in a hole with a spring on the bottom. The spring is just stiff enough so that only one plate is visible. Plates may be added ("pushed down") or removed from the stack only at the top of the stack. By analogy to such a stack of dinner plates, the leftmost symbol of a pushdown store is frequently referred to as the *top* symbol.

A pda is, intuitively, a finite-state acceptor which has a pushdown store attached to it. The input to a pda is a string of symbols written on an input tape much like a Turing machine tape. A tape head on this input tape is connected to a finite-state control so that the finite-state control can read one symbol of the input at a time. The tape head can read but cannot write on the input tape. At the start of a computation, the input tape head is at the left end of the input. The finite-state control can move the input tape head to the right but cannot move it to the left. So, like a one-way finite-state acceptor, the pda only gets one look (one "pass") at the input. The finite-state control can also read the top symbol on the pushdown store and may add (*push*) or delete (*pop*) symbols from the top of the pushdown store. At a typical point in a computation the finite-state control is in some state, the input tape head is scanning some symbol and there is some symbol on top of the pushdown store. On the basis of this information it will change the state of the finite-state control, pop the top symbol of the pushdown store, place (push) a finite number of symbols on to the pushdown store, and may or may not move the input tape head one square to the right. Like finite-state acceptors, pda's may be nondeterministic. So there are frequently several possible moves for a pda in a given configuration.

This may seem like a rather strange model at first glance, but many compiler programs do make use of a pushdown store and, as we shall see, a pushdown store is an excellent device to use in constructing parse trees. We now make these notions formal.

DEFINITIONS AND EXAMPLES

9.1 Definition

A *pushdown automaton* (*pda*) is a seven-tuple $M = (S, \Sigma, \Gamma, \delta, s, Z_0, Y)$ where S is a finite set of *states*, Σ and Γ are finite sets of symbols referred to as the *input alphabet* and *pushdown alphabet* respectively, s is an element of S called the *start state*, Z_0 is an element of Γ called the *start symbol*, and Y is a subset of S called the set of *accepting states*. The fourth element δ is a mapping from $S \times (\Sigma \cup \{\Lambda\}) \times \Gamma$ into finite subsets of $S \times \Gamma^*$. The mapping δ is called the *transition function*. As with previous definitions of machines, we will employ the following notation: States$(M) = S$, Input-alph$(M) = \Sigma$, Push-alph$(M) = \Gamma$, Instructions$(M) = \delta$, Start-state$(M) = s$, Start-symbol$(M) = Z_0$, and Accepting-states$(M) = Y$.

The intuitive meaning of these items is as follows. States(M) are the possible states of the finite-state control, Input-alph(M) is the alphabet used for the input tape, and Push-alph(M) is the alphabet used for the pushdown store; at the start of a computation the finite-state control is placed in Start-state(M) and the pushdown store contains only the one symbol Start-symbol(M); Accepting-states(M) serve approximately the same function that accepting states of Turing machines do. If $\delta(q, a, C) = \{(p_1, \gamma_1), (p_2, \gamma_2) \ldots \ldots (p_m, \gamma_m)\}$, where a is in Σ, this is interpreted to mean that if the finite-state control is in state q, the input tape head is scanning a and C is on top of the pushdown store, then M may perform any of the moves (p_i, γ_i), $1 \leqslant i \leqslant m$. To perform the move (p_i, γ_i), M removes (pops) C from the pushdown store and places (pushes) γ_i on the pushdown store (the leftmost symbol of γ_i goes on top); M then advances the input head past a and changes the state of the finite-state control to p_i. If $a = \Lambda$, the interpretation is similar. The set of instructions $\delta(q, \Lambda, C)$ is applicable whenever the finite-state control is in state q and C is on top of the pushdown store. In this case, it does not matter what input symbol is being read. In fact, the pda may move according to an instruction in $\delta(q, \Lambda, C)$ even if there is not input left. If $a = \Lambda$, then the moves (p_i, γ_i) have the same interpretation as they do when a is in Σ, except that in the case $a = \Lambda$ the input tape head is not advanced. If the pushdown store is empty, then no instruction is applicable and the computation ends.

Note that a pda is a nondeterministic machine. In any one situation there may be several instructions that are applicable. If the pda has its finite-state control in q, its input tape head scanning symbol a out of Σ, and has the symbol C on top of its pushdown store, then all instructions in the set $\delta(q, a, C)$ are applicable. Also, all instructions in the set $\delta(q, \Lambda, C)$ are applicable. Which instruction does the machine follow? The situation is exactly analogous to that of nondeterministic finite-state acceptors. We can think of the machine as replicating itself to make one copy for each instruction and then having each copy follow a different instruction. The various copies of the machine then compute in parallel. An equivalent and sometimes more useful intuition is to think of the machine as "guessing" at one instruction to follow.

These pda's accept languages consisting of strings over the input alphabet. The language accepted by a pda is just the set of all input strings accepted. The pda model has two different notions of accepting an input called *accepting by final state* and *accepting by empty store*. So every pda defines two, possibly different, languages: the language accepted by final state and the language accepted by empty store. A computation of a pda starts with the input written on the input tape, the input head scanning the first (leftmost) symbol of the input string, the finite-state control in the start state, and the pushdown store containing only the start symbol. The machine then follows the instructions determined by the transition function δ in the manner outlined above. The input is said to be *accepted by final state* if one of the parallel machines (equivalently one of the computations resulting from some sequence of guesses) gets to a configuration where the entire input has been read and the finite-state control is in an accepting state. The input is said to be *accepted by empty store* if the pda can get to a configuration where the entire input has been read and the pushdown store is empty; in this case, it does not matter whether the finite-state control is in an accepting state or not. Notice that an input is not accepted until after it is completely read. A final state at some point before the input is completely read has no significance. An empty store before the input is completely read will similarly not indicate acceptance. Acceptance by final state has a clear intuitive meaning. Acceptance by empty store turns out to be at least as important. As we shall see, pda's accept exactly the context-free languages. This is true whether we use acceptance by empty store or acceptance by final state. Intuitively, the pda accepts an input by constructing something analogous to the parse tree for the input. This type of acceptance by parsing is most naturally modeled using acceptance by empty store. Before formalizing these notions it will be helpful to look at some examples of pda's.

9.2 Examples

9.2.1 The pda M described below accepts the language $L = \{w \cent w^R \mid w \in \{0, 1\}^*\}$ by both final state and empty store. As before, w^R denotes w written backwards.

> States(M) = {<push>, <pop>, <accept>}
> Accepting-states(M) = {<accept>}
> Input-alph(M) = {0, 1, $\cent$}
> Push-alph(M) = {0, 1, Z_0}
> Start-state(M) = <push>
> Start-symbol(M) = Z_0
> Instructions(M) = δ, defined below

We will design δ so that, given an input $w \cent w^R$ in L, M will push w on the pushdown store staying in state <push>. When it reads the symbol $\cent$ it will change to state <pop> and will pop the symbols off the pushdown store one at a time comparing them to w^R. Notice that when the symbol $\cent$ is read, the pushdown store contains w but the last (rightmost) symbol of w is on top. So the symbols in the pushdown store are in the correct order to allow comparison with w^R. If the symbols all match, and the pda gets to the last symbol Z_0 in the pushdown store, then it pops Z_0 and goes to the accepting state. If the input is not in L, then the above procedure of pushing then comparing will fail and the input will not be accepted. With this intuition in mind, we now define δ.

$$\delta(<\text{push}>, 1, X) = \{(<\text{push}>, 1X)\}, \quad X = 0, 1 \text{ or } Z_0$$
$$\delta(<\text{push}>, 0, X) = \{(<\text{push}>, 0X)\}, \quad X = 0, 1 \text{ or } Z_0$$
$$\delta(<\text{push}>, \text{¢}, X) = \{(<\text{pop}>, X)\}, \quad X = 0, 1 \text{ or } Z_0$$
$$\delta(<\text{pop}>, Y, Y) = \{(<\text{pop}>, \Lambda)\}, \quad Y = 0, \text{ or } 1$$
$$\delta(<\text{pop}>, \Lambda, Z_0) = \{(<\text{accept}>, \Lambda)\}$$

All other arguments are mapped onto the empty set by δ.

There are a number of things to notice about the definition of δ. Our definition of pda's required that the top symbol always be popped. So, in the first instruction, in order to accomplish the act of simply pushing a 1 on the pushdown store, the pda first pops the symbol X, which is on top, and then pushes the two symbols: X followed by 1. The net effect is to add a 1 to the pushdown store. Another thing to note is that this pda is deterministic in the sense that, in any configuration, there is at most one applicable instruction. Finally, observe how the pda computation proceeds on the inputs 10¢01 and 10¢011. In the first case, the pda pushes 1 then pushes 0 and changes to state $<\text{pop}>$. At this point the pushdown store contains $01Z_0$ with the 0 on top, and the input still remaining to be read is 01. It then pops 0 and pops 1 and has read the entire input. Even though the entire input is read, it can still make one move defined by $\delta(<\text{pop}>, \Lambda, Z_0)$. This move pops Z_0, leaving the stack empty and puts the finite-state control into state $<\text{accept}>$. So 10¢01 is accepted by empty store and is accepted by final state. On input 10¢011, the pda would compute exactly as it did on 10¢01. With input 10¢011, the computation would end with an empty store and with the finite-state control in an accepting state. However, 10¢011 is not accepted since the entire input is not read. The final 1 will never be read; that is, the input head will never be advanced past this final 1. We do not consider a symbol to be read until after the input head advances past the symbol.

9.2.2 The pda M described below accepts the language $L = \{ww^R \mid w \in \{0, 1\}^* \text{ and } w \neq \Lambda\}$ both by empty store and by final state. M is similar to the pda of 9.2.1, but now there is no ¢ to tell the pda when to stop pushing and start popping. So it will use nondeterminism to guess when it has found the middle of the input.

$$\text{States}(M) = \{<\text{push}>, <\text{pop}>, <\text{accept}>\}$$
$$\text{Accepting-states}(M) = \{<\text{accept}>\}$$
$$\text{Input-alph}(M) = \{0, 1\}$$
$$\text{Push-alph}(M) = \{0, 1, Z_0\}$$

Start-state(M) = <push>
Start-symbol(M) = Z_0
Instruction(M) = δ where
$\delta($<push>$, 1, X)$ = {(<push>$, 1X)$, (<pop>$, 1X)$}
$\delta($<push>$, 0, X)$ = {(<push>$, 0X)$, (<pop>$, 0X)$}
  X = 1, 0 or Z_0
$\delta($<pop>$, Y, Y)$ = {(<pop>$, \Lambda)$}, Y = 0 or 1
$\delta($<pop>$, \Lambda, Z_0)$ = {(<accept>$, \Lambda)$)}
and δ maps all other arguments onto the empty set.

9.2.3 The pda M described below accepts $L_1 = \{w¢w^R \mid w \in \{0, 1\}^*\}$ by empty store and $L_2 = \{w¢w^R¢ \mid w \in \{0, 1\}^*\}$ by final state. M is exactly the same as in 9.2.1 except that δ is defined slightly differently.

$$\delta(\text{<push>}, 1, X) = \{(\text{<push>}, 1X)\}, \quad X = 0, \text{ 1 or } Z_0$$
$$\delta(\text{<push>}, 0, X) = \{(\text{<push>}, 0X)\}, \quad X = 0, \text{ 1 or } Z_0$$
$$\delta(\text{<push>}, ¢, X) = \{(\text{<pop>}, X)\}, \quad X = 0, \text{ 1 or } Z_0$$
$$\delta(\text{<pop>}, Y, Y) = \{(\text{<pop>}, \Lambda)\}, \quad Y = 0, \text{ or } 1$$
$$\delta(\text{<pop>}, \Lambda, Z_0) = \{(\text{<pop>}, \Lambda)\}$$
$$\delta(\text{<pop>}, ¢, Z_0) = \{(\text{<accept>}, Z_0)\}$$

All other arguments are mapped onto the empty set by δ.

Notice that even though each value of δ contains at most one instruction, M is still nondeterministic. In state <pop>, scanning input symbol ¢, with Z_0 on top of the stack, there are two applicable instructions:

$$\delta(\text{<pop>}, \Lambda, Z_0) \text{ and } \delta(\text{<pop>}, ¢, Z_0)$$

We now formalize the notions of computation and acceptance.

9.3 Definition

Let M be a pda and adopt the notation of Definition 9.1.

9.3.1 An *instantaneous description* (*id*) of M is a triple (x, p, γ), where x is a string of input symbols in Σ^*, p is a state in S and γ is a string of pushdown store symbols in Γ^*.

The intuitive interpretation of (x, p, γ) is that the finite-state control of M is a state p, γ is in the pushdown store with the leftmost symbol of γ on top, and x is the string of input symbols that have not yet been read. So if x is not empty, then the input tape head is scanning the first symbol in x. It is important to note that x is not necessarily the entire input string but is only that portion of the input which has not yet been read.

To aid readability we will, when discussing *pda*'s, adopt the convention that the variables w, x, y and z range over strings of input symbols, that lower-case Greek letters α, β, γ, ... range over strings of pushdown store symbols, that a, b, c usually range over single input symbols (and sometimes may take on the value Λ), and that variables which range over pushdown store symbols are usually chosen to be capital roman letters.

9.3.2 The *next step relation* $\vdash_{\overline{M}}$ is a binary relation on id's of M and is defined to hold in the following situation:

$$(ay, q, X\beta) \vdash_{\overline{M}} (y, p, \gamma\beta) \text{ provided } (p, \gamma) \text{ is in } \delta(q, a, X)$$

Notice that a can be either Λ or an element of the input alphabet Σ. As usual, $\vdash_{\overline{M}}^{*}$ denotes any finite number, possibly zero, of applications of $\vdash_{\overline{M}}$. When it is clear from context, we will omit the subscript M in $\vdash_{\overline{M}}$ and $\vdash_{\overline{M}}^{*}$.

9.3.3 The *language accepted* by M *by final state* is denoted $A(M)$ and is defined by $A(M) = \{w \mid (w, s, Z_0) \vdash_{\overline{M}}^{*} (\Lambda, p, \gamma) \text{ for some } p \text{ in } Y \text{ and some } \gamma \text{ in } \Gamma^* \}$. Recall that $s = $ Start-state(M), $Z_0 = $ Start-symbol(M), $Y = $ Accepting-state(M), and $\Gamma = $ Push-alph(M).

9.3.4 The *language accepted* by M *by empty store* is denoted $E(M)$ and is defined by $E(M) = \{w \mid (w, s, Z_0) \vdash_{\overline{M}}^{*} (\Lambda, p, \Lambda) \text{ for some state } p\}$. The notation is as in 9.3.3. Notice that in this case, p need not be an accepting state.

9.4 Example

In Figure 9.1 we give, in diagrammatic form, all the id's which can arise from computations of the pda in Example 9.2.2 on the input 1001. The diagram exhibits the nondeterministic behavior in a way analogous to that used to illustrate a nondeterministic finite-state acceptor's action in Figure 3.4. A path through the tree from the root node (start configuration) to a leaf of the tree is called a computation. In this case, there are five computations. One is an accepting computation and four are not. The input is accepted (by both empty store and final state in this case) because at least one computation is an accepting computation; that is, it ends in an accepting configuration.

EQUIVALENCE OF PDA's AND CONTEXT-FREE GRAMMARS

We now proceed to show that the class of context-free languages is the same as the class of languages accepted by pda's by empty store which, in turn, is the same as the class of languages accepted by pda's by final state.

9.5 Theorem If L is a context-free language, then there is some pda M such that $L = E(M)$.

PROOF Let $G = (N, T, P, S)$ be a context-free grammar in Chomsky normal form such that $L(G) = L$. We will construct a pda M such that $E(M) = L(G) = L$. In some intuitive sense, the pda tries to construct a parse tree for the input. If it succeeds, then it accepts the input. More specifically, but still intuitively, the pda uses its pushdown store to try to construct a leftmost derivation of the input string. The formal definition of M is:

$$\text{States}(M) = \{q\}, \text{ where } q \text{ is arbitrary.}$$
$$\text{Start-state}(M) = q.$$
$$\text{Start-symbol}(M) = S, \text{ the start symbol of } G.$$

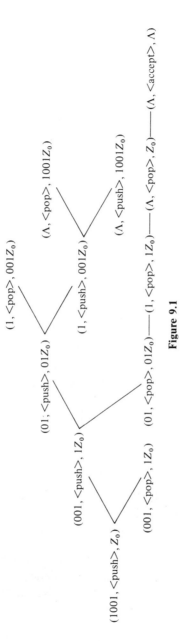

Figure 9.1

Input-alph$(M) = T = $ Terminals(G).
Push-alph$(M) = $ N $\cup$ $T = $ Symbols(G).
Accepting-states(M) is irrelevant to this proof.
Instructions$(M) = \delta$, defined below.

There are two cases, when the top symbol on the pushdown store is in N and when it is in T.

1. $\delta(q, \Lambda, A) = \{(q, \beta) \mid A \to \beta$ is in $P\}$, for A in $N = $ Nonterminals(G).
2. $\delta(q, a, a) = \{(q, \Lambda)\}$, for a in $T = $ Terminals(G).

For all other arguments δ is empty. To see that $E(M) = L(G)$, we make a series of observations. First recall that the grammar is in Chomsky normal form. Hence, if $A \overset{*}{\Rightarrow} \beta$ by a leftmost derivation and the leftmost symbol of β is a nonterminal, then every symbol in β is a nonterminal. We now go on to some more fundamental observations.

3. If $S \overset{*}{\Rightarrow} \beta$ by a leftmost derivation and the leftmost symbol (and hence every symbol) of β is a nonterminal, then $(w, q, S) \overset{*}{\vdash} (w, q, \beta)$ for any input w.

More generally, for any nonterminal A,

4. If $A \overset{*}{\Rightarrow} \beta$ by a leftmost derivation and the leftmost symbol (and hence every symbol) of β is a nonterminal, then $(x, q, A\gamma) \overset{*}{\vdash} (x, q, \beta\gamma)$, for any string of input symbols x and any string of stack symbols γ.

To see (3) and (4), simply note that the pda can change the top pushdown store symbol, S or A, to β by a suitable choice of instructions of type (1).

Now suppose $w = a_1a_2...a_n$ is in $L(G)$, where the a_i are single symbols. Then w has a leftmost derivation in G that can be decomposed to look like the following:

5. $S \overset{*}{\Rightarrow} A_1\alpha_1 \overset{*}{\Rightarrow} a_1A_2\alpha_2 \overset{*}{\Rightarrow} a_1a_2A_3\alpha_3 \overset{*}{\Rightarrow} a_1a_2a_3A_4\alpha_4 \overset{*}{\Rightarrow}...$
   $... \Rightarrow a_1a_2... a_{n-1}A_n \Rightarrow a_1a_2...a_n = w$

where the A_i are nonterminals and the α_i are strings of nonterminals. We know that the symbols a_1, a_2, ..., a_n will be generated one at a time and in that order, because we know that G is in Chomsky normal form and that the derivation is leftmost. The only importance of the Chomsky normal form is that it ensures us that every terminal a_i is produced by a rule of the form $A_i \to a_i$, and even this is a notational convenience rather than a necessity.

Now, combining (2), (3), (4), and (5), we see that

6. $(a_1a_2...a_n, q, S) \overset{*}{\vdash} (a_1a_2...a_n, q, A_1\alpha_1) \overset{*}{\vdash}$
   $(a_1a_2...a_n, q, a_1A_2\alpha_2) \vdash (a_2a_3...a_n, q, A_2\alpha_2) \overset{*}{\vdash}$
   $(a_2a_3...a_n, q, a_2A_3\alpha_3) \vdash (a_3a_4...a_n, q, A_3\alpha_3) \overset{*}{\vdash}$
   $(a_3a_4...a_n, q, a_3A_4\alpha_4) \vdash ... (a_n, q, A_n) \vdash (a_n, q, a_n) \vdash (\Lambda, q, \Lambda)$

Since w was an arbitrary nonempty string in $L(G)$ and (6) holds for

$w = a_1 a_2 ... a_n$, we conclude that the following holds for all nonempty strings w:

7. If w is in $L(G)$, then w is in $E(M)$.

It is straightforward to check that the empty string is in $L(G)$ if and only if it is in $E(M)$. We must still show that, for nonempty strings w,

8. *Claim*: If w is in $E(M)$, then w is in $L(G)$.

To see that (8) is true, we proceed by another series of observations. By definition of δ we see that

9. If $(x, q, A\gamma) \models^* (x, q, \beta\gamma)$ then $A \overset{*}{\Rightarrow} \beta$. Here A is a nonterminal.

Now suppose $w = a_1 a_2 ... a_n$ is in $E(M)$; then

10. $(a_1 a_2 ... a_n, q, S) \models^* (a_1 a_2 ... a_n, q, a_1 B_1 \beta_1) \models$
$(a_2 a_3 ... a_n, q, B_1 \beta_1) \models^* (a_2 a_3 ... a_n, q, a_2 B_2 \beta_2) \models$
$(a_3 a_4 ... a_n, q, B_2 \beta_2) \models^* (a_3 a_4 ... a_n, q, a_3 B_3 \beta_3) \models ...$
$... (a_{n-1} a_n, q, a_{n-1} B_{n-1} \beta_{n-1}) \models (a_n, q, B_{n-1} \beta_{n-1})$
$\models^* (a_n, q, a_n) \models (\Lambda, q, \Lambda)$

Combining (9) and (10), we see that

11. $S \overset{*}{\Rightarrow} a_1 B_1 \beta_1 \overset{*}{\Rightarrow} a_1 a_2 B_2 \beta_2 \overset{*}{\Rightarrow} a_1 a_2 a_3 B_3 \beta_3 \overset{*}{\Rightarrow} ...$
$... \overset{*}{\Rightarrow} a_1 a_2 ... a_{n-1} B_{n-1} \beta_{n-1} \overset{*}{\Rightarrow} a_1 a_2 ... a_n .$

(It is always the case that $\beta_{n-1} = \Lambda$ but we include it in order to keep the notation uniform). By (11), w is in $L(G)$. Thus we have established (8). (7) and (8) yield the desired equality $L(G) = E(M)$. $\square$

This completes the proof but, before leaving it, a few remarks are in order. First, the construction works even if the grammar is not in Chomsky normal form. The only reason we took the grammar in this form was to make the notation, particularly in (5), easier to handle. Of course, we know that we can always take the grammar to be in this form and so for convenience we have. Second, the above proof is rather informal. However, it is not too difficult to convert it to a formal inductive proof. Finally, it is interesting to note that the pda need have only one state.

We now proceed to show that if a language is accepted by a pda by empty store, then it is a context-free language. The proof is in two parts. First, we show that if $L = E(M)$ for some pda M, then $L = E(M_1)$ for some pda M_1 with just one state. We then show that if $L = E(M_1)$ for some one state pda M_1, then $L = L(G)$ for some context-free grammar G. The grammar G is obtained from M_1 by essentially the reverse of the process used to prove Theorem 9.5.

9.6 Theorem If M is any pda, then we can find a pda M_1 such that M_1 has only one state and $E(M_1) = E(M)$.

PROOF We will first describe M_1 informally and then give the formal construction of M_1. M_1 operates by simulating M step by step. In order to do this, M_1 will store the simulated state of M in its pushdown store. More specifically, we can think of M_1's pushdown store as having three tracks. So each pushdown store symbol of M_1 will contain three pieces of information. These three pieces of information will code a pushdown store symbol of M and two states of M. Let us denote a pushdown store symbol of M_1 by $<A, p, q>$, where A is a pushdown store symbol of M and both p and q are states of M. If at some point in a computation M_1 is simulating M in state p with $A_1 A_2 ... A_l$ in its pushdown store and with A_1 on top of the pushdown store, then the pushdown store of M_1 will contain

1. $<A_1, p, q_2> \ <A_2, q_2, q_3> \ <A_3, q_3, q_4> \ ... \ <A_l, q_l, q_{l+1}>$

where the states q_i were chosen nondeterministically at some previous moves, and $<A_1, p, q_2>$ is on top of the pushdown store. At some later time, $<A_2, q_2, q_3>$ may be on top of the pushdown store. When this occurs, A_2 will be the simulated top symbol of M's pushdown store and q_2 will be the simulated state of M. The third element of $<A_1, p, q_2>$ is equal to this state q_2. Similarly, the third element of $<A_2, q_2, q_3>$ is equal to the second element of the symbol $<A_3, q_3, q_4>$ below it and so forth. The state q_{l+1} is chosen nondeterministically at the start of the computation.

Now the state p, pushdown store symbol A_1 and current input symbol determine the possible moves of M. Suppose one such move replaces A_1 by BC with B on top and changes the state of M to p'. Then one possible move of M_1 will be to replace $<A_1, p, q_2>$ by $<B, p', q_1> \ <C, q_1, q_2>$. The state q_1 is chosen nondeterministically. So this one possible move of M gives rise to as many possible nondeterministic moves of M_1 as there are states of M. Notice that after such a move, the pushdown store of M_1 will contain

$<B, p', q_1> \ <C, q_1, q_2> \ <A_2, q_2, q_3> \ <A_3, q_3, q_4> \ ... \ <A_l, q_l, q_{l+1}>$

Hence, after one such move, the pushdown store of M_1 will contain a coding of the simulated pushdown store of M, plus a coding of the correct simulated state of M on top of the pushdown store, plus some nondeterministically chosen codings of states of M. In this way M_1 can easily simulate those moves of M which do not cause the pushdown store to become shorter.

Suppose that one possible move of M determined by the state p, pushdown store symbol A_1 and current input symbol were, instead, a move that pops A_1, adds nothing to the pushdown store and leaves the finite-state control of M in state p'. Suppose further, that the pushdown store of M_1 contains the string (1). There are two cases, $p' \neq q_2$ and $p' = q_2$. If $p' \neq q_2$, then this move of M gives rise to no moves of M_1. Intuitively, M_1 guessed incorrectly when it guessed q_2. If this move is the only possible move for M, then the computation of M_1 is aborted. If $p' = q_2$, then M_1 guessed correctly when it chose q_2. In this case, one possible move of M_1 is to pop $<A_1, p, q_2>$. This leaves $<A_2, q_2, q_3>$ on top of the pushdown store. Note that in this case, q_2 records the correct simulated state of M. If $<A_1, p, q_2>$ is the only symbol in the pushdown store ($l = 1$), then this move allows M_1 to empty its pushdown store and correctly simulate M, provided $p' = q_2$. Since one possible nondeterministic guess for q_2 was $q_2 = p'$, M_1 can perform a faithful simulation of M in this case as well. By these techniques, M_1 can use its pushdown store to simulate both the pushdown store of M and the finite-state control of M. We now give a formal definition of M_1 in terms of M.

States(M_1) = $\{q_0\}$ where q_0 is arbitrary. Input-alph(M_1) = Input-alph(M). Push-alph(M_1) = $\{<A, p, q> \mid A$ in Push-alph(M); p and q in States$(M)\} \cup \{Z_1\}$, where Z_1 is a new symbol. Start-state(M_1) = q_0; Start-symbol(M_1) = Z_1. The accepting states of M_1 are irrelevant to this proof. The transition function δ_1 of M_1 is defined by cases. At the start of a computation, the pushdown store of M_1 is initialized by a move defined by $\delta_1(q_0, \Lambda, Z_1)$ = $\{(q_0, <Z_0, s, q>) \mid q$ in States$(M)\}$ where s is the start state of M and Z_0 is the start pushdown store symbol of M. [This is the move which nondeterministically guesses the state q_{l+1} in (1).] In all other cases, δ_1 is defined in terms of the transition function δ of M. For any a equal to either Λ or an input symbol, any pushdown store symbol A of M, and any states p and q of M, $\delta_1(q_0, a, <A, p, q>)$ is the set of all pairs (q_0, β), where β is any string of pushdown symbols of M_1 satisfying one of the following two conditions:

1. $(p', B_1B_2...B_t) \in \delta(p, a, A)$, $t \geq 1$ and
   $\beta = <B_1, p_1, p_2> <B_2, p_2, p_3> ... <B_t, p_t, p_{t+1}>$ where $p_1 = p'$, $p_{t+1} = q$ and the p_i, $2 \leq i \leq t$, are any states of M.
2. $(p', \Lambda) \in \delta(p, a, A)$, $p' = q$ and $\beta = \Lambda$.

M_1 defined in this way will compute in the manner outlined in our intuitive description of M_1 at the start of this proof. So M_1 will simulate M step by step and hence $E(M_1) = E(M)$. A formal proof that $E(M_1) = E(M)$ would be little more than a restatement of the intuitive ideas which opened this proof and so will not be given. □

9.7 Lemma If M is any one state pda, then we can find a context-free grammar G such that $L(G) = E(M)$.

PROOF Without loss of generality, assume that Push-alph(M) and Input-alph(M) are disjoint. G is obtained from M by a process which intuitively is almost the reverse of the construction used in the proof of Theorem 9.5 to obtain a one-state pda from a cfg. Terminals(G) = Input-alph(M), Nonterminals(G) = Push-alph(M), Start(G) = Start-symbol(M), and the productions of G are defined in terms of the transition function δ of M. The productions of G consist of all rewrite rules $A \rightarrow a\gamma$ such that (q, γ) is in $\delta(q, a, A)$, where q is the unique state of M. Here a may be either a symbol or Λ. The fact that $L(G) = E(M)$ follows easily from the claim below. In the claim, x is a string of terminal symbols of G, β is a string of nonterminals, A is a single nonterminal and q is the single state of M.

Claim: $A \overset{*}{\Rightarrow} x\beta$ by a leftmost derivation in G if and only if $(x, q, A) \vdash^{*}_{M}$

(Λ, q, β), where q is the unique state of M.

The claim is easily proved by induction on the number of steps in the derivation and by induction on the number of steps in the computation of M. The details are left as an exercise. To see that $L(G) = E(M)$, notice that, by the claim, the following chain of statements are equivalent: A string w is in $L(G)$; $S \overset{*}{\Rightarrow} w$ by a leftmost derivation, where S is the start symbol of G; $(w, q, S) \overset{*}{\underset{M}{\vdash}} (\Lambda, q, \Lambda)$; w is in $E(M)$. $\square$

Notice that the grammar G produced in the proof of Lemma 9.7 has a special form. Every production is of the form $A \rightarrow a\gamma$, where a is either a terminal symbol or Λ and γ is a (possibly empty) string of nonterminals. Hence, in any leftmost derivation of G the terminals are produced from left to right.

Combining Theorem 9.6 and Lemma 9.7, we get Theorem 9.8.

9.8 Theorem If M is any pda, then we can find a context-free grammar G such that $L(G) = E(M)$.

Theorems 9.5 and 9.8 say that pda's accept exactly the context-free languages, provided that acceptance is by empty store. Our next result shows that acceptance by empty store and acceptance by final state are, in some sense, equivalent.

9.9 Theorem $L = E(M_1)$ for some pda M_1 if and only if $L = A(M_2)$ for some pda M_2.

PROOF We will describe the idea behind the proof and leave the formalizing of the proof as an exercise.

Suppose we have a pda M_1 and we wish to construct a pda M_2 such that $A(M_2) = E(M_1)$. We must, in some sense, translate acceptance by empty store into acceptance by final state. This can be done as follows. M_2 is very similar to M_1, but it has one extra pushdown store symbol X and two extra states q_1, q_2; q_1 is the start state of M_2, q_2 is the only accepting state of M_2, and X is the start pushdown store symbol of M_2. The transition function for M_2 is the same as the transition function for M_1, except that it is now extended to have instructions for these two new states and the new stack symbol. At the start of a computation, M_2 places Z_0 on top of X in the pushdown store and goes to state s. Here s is the start state of M_1 and Z_0 the start pushdown store symbol of M_1. M_2 then computes exactly the same as M_1 until it finds the X on top of its pushdown store. That means that M_1 would have emptied its pushdown store at this point. So when M_2 finds X on top of its pushdown store it goes to the accepting state q_2 and halts. In this way we can ensure that $A(M_2) = E(M_1)$.

Conversely, suppose we have a pda M_2 and wish to construct a pda M_1 such that $E(M_1) = A(M_2)$. Again, we can construct M_1 to be almost the same as M_2. To convert acceptance by final state into acceptance by empty store, make M_1 the same as M_2 but add some additional states so that whenever M_1 enters an accepting state (of M_2) it can nondeterministically go to a state which will cause it to empty the pushdown store. Since an accepting state can be entered before the end of the input is read, it is important to allow the machine to be nondeterministic so that it has the option of either emptying its pushdown store or behaving like M_2 when it is in an accepting state of M_2. This guarantees that M_1 can empty its pushdown store when it should. To ensure that $E(M_1) = A(M_2)$, you must also ensure that M_1 does not empty its pushdown store when it should not. To ensure this, add an additional pushdown symbol that always stays at the bottom of the pushdown store until M_1 decides that it should empty the pushdown store. □

The next theorem summarizes the equivalence of pda's and context-free languages which we have proven in the previous results.

9.10 Theorem For any language L, the following are equivalent:

1. L is a context-free language.
2. $L = E(M)$ for some pda M.
3. $L = A(M)$ for some pda M.

The pda model gives us an alternate characterization of the context-free languages. As the examples indicate, it is frequently just as easy to prove a language is context-free by describing a pda to accept it as it is to prove it is context-free by describing a grammar to generate it. Some examples given in the exercises show that sometimes it is even easier to give a pda description of a language than it is to give a grammar description. Also, the pda model sometimes makes it easier to prove properties about context-free languages, as illustrated by our next theorem.

9.11 Theorem If L is a context-free language and R is a finite-state language, then $L \cap R$ is a context-free language.

PROOF The intuitive idea of the proof is very simple. If L is a context-free language and R is a finite-state language, then there is a pda M_L and a (one-way) finite-state acceptor M_R such that $L = A(M_L)$ and $R = A(M_R)$. We can combine M_L and M_R to make a pda M such that $A(M) = A(M_L) \cap A(M_R) = L \cap R$. Intuitively, M consists of M_L and M_R running in parallel. We will give a formal definition of M. The proof that M has the desired properties is an easy exercise.

Input-alph(M) = Input-alph$(M) \cap$ Symbols(M_R)
States(M) = State$(M_L) \times$ States(M_R)
Start-state(M) = (Start-state(M_L), Start(M_R))
Push-alph(M) = Push-alph(M_L)
Start-symbol(M) = Start-symbol(M_L)
Accepting-states(M) = $\{(p, q) \mid p$ in Accepting-states(M_L)
    and q in Accepting-states$(M_R)\}$
Instructions(M) = δ, where δ is defined below in terms
    of $δ_L$ = Instructions(M_L) and $δ_R$ = Instructions(M_R).

For any input symbol a, pushdown store symbol A and state (p, q) of M:

$$\delta((p, q), a, A) = \{((p', q'), \beta) \mid (p', \beta) \text{ is in}$$
$$\delta_L(p, a, A) \text{ and } q' \text{ is in } \delta_R(q, a)\} \text{ and}$$
$$\delta((p, q), \Lambda, A) = \{((p', q), \beta) \mid (p', \beta) \text{ is in } \delta_L(p, \Lambda, A)\}. \quad \square$$

Notice that Theorem 9.11 is not true if we only require that R be a context-free language. This follows from Exercise 2-3. The proof of the next theorem shows one of the uses that can be made of Theorem 9.11.

9.12 Theorem There are context-free languages L with the following property. If Σ is any alphabet such that $L \subseteq \Sigma^*$, then $\Sigma^* - L$ is not a context-free language.

PROOF Let $L = \{a^i b^j c^k \mid i \neq j \text{ or } j \neq k\}$. We leave it as an exercise to show that L is a context-free language. Let Σ be any alphabet such that $\Sigma^* \supseteq L$. We wish to show that $\Sigma^* - L$ is not a context-free language. Suppose $\Sigma^* - L$ were a context-free language. We will derive a contradiction. Let $L' = (\Sigma^* - L) \cap \{a^i b^j c^k \mid \text{any } i, j, k\}$.

It is easy to see that $\{a^i b^j c^k \mid \text{any } i, j, k\}$ is a finite-state language. So, by Theorem 9.11, L' is a context-free language. But $L' = \{a^n b^n c^n \mid n \geqslant 0\}$ and hence, by Theorem 2.18, L' is not a context-free language. So we have derived a contradiction. Hence it follows that $\Sigma^* - L$ cannot be a context-free language. $\square$

We conclude this section with a result whose proof makes efficient use of the notion of a pda.

9.13 Theorem If L is a cfl and f is a finite-state transduction, then $f(L) = \{f(w) \mid w \text{ in } L\}$ is also a cfl.

PROOF Suppose M_L is a pda that accepts L by final state and that M_f is a finite-state transduction that computes f. We will define a pda M that accepts $f(L)$ by final state. Intuitively, M operates as follows. Given an input z, M guesses a string w one symbol at a time. As it guesses w it does two things in parallel. It simulates M_f to see if $f(w) = z$ and it simulates M_L to see if w is in L. More formally, M is defined as follows.

Input-alph(M) = Out-symbols(M_f);   Push-alph(M) = Push-alph(M_L); States$(M) = \{(p, q) \mid p \in \text{States}(M_f) \text{ and } q \in \text{States}(M_L)\}$; Start-symbol$(M)$ = Start-symbol(M_L);   Start-state$(M) = (s_f, s_L)$, where s_f is the start state of M_f and s_L is the start state of M_L; Accepting-states$(M) = \{(p, q) \mid p \in \text{Accepting-states}(M_f) \text{ and } q \in \text{Accepting-states}(M_L)\}$. The transition function δ of M is defined in terms of the transition function δ_f of M_f and the transition function δ_L of M_L as follows:

Let (p, q) be a state of M, let a be an element of Input-alph$(M) \cup \{\Lambda\}$ = Out-symbols$(M_f) \cup \{\Lambda\}$, and let A be an element of Push-alph(M) = Push-alph(M_L). Define $\delta((p, q), a, A)$ to be the set of all instructions satisfying (1), (2), or (3) below.

1. All instructions $((p', q'), \gamma)$ such that there is a c for which all of the following hold:
   a. $c \in$ In-symbols$(M_f) \cap$ Input-alph(M_L)
   b. $\delta_f(p, c) = (p', a)$ and
   c. $\delta_M(q, c, A) = (q', \gamma)$
2. All instructions $((p', q), A)$ such that $\delta_f(p, \Lambda) = (p', a)$
3. If $a = \Lambda$, then also include all instructions $((p, q'), \gamma)$ such that $\delta_M(q, \Lambda, A) = (q', \gamma)$.

The proof that $A(M) = f(L)$ is left as an exercise. In order to get the idea of the proof, it might be helpful to first prove it for the special case where both M_f and M_L advance their input head past a symbol on every move. In this special case, there are no instructions of type (2) or (3). After doing that special case, it should be easier to understand the general case. $\square$

* PUSHDOWN TRANSDUCERS

Since a pda is in some sense a model for compilers, and since compilers are programs with output, we will make a few informal observations about pda's with output. Such machines are called pushdown transducers.

A *pushdown transducer (pdt)* is a pda that has been provided with an output tape. That is, there is another tape like the tape of a Turing machine attached to the finite-state control. The pdt may write on this tape but cannot read from the tape. The tape is only for output and cannot be used for storing information. To keep the pdt from changing its mind about output, we insist that the output head must shift right after printing a symbol and that it can never shift left (back up). Since we will not be developing any elaborate theory for pdt's, we will not give a formal definition of a pdt but will only talk informally about the model.

The one observation we want to make about pdt's is that given any context-free grammar G, we can construct a pdt M with the property that, given any input string w in $L(G)$, the pdt will read all of w while outputting a parse tree for w and then will halt with an empty pushdown store. If w is not in $L(G)$, then the pdt will not accept w, that is, will not have an empty pushdown store after reading all of w. Thus M accepts $L(G)$ by empty store and parses all strings in $L(G)$. Since a linear tape cannot hold a two-dimensional picture of a parse tree, we should say a word about how the parse tree is outputted. We know that parse trees are equivalent to leftmost derivations. So we will be satisfied if the pdt M outputs a leftmost derivation of every string in $L(G)$. To accomplish this, M will have one symbol associated with each production in G, in other words, one symbol to name each production. Given input w in $L(G)$, the pdt will output the name of each production used in a leftmost derivation of w. The names of productions will be written on the output tape in exactly the order that the productions are applied in the leftmost derivation. In particular, the name of a production will occur exactly as many times as it is used in the derivation.

The construction of M has already been given, at least implicitly, in the proof of Theorem 9.5. To obtain M from G, construct the pda obtained from G as in the proof of Theorem 9.5. Provide the pda with an output tape so that it is a pdt and design the instructions so that they output every production used.

To be a little more precise, suppose δ is the transition function of M and that (p, β, c) in $\delta(q, a, A)$ means that in state q scanning input symbol a and with A on top of the pushdown store, M may change the state of its finite-state control to state p, replace A by β, print c on the output tape, and advance the output tape one square to the right. If $a = \Lambda$, then this will be treated exactly as it was for pda's; the move is independent of the input symbol scanned and the input head is not advanced. The third element c may be either a symbol or Λ. If it is Λ, then the machine behaves as described above except that nothing is written on the output tape and the head on the output tape is not moved. M has only one state q. Now if we use $<A \rightarrow \beta>$ to denote a symbol to name the production $A \rightarrow \beta$ and let P be the set of productions of G, then δ is defined as follows:

$\delta(q, \Lambda, A) = \{(q, \beta, <A \rightarrow \beta>) \mid A \rightarrow \beta$ is in $P\}$, for all nonterminals A of G.

$\delta(q, a, a) = \{(q, \Lambda, \Lambda)\}$, for all terminals a of G.

It is a good exercise to check that this construction works even if G is not in Chomsky normal form.

One characteristic of the pdt M described above is that it is nondeterministic. A given input can give rise to more than one computation and more than one output. If the grammar G is ambiguous, and w in $L(G)$ has m distinct parse trees, then there will be m different computations of M on input w, each one outputting a different leftmost derivation. There will be even more than m computations on w, but the other computations will not accept w by empty store and so we will not consider what is on the output tape as a valid output in these other cases. An interesting topic is the question of when the pdt M can be made deterministic. In the next section we will study deterministic pda's and gain some insight into this question. We will not, however, spend any time on deterministic pdt's as such, but will leave that topic for more advanced texts.

DETERMINISTIC PDA'S

We have seen that pda's exactly characterize the context-free languages. Furthermore, a variant of the pda model, namely the pdt, can be used to obtain procedures to parse the strings generated by an arbitrary, given context-free grammar. Since the context-free languages are an important class of languages which include many programming languages, this means that pda's are an important class of procedures for handling programming languages. There is, however, one undesirable feature of the pda model. It is a nondeterministic model. It would be nice to be able to show that every context-free language is accepted by a deterministic pda. As we shall see shortly, it is not possible to prove such a theorem.

9.14 Definition

9.14.1 A pda M is said to be *deterministic* provided the following conditions are satisfied by $\delta = $ Instructions(M).

1. For any state q, input symbol a, and pushdown store symbol A, $\delta(q, a, A)$ contains at most one instruction.
2. For any state q and pushdown store symbol A, $\delta(q, \Lambda, A)$ contains at most one instruction.
3. For any state q and pushdown store symbol A, if $\delta(q, \Lambda, A)$ is not empty, then $\delta(q, a, A)$ is empty for all input symbols a.

Intuitively, a pda is deterministic provided there is at most one applicable instruction for each machine configuration. To see why we must include condition (3), look at Example 9.2.3. Since, for deterministic pda's $\delta(q, a, A)$ never contains more than one instruction, we will simplify our notation by writing $\delta(q, a, A) = (p, \beta)$ instead of $\delta(q, a, A) = \{(p, \beta)\}$.

9.14.2 L is said to be a *deterministic context-free language (deterministic cfl)* provided $L = A(M)$, for some deterministic pda M.

When studying deterministic pda's, it is usual to consider only acceptance by final state. This is because of a peculiarity in the definition of pda's. As commonly defined, and as we have defined them, pda computations halt whenever the pushdown store is empty. Since a deterministic pda has a unique computation for each input string, that means that if a deterministic pda accepts an input x by empty store, then it cannot accept any string of the form xy by empty store, where $y \neq \Lambda$. This seems like an unnatural restriction. Hence, when discussing deterministic pda's, we will only consider acceptance by final state. This point is important to the formal mathematical development of the theory but has little intuitive importance. We could change the definition of acceptance by empty store in a number of ways that would allow our model to accommodate procedures which intuitively are deterministic procedures and which accept by empty store. Furthermore, we could do it in such a way that the pda can accept both a string x and a string xy. For example, one such change would be to add a special end marker symbol which is placed at the end of each input string. We will, however, follow common usage and only consider deterministic pda's as accepting by final state.

We have already seen that there are context-free languages whose complement is not a context-free language. Our next result shows that the class of deterministic context-free languages is better behaved in this respect. It is closed under taking complements.

9.15 Theorem If M is a deterministic pda with input alphabet Σ, then there is a deterministic pda M' such that $\Sigma^* - A(M) = A(M')$.

The basic intuition for why Theorem 9.15 holds is quite simple. Given a deterministic pda M, to get a deterministic pda M' such that $A(M') = \Sigma^* - A(M)$, do something like the following: Make M' the same as M but with the notions of accepting and nonaccepting states interchanged. Unfortunately, simply interchanging the notions of accepting and nonaccepting states will not quite work to give $A(M') = \Sigma^* - A(M)$. Two situations can cause problems. One problem is that for some inputs w, M may not read all of w, either because it reaches a configuration where no move is possible or because it enters an infinite loop that does not advance the input head. All such inputs should be accepted by M', but M' cannot accept an input unless it reads all of the input. The second problem is that M may make moves after it has read all of the input. M may be in an accepting state after some of these moves and in a nonaccepting state after others. Simply interchanging accepting and nonaccepting states could thus produce an M' that accepts an input in $A(M)$. To eliminate these problems, we will use the next two lemmas.

9.16 Lemma Given a deterministic pda M, we can find another deterministic pda M_1 such that $A(M_1) = A(M)$ and such that the following hold. Given any input string w, M_1 will read all of w in the computation starting from the usual start configuration with input w. Every computation of M_1 eventually reaches a halting configuration.

PROOF Without loss of generality, we will assume that in every configuration M has a next move. If this is not true of M, then we can easily modify M to make it true. The modification consists of adding a new pushdown store symbol Z and a new state q. At the start of every computation, Z is put on the bottom of the pushdown store. Z is then never removed. This ensures that the pushdown store is never empty. The transition function is then extended so that, in any configuration in which the original machine has no next move, the modified machine will go to state q, advance the input, but not change the pushdown store. Once the machine enters state q, it remains in state q, advancing the input but leaving the pushdown store unaltered. The state q is not an accepting state.

Since M now has a next move in each configuration, the only situation in which M would not read its entire input is when M makes an infinite number of moves without advancing its input head. To aid in the construction of M_1, we now analyze what happens when M enters such an infinite loop. We distinguish two cases, when the pushdown store grows arbitrarily large and when it remains bounded. Let s be the number of states of M, t the number of pushdown store symbols of M, and u the maximum number of symbols M can place on the pushdown store in one move.

Claim: For any input string x, states q_1, q_2 and strings of pushdown store symbols β_1, β_2: If $(x, q_1, \beta_1) \vert_{\overline{M}}^* (x, q_2, \beta_2)$ and length(β_2)−length$(\beta_1) > stu$, then starting in configuration (x, q_1, β_1) the pushdown store of M will grow arbitrarily large and the input head will not be advanced.

To see that the claim is true, note that it takes at least st steps to increase the pushdown store height (length) by stu symbols. So the partial computation mentioned in the claim includes at least st steps and hence includes at least $st+1$ id's. In fact it includes at least $st+1$ id's such that, in this partial computation, no symbol in the pushdown store, other than the top symbol, is ever removed from the pushdown store. But there are only st state/pushdown-store-symbol combinations. So two such id's must have the same state and the same symbol on top of the pushdown store. Hence, there must be id's $(x, q, A\gamma_1)$ and $(x, q, A\gamma_2\gamma_1)$ such that

1. $(x, q_1, \beta_1) \mathrel{\overset{*}{\vdash}} (x, q, A\gamma_1) \mathrel{\overset{*}{\vdash}} (x, q, A\gamma_2\gamma_1) \mathrel{\overset{*}{\vdash}} (x, q_2, \beta_2)$.
2. No symbol of γ_1 is removed from the pushdown store during the partial computation $(x, q, A\gamma_1) \mathrel{\overset{*}{\vdash}} (x, q, A\gamma_2\gamma_1)$.
3. γ_2 is not empty.

From these facts it follows that

$$(x, q_1, \beta_1) \mathrel{\overset{*}{\vdash}} (x, q, A\gamma_1) \mathrel{\overset{*}{\vdash}} (x, q, A\gamma_2^n\gamma_1)$$

for all n and so the claim is established.

By the claim, we see that the pushdown store will grow arbitrarily large without M advancing its input head if and only if it increases by more than stu symbols, while the input head remains fixed. To check for this type of infinite loop, we need only check to see if the pushdown store increases by more than stu symbols.

Next we consider how it is possible to detect when M is in an infinite loop in which the pushdown store remains bounded in length while the input head does not advance. In this situation we know, by the claim, that the difference between the lengths of the shortest and subsequent longest pushdown store contents, occurring in the infinite loop, is at most stu. Consider that part of the infinite loop which occurs after the pushdown store length reaches its minimum. This part of the infinite loop can contain no more than $s(t+1)^{stu}$ distinct machine configurations. By similar reasoning, if M makes more than $s(t+1)^{stu}$ moves without advancing its input head and without increasing the length of the pushdown store by more than stu symbols, then it must repeat a machine configuration and hence must be in an infinite loop in which the pushdown store remains bounded.

We are now ready to describe the pda M_1 with the properties given in Lemma 9.16. M_1 has the same input and pushdown store symbols as M. States$(M_1) = \{<q, i, j> \mid q$ in States(M), $0 \leqslant i \leqslant stu$, $0 \leqslant j \leqslant s(t+1)^{stu}\} \cup \{<$loop-detected$>\}$, where $<$loop-detected$>$ is a new state. Accepting-states$(M_1) = \{<q, i, j> \mid q$ in Accepting-states$(M)\}$. Start-state$(M_1) = <q_0, 0, 0>$, where q_0 is the start state of M.

M_1 will simulate M while checking for infinite loops in M's computation. The integer i in the state $<q, i, j>$ will record the difference in length between the current string in the pushdown store and the shortest string that was in the pushdown store since the last time the input head was advanced. The integer j will record the number of moves since either the last advance of the input head or the last time the length of the pushdown store fell to a new minimum (since advancing the input head). The state $<$loop-detected$>$ will be entered whenever it is detected that M would have entered an infinite loop without advancing its input head. With this in mind, we now define δ_1, the transition function of M_1 in terms of δ, the transition function of M.

1. If $\delta(q, a, C) = (p, \beta)$ and a is an input symbol, then
   $\delta'(<q, i, j>, a, C) = (<p, 0, 0>, \beta)$ for all i and j.
2. If $\delta(q, \Lambda, C) = (p, \beta)$ and $n = \text{length}(\beta)$, then $\delta'(<q, i, j>, \Lambda, C)$ is defined by cases.
   a. If $0 \leqslant i+n-1 \leqslant stu$ and $j+1 \leqslant s(t+1)^{stu}$, then
      $\delta'(<q, i, j>, \Lambda, C) = (<p, i+n-1, j+1>, \beta)$.
   b. If $i+n-1 < 0$, then $\delta'(<q, i, j>, \Lambda, C) = (<p, 0, 0>, \beta)$.
   c. If $i+n-1 > stu$ or if $j+1 > s(t+1)^{stu}$, and case (b) does not apply, then $\delta'(<q, i, j>, \Lambda, C) = (<$loop-detected$>, C)$.
3. $\delta'(<$loop-detected$>, a, C) = (<$loop-detected$>, C)$, for all input symbols a and pushdown store symbols C.

Rules 1, 2a, and 2b ensure that i and j record the desired information. Rules 2c and 3 ensure that, if M would enter an infinite loop, then M_1 would instead advance the input head to the end of the input but not accept the input. It should be clear that M_1 has the desired properties and we leave a formal proof of this fact as an exercise. $\square$

9.17 Lemma Given a deterministic pda M, we can find another deterministic pda M_2, such that:

1. $A(M_2) = A(M)$.
2. Given any input string w, M_2 will read all of w in the computation starting from the usual start configuration on input w.
3. Every computation of M_2 eventually reaches a halting configuration.
4. For any input string w, w is accepted by M_2 if and only if the computation of M_2, on input w, halts in an accepting state.

PROOF Without loss of generality, we will assume that M already satisfies the conditions (2) and (3) which we want our new pda M_2 to satisfy. This is possible by Lemma 9.16. M_2 is defined to simulate M and to keep track of whether or not M would have entered an accepting state since the last time it advanced the input head.

The input and pushdown store alphabets of M_2 are the same as M. States$(M_2) = \{<q, i>\} \mid q$ is a state of M and i is either 0 or 1$\}$. If $i = 1$, this will indicate that, in the computation of M, an accepting state was entered since the last time the input head was advanced. Accepting-States(M_2) = $\{<q, 1> \mid q$ is any state of $M\}$. The transition function δ_2 of M_2 is defined in terms of the transition function δ of M as follows. Let a be a member of the input alphabet, q a state of M, and C a pushdown store symbol.

1. Suppose $\delta(q, a, C) = (p, \beta)$.
   a. If p is an accepting state of M, then $\delta_2(<q, 0>, a, C) = \delta_2(<q, 1>, a, C) = (<p, 1>, \beta)$.
   b. If p is not an accepting state of M, then $\delta_2(<q, 0>, a, C) = \delta_2(<q, 1>, a, C) = (<p, 0>, \beta)$.
2. Suppose $\delta(q, \Lambda, C) = (p, \beta)$.
   a. If p is an accepting state of M, then
   $\delta_2(<q, 0>, \Lambda, C) = \delta_2(<q, 1>, \Lambda, C) = (<p, 1>, \beta)$.
   b. If p is not an accepting state of M, then $\delta_2(<q, i>, \Lambda, C) = (<p, i>, \beta)$ for $i = 0, 1$.

Clearly, M_2 has the desired properties. $\square$

Proof of Theorem 9.15

Without loss of generality, assume that M satisfies the conditions (1) through (4) of Lemma 9.17. M' is basically the same as M but has two copies of each state. States(M') = States$(M) \cup \{q' \mid q$ in States$(M)\}$, Input-alph(M') = Input-alph(M), Push-alph(M') = Push-alph(M), Start-state(M') = Start-state(M), and Start-symbol(M') = Start-symbol(M). Here each q' is a new state that intuitively is a second copy of the state q. The transition function δ' of M' is defined in terms of the transition function δ of M. The definition of δ' is designed so that M' computes exactly like M using the states q of States(M), so long as the input head is not advanced. When M would be in a state q and would be about to advance its input head, M' will change to state q' before advancing its input head. In state q', M' behaves like M in state q and so, among other things, M' advances its input head. With this intuition in mind, we now define δ'. Let q be a state of M, a an input symbol, and C a pushdown store symbol.

1. If $\delta(q, \Lambda, C)$ is nonempty, then $\delta'(q, \Lambda, C) = \delta(q, \Lambda, C)$.
2. If $\delta(q, \Lambda, C)$ is empty, then $\delta'(q, \Lambda, C) = (q', C)$.
3. $\delta'(q', a, C) = \delta(q, a, C)$, for a in Input-alph(M).
4. For all other types of arguments, δ' yields the empty set.

Notice that, given any input string w, the computation of M' on input w halts in state q' if and only if the computation of M on input w halts in state q. Also M satisfies condition (4) of Lemma 9.17. So if we set Accepting-states(M') = $\{q' \mid q$ is not in Accepting-states$(M)\}$, then $A(M')$ = $\Sigma^* - A(M)$. Hence the theorem is proven. $\square$

Using Theorem 9.15, we can show that there are context-free languages which are not deterministic context-free languages.

9.18 Theorem There are context-free languages L such that L is not equal to $A(M)$ for any deterministic pda M.

PROOF Let L be any context-free language such that $\Sigma^* - L$ is not a context-free language, whenever Σ is an alphabet such that $L \subseteq \Sigma^*$. For example, take L to be the language given in Theorem 9.12. This L is not equal to $A(M)$ for any deterministic pda M. To see this, suppose $L = A(M)$ for some deterministic pda M. Then $\Sigma^* - L$ would be accepted by some deterministic pda, where Σ is the input alphabet of M. So $\Sigma^* - L$ is a context-free language. But this contradicts what we know about L. So no such M can exist. □

EXERCISES

1. Describe pda's to accept each of the following languages by empty store and also describe pda's to accept each language by final state.
    a. $\{a^n b^n \mid n \geqslant 0\}$
    b. $\{a^n b^n \mid n \geqslant 0\} \cup \{a^n b^{2n} \mid n \geqslant 0\}$
    c. $\{w \mathcal{c} u_1 \mathcal{c} u_2 \mathcal{c} ... \mathcal{c} u_n \mid n \geqslant 1 \text{ and } w = u_i^R \text{ for some } i; \ w, u_j \in \{a, b\}^*\}$
    d. $\{a^i b^j c^k \mid i = j \text{ or } j = k\}$
    e. $\{a^i b^j c^k \mid i \neq j \text{ or } j \neq k\}$
    f. $\{x \mathcal{c} y \mid x, y \in \{a, b\}^* \text{ and } x \neq y\}$

2. Describe deterministic pda's to accept each of the following languages:
    a. $\{a^n b^n \mid n \geqslant 0\}$
    b. $\{w \mid w \in \{a, b\}^* \text{ and } w \text{ contains more } a\text{'s than } b\text{'s}\}$
    c. The set of all well-formed strings of parentheses
    d. $\{a, b\}^*$

3. Prove that the construction given in the proof of Theorem 9.5 works, i.e., $E(M) = L(G)$, even if the grammar G is not in Chomsky normal form.

4. Complete the proof of Lemma 9.7 by proving the claim whose proof was left as an exercise.

5. Give a detailed formal proof of Theorem 9.9.

6. Complete the proof of Theorem 9.11 by showing that the pda M has the properties claimed.

7. Complete the proof of Theorem 9.13 by proving that $A(M) = f(L)$.

8. Complete the proof of Lemma 9.16 by showing that the pda M_1 has the properties claimed.

9. A *two pushdown machine* is the same as a pda except that it has two pushdown stores. A move is defined in the same way as it is for a pda except that each move depends on two pushdown store symbols and gives two, possibly different, pushdown store actions instead of just one. Prove: L is accepted by final state by a two pushdown machine if and only if L is recursively enumerable.

10. Prove: If L is a deterministic cfl and R is a finite-state language, then $L \cap R$ is a deterministic cfl. (*Hint*: Model your proof after the proof of Theorem 9.11.)

11. Give an example of a deterministic cfl L and a deterministic finite-state transduction f such that $f(L)$ is not a deterministic cfl. Recall that $f(L) = \{f(w) \mid w \text{ in } L\}$.

12. Prove: If L is a deterministic language, then there is an unambiguous cfg G such that $L(G) = L$.

Chapter
Ten

Unsolvable
Questions About
Context-Free
Languages

In Chapter 6 we saw some examples of tasks which cannot be done by any computer program. Such tasks are frequently said to be *unsolvable*, meaning that they cannot be solved by any computer program. The most interesting unsolvable problem we saw there was the halting problem for Turing machines (Theorem 6.7). You will recall that we proved it to be unsolvable by first proving that another task was unsolvable (Theorem 6.5). After that, we showed that if the halting problem were solvable, then this other task would be solvable. So assuming the halting problem is solvable leads to a contradiction. For this reason, we concluded that the halting problem was unsolvable. This general idea of showing that if problem X is solvable, then it can be used to solve problem Y is sometimes referred to as *reducing* problem Y to problem X. If we reduce problem Y to problem X and we know Y is unsolvable, then we can conclude that X is unsolvable. In this chapter we will show that a number of questions about context-free languages are unsolvable. We will do this by means of the reduction technique just described. However, the halting problem is not a convenient unsolvable problem to use for showing that such language problems are unsolvable. We will first consider a problem called the *Post correspondence problem*. We will show it is unsolvable by reducing the halting problem to it. We will then use the unsolvability of the Post correspondence problem to show that these various language questions are unsolvable.

THE POST CORRESPONDENCE PROBLEM

10.1 Definition Let $A = (x_1, x_2, ..., x_k)$ and $B = (y_1, y_2, .., y_k)$ be two ordered k tuples of nonempty words with k some positive integer. Less formally, A and B are two lists of words and the two lists have the same length k. We say that this *instance of the Post correspondence problem has a solution* if there is a nonempty sequence of integers $i_1, i_2, ..., i_m$ such that

$$x_{i_1} x_{i_2} ... x_{i_m} = y_{i_1} y_{i_2} ... y_{i_m}$$

10.2 Examples

10.2.1 Let $A = (1, 1110, 110)$ and $B = (11, 10, 101)$. For notational convenience, set $(x_1, x_2, x_3) = A$ and $(y_1, y_2, y_3) = B$. Then $i_1 = 1$, $i_2 = 3$, $i_3 = 1$, and $i_4 = 2$ is a solution to this instance of the Post correspondence problem because

$$x_1 x_3 x_1 x_2 = y_1 y_3 y_1 y_2 = 111011110$$

10.2.2 Let $A = (00, 11, 01)$ and $B = (11, 110, 10)$. Again for notational convenience, let $(x_1, x_2, x_3) = A$ and $(y_1, y_2, y_3) = B$. This instance of the Post correspondence problem has no solution. To see this, note that if there were a solution, it must have $i_1 = 2$, since x_1 and y_1 have different first letters and since x_3 and y_3 have different first letters. Any possible solution must start with $x_2 = 11$ and $y_2 = 110$. That means x_{i_2} must start with 0. So i_2 must be 1 or 3. If we try $i_2 = 1$, we get $x_2 x_1 = 1100$ and $y_2 y_1 = 11011$. There is no way to complete the sequence to a solution, since the fourth letters do not match. So we must have $i_2 = 3$. If we try $i_2 = 3$, we get $x_2 x_3 = 1101$ and $y_2 y_3 = 11010$. Similar reasoning shows that, in any possible solution, i_3 must be 3 and i_4 must be 3 and so forth. Since this is the only way to possibly obtain a solution and since this process does not terminate, we know that no solution is possible.

10.3 Definition

The *(general) Post correspondence problem* over an alphabet Δ is the following task: Given any two nonempty, equally long lists A and B of nonempty strings over Δ, determine whether or not this instance of the Post correspondence problem has a solution.

As it turns out, the general Post correspondence problem is unsolvable and that result is formalized in the next theorem.

10.4 Theorem (Unsolvability of the Post correspondence problem) Let Δ be an alphabet with at least two elements. Let $<$yes$>$ and $<$no$>$ be two distinct elements. Let $\mathbb{c}$ be a symbol not in Δ and set $\Sigma = \Delta \cup \{\mathbb{c}\}$. Let p be any partial function with domain Σ^* which satisfies the following for all $k \geqslant 1$ and all nonempty strings $x_1, x_2, ..., x_k, y_1, y_2, ..., y_k$ in Δ^*: $p(x_1 \mathbb{c} x_2 ... \mathbb{c} x_k \mathbb{c}\mathbb{c} y_1 \mathbb{c} y_2 ... \mathbb{c} y_k) = <yes>$, provided that the instance $A = (x_1, x_2, ..., x_k)$ and $B = (y_1, y_2, .., y_k)$ of the Post correspondence problem has a solution and $p(x_1 \mathbb{c} x_2 ... \mathbb{c} x_k \mathbb{c}\mathbb{c} y_1 \mathbb{c} y_2 ... \mathbb{c} y_k) = <no>$ otherwise. Under these conditions, p is not a computable function.

Theorem 10.4 is stated in the usual formalism that we have been using. For the remainder of this chapter, including the proof of Theorem 10.4, we will be much more informal. We will use informal notions like problem and algorithm rather than formally defined notions like computable function. The translation to very formally stated theorems and proofs is routine and the informal presentation should be easier to follow. In this informal language, Theorem 10.4 says the following: There is no algorithm which can tell, for any two equally long lists A and B of nonempty strings over the alphabet Δ, whether or not the Post correspondence problem for A and B has a solution. For ease of reading we will usually present the lists A and B as pairs of corresponding entries. For example, the lists $A = (1, 1110, 110)$ and $B = (11, 10, 101)$ of Example 10.2.1 would be presented as follows:

$$1 \longleftrightarrow 11$$
$$1110 \longleftrightarrow 10$$
$$110 \longleftrightarrow 101$$

The first entries are from list A, the second entries are from list B, and the double arrows indicate which entries are corresponding. We are now ready to proceed with the proof of Theorem 10.4. The next lemma is the heart of the proof. Ignoring some technical details about the sizes of alphabets, the lemma says that if we could solve the Post correspondence problem, then we could solve the halting problem. We know that the halting problem is unsolvable. So in order to get a complete proof of the unsolvability of the Post correspondence problem, all we need do is clear up these details about alphabet size. We now proceed with the lemma.

10.5 Lemma Let Δ be any alphabet with n letters and suppose we have an algorithm for the Post correspondence problem over Δ. We can then find an algorithm to decide the halting problem for all (deterministic) simple Turing machines such that the number of states plus the number of tape symbols for the Turing machine is at most $n/2 - 5/2$.

PROOF We will present an algorithm which, given any simple Turing machine M with s states and t tape symbols together with an input string w, will produce two lists $A(M, w)$ and $B(M, w)$ over an alphabet Σ with $2(s + t) + 5$ symbols and with the following property:

1. M halts on input w if and only if there is a solution to the Post correspondence problem for $A(M, w)$ and $B(M, w)$.

Once we give the algorithm to produce the two lists and we establish (1), we will have completed the proof of the lemma. To see this, note that $2(s + t) + 5 \leqslant n$ is equivalent to $s + t \leqslant n/2 - 5/2$. So, as long as $s + t \leqslant n/2 - 5/2$, we may replace the alphabet Σ by the alphabet Δ. In that case, we can test to see if M halts on w by using our hypothesized algorithm to test for a solution to the Post correspondence problem for the lists $A(M, w)$ and $B(M, w)$. We now proceed to explain and present the algorithm to produce these two lists.

Let M be a simple Turing machine and w an input string for M. We can always modify M so that its states are actually symbols and so we will assume that they are. We also assume that $\text{States}(M)$ and $\text{Symbols}(M)$ are disjoint. (Recall $\text{Symbols}(M)$ denotes the set of tape symbols in M.) We have usually represented id's of M as pairs $(p, \alpha \triangleright \beta)$ where p is a state and $\alpha \triangleright \beta$ is a tape configuration. For this proof we will represent the id $(p, \alpha \triangleright \beta)$ by the string $\alpha p \beta$ and we will refer to the string $\alpha p \beta$ as an id. A halting computation of M on w can be represented by a string of the form

2. $\# \alpha_1 p_1 \beta_1 \# \alpha_2 p_2 \beta_2 \# \ ... \ \# \alpha_h p_h \beta_h \#$

where $\alpha_1 p_1 \beta_1 = q_0 w$ with q_0 the start state of M, where $\alpha_i p_i \beta_i \vdash \alpha_{i+1} p_{i+1} \beta_{i+1}$ for $i < h$, where $\alpha_h p_h \beta_h$ is a halting id and where $\#$ is a new symbol. We will show how to obtain two lists $A(M, w) = (x_1, x_2, ..., x_k)$ and $B(M, w) = (y_1, y_2, .., y_k)$ which satisfy (1). It will turn out that if $i_1, i_2, ..., i_m$ is a solution to the Post correspondence problem for these two lists, then $x_{i_1} x_{i_2} ... x_{i_m} = y_{i_1} y_{i_2} ... y_{i_m}$ will be a string which represents the halting computation of M on w in a way very similar to, but not identical to, (2). For this purpose, it will be helpful to have two copies each of $\text{States}(M)$ and $\text{Symbols}(M)$. Let $\overline{\text{States}}(M) = \{\overline{q} \mid q \text{ in States}(M)\}$ and $\overline{\text{Symbols}}(M) = \{\overline{a} \mid a \text{ in Symbols}(M)\}$. Here each $\overline{q}$ and each $\overline{a}$ is a new symbol to serve as a second copy of q or a. Let $\Sigma = \text{States}(M) \cup \overline{\text{States}}(M) \cup \text{Symbols}(M) \cup \overline{\text{Symbols}}(M) \cup \{\$, \#, \overline{\#}, E, \overline{E}\}$ where $\$, \#, \overline{\#}, E$, and $\overline{E}$ are five more new symbols. The strings in the lists will be strings over the alphabet Σ. If $\alpha p \beta$ is an id of M, then $\overline{\alpha} \overline{p} \overline{\beta}$ will denote the string of symbols obtained from $\alpha p \beta$ by placing bars over all symbols. So $\overline{\alpha} \overline{p} \overline{\beta}$ is a string over $\overline{\text{States}}(M) \cup \overline{\text{Symbols}}(M)$. We now describe the lists $A(M, w)$ and $B(M, w)$. In order to make the presentation more readable, we will talk about corresponding pairs of strings $x_i \longleftrightarrow y_i$ rather than lists.

The following are the corresponding pairs for $A(M, w)$ and $B(M, w)$ arranged into three groups.

Group 1:

$\$\# \longleftrightarrow \$\# B q_0 w B \overline{\#} \overline{B}$, where q_o is the start state of M and B is the blank symbol for M.

$a_1 \longleftrightarrow \overline{a}_1, \quad \overline{a}_1 \longleftrightarrow a_1$

$a_2 \longleftrightarrow \overline{a}_2, \quad \overline{a}_2 \longleftrightarrow a_2$

$\vdots \qquad\qquad \vdots$

$a_l \longleftrightarrow \overline{a}_l, \quad \overline{a}_l \longleftrightarrow a_l$, where $\text{Symbols}(M) = \{a_1, a_2, ..., a_l\}$

$\# \longleftrightarrow B \overline{\#} \overline{B}, \quad \overline{\#} \longleftrightarrow \overline{B} \# B$, where again B is the blank symbol for M.

The next set of corresponding pairs depends on the transition function δ of M.

Group 2:

For all states p, q and all tape symbols a, b, and c of M, we have the following corresponding pairs:

$$pa \longleftrightarrow \overline{qb}, \qquad \overline{pa} \longleftrightarrow qb$$
$$\text{provided} \quad \delta(p, a) = (q, b, \downarrow)$$
$$pa \longleftrightarrow \overline{bq}, \qquad \overline{pa} \longleftrightarrow bq$$
$$\text{provided} \quad \delta(p, a) = (q, b, \rightarrow) \quad \text{and}$$
$$cpa \longleftrightarrow \overline{qcb}, \qquad \overline{cpa} \longleftrightarrow qcb$$
$$\text{provided} \quad \delta(p, a) = (q, b, \leftarrow)$$

Group 3:

For all states p and tape symbols a, the following corresponding pairs are included provided $\delta(p, a)$ is undefined:

$$pa \longleftrightarrow \overline{Ea}, \quad \overline{pa} \longleftrightarrow Ea$$
$$Ea \longleftrightarrow \overline{E}, \quad \overline{Ea} \longleftrightarrow E$$
$$aE \longleftrightarrow \overline{E}, \quad \overline{aE} \longleftrightarrow E$$
$$\# \longleftrightarrow \overline{\#}, \quad \overline{\#} \longleftrightarrow \#$$

Finally, Group 3 also contains

$$\#E\overline{\#} \longleftrightarrow \overline{\#}, \quad \overline{\#}\overline{E}\# \longleftrightarrow \#$$

Note that if for some corresponding pair $x_i \longleftrightarrow y_i$ we had $x_i = y_i$, then we would have a trivial solution to the Post correspondence problem. The reason for putting in the barred symbols is to exclude this trivial type of solution. One side effect of these barred symbols is that when we get computations coded in a form similar to (2) above, every other id will be formed out of barred symbols. There will also be two other differences between the codings we obtain and (2). Namely, our coding will have the symbol $ tacked on the front and some extra symbols tacked on the end. Also, the coding we obtain will have extra leading and trailing blanks inserted into each id. However, since we have always identified id's that differ only by leading or trailing blanks, this will cause no problems. Also note that in any solution to this instance of the Post correspondence problem $\$\# \longleftrightarrow \$\#Bq_0wB\overline{\#}\overline{B}$ must be the first pair chosen. The symbol $ will guarantee that this pair is never used except as the first pair in a solution.

It remains to establish (1). With this goal in mind, suppose M does halt on w and that

3. $Bq_0wB = \alpha_1 p_1 \beta_1 \mid - \alpha_2 p_2 \beta_2 \mid - \ldots \mid - \alpha_h p_h \beta_h$

is the halting computation of M on input w. The extra blank symbols B in the first id are there for technical reasons. They guarantee that if w is the empty word, then the symbol scanned by the tape head is explicitly written in the id and that, if the head shifts left on the first move, then the symbol it shifts to is explicitly written in the id.

For notational convenience assume h is even. The proof is the same for h even or odd but it is notationally easier to consider only one of the two cases. We will exhibit a solution to the Post correspondence problem for the lists $A(M, w)$ and $B(M, w)$. That is, we will choose pairs $x_{i_1} \longleftrightarrow y_{i_1}$, $x_{i_2} \longleftrightarrow y_{i_2}$, ..., $x_{i_m} \longleftrightarrow y_{i_m}$ from the above three groups so that $x_{i_1} x_{i_2}...x_{i_m} = y_{i_1} y_{i_2}...y_{i_m}$. Choose $\$\# \longleftrightarrow \$\#Bq_0 wB\#\overline{B}$ for $x_{i_1} \longleftrightarrow y_{i_1}$. We then choose pairs from Groups 1 and 2 so that the first d pairs produce:

4. $x_{i_1} x_{i_2}...x_{i_d} = \$\#Bq_0 wB\#$
   $y_{i_1} y_{i_2}...y_{i_d} = \$\#Bq_0 wB\#\overline{\alpha}_2\overline{p}_2\overline{\beta}_2\#B$

Here $d \leqslant m$ is just whatever number of pairs we need to choose in order to get this situation. Recall that we chose $x_{i_1} \longleftrightarrow y_{i_1}$ to be $\$\# \longleftrightarrow \$\#Bq_0 wB\#\overline{B}$. So $x_{i_1} = \$\#$ and $y_{i_1} = \$\#Bq_0wB\#\overline{B}$. To get (4) we choose pairs from Groups 1 and 2 which match the beginning of $Bq_0 wB$. For example, if a is the first letter of w and $\delta(q_0, a) = (p_2, b, \downarrow)$, we choose $B \longleftrightarrow B$ and $q_0 a \longleftrightarrow \overline{p}_2\overline{b}$ for $x_{i_2} \longleftrightarrow y_{i_2}$ and $x_{i_3} \longleftrightarrow y_{i_3}$. This guarantees that what comes after the $\#$ in $y_{i_1}y_{i_2}...y_{i_m}$ is the start of the correct next id $\overline{\alpha}_2\overline{p}_2\overline{\beta}_2$. We then choose pairs from Group 1 which "copy" the rest of $Bq_0 wB\#$ onto the string $x_{i_1} x_{i_2}...x_{i_d}$. The result is (4). Similarly, we can "copy" $\overline{\alpha}_2\overline{p}_2\overline{\beta}_2$. onto the string of x's by choosing suitable pairs from Groups 1 and 2. This will produce the correct id $\alpha_3 p_3 \beta_3$ on the string of y's. We can then copy the $\alpha_3 p_3 \beta_3$ and so forth until we get the following representation of the halting computation (3). Here B is the blank symbol.

5. $x_{i_1} x_{i_2}...x_{i_g} = \$\#\alpha_1 p_1 \beta_1 \#\overline{\alpha}_2\overline{p}_2\overline{\beta}_2\# \alpha_3 p_3 \beta_3 \#... \# \alpha_{h-1}p_{h-1}\beta_{h-1}\#$
   $y_{i_1} y_{i_2}...y_{i_g} = \$\#\alpha_1 p_1 \beta_1 \#\overline{\alpha}_2\overline{p}_2\overline{\beta}_2\# \alpha_3 p_3 \beta_3 \#...... \#\overline{\alpha}_h \overline{p}_h \overline{\beta}_h \#B$

Notice that, in (5), $\alpha_{i+1}p_{i+1}\beta_{i+1}$ is always longer than $\alpha_i p_i \beta_i$. This is because an extra leading blank and an extra trailing blank have been added. These extra blanks ensure that if a blank is ever needed in an id, then it is explicitly there. (We could keep the id's shorter by sometimes using the pair $\# \longleftrightarrow \overline{\#}$ or $\overline{\#} \longleftrightarrow \#$ from Group 3 instead of the pair $\# \longleftrightarrow B\#\overline{B}$ or $\overline{\#} \longleftrightarrow \overline{B}\#B$ from Group 1. Among other things, this could eliminate the extra blank symbol B at the end of the string of y_i's. However, there is no need for this added refinement.)

In order to complete a solution to the Post correspondence problem, we then choose pairs from Groups 1 and 3 which "erase" the halting id $\overline{\alpha}_h\overline{p}_h\overline{\beta}_h$ one symbol at a time. For example, say $\overline{\alpha}_h\overline{p}_h\overline{\beta}_h = \overline{qa}$, where q is a state and a is a tape symbol. (Because of the extra leading and trailing blanks, $\overline{\alpha}_h\overline{p}_h\overline{\beta}_h$ will not really be this short. However, the idea is the same no matter how long it is and we want to have a short example.) For this example, we would choose the following pairs: $\overline{qa} \longleftrightarrow Ea$, $\# \longleftrightarrow \overline{\#}$, $B \longleftrightarrow \overline{B}$, $Ea \longleftrightarrow \overline{E}$, $\overline{\#} \longleftrightarrow \#$, $\overline{BE} \longleftrightarrow E$ and $\#E\# \longleftrightarrow \overline{\#}$. This yields the following solution to the Post correspondence problem:

$$x_{i_1} x_{i_2} ... x_{i_{g+7}} = y_{i_1} y_{i_2} ... y_{i_{g+7}} =$$

$$\$\# \, \alpha_1 p_1 \beta_1 \overline{\#} \overline{\alpha}_2 \overline{p}_2 \overline{\beta}_2 \# \; ... \; \# \alpha_{h-1} p_{h-1} \beta_{h-1} \overline{\#} \overline{qa} \# BEa \, \overline{\#} \, \overline{BE} \# E \overline{\#}$$

Similarly, for any other value of the halting id $\overline{\alpha}_h \overline{p}_h \overline{\beta}_h$, we can complete a solution to the Post correspondence problem using pairs from Groups 1 and 3. Hence, if M halts on w, then there is a solution to the Post correspondence problem for $A(M, w)$ and $B(M, w)$.

Conversely, if M does not halt on w, then there is no solution to the Post correspondence problem for $A(M, w)$ and $B(M, w)$. To see this, note that any partial solution must start with the pair $\$\# \longleftrightarrow \$\# Bq_o wB\overline{\#}\overline{B}$. By a partial solution we mean a sequence $i_1, i_2, ..., i_g$ such that one of $x_{i_1} x_{i_2} ... x_{i_g}$ and $y_{i_1} y_{i_2} ... y_{i_g}$ is an initial substring of the other. Unless M halts on input w, the only partial solutions possible are essentially of the form shown in (5) with $\overline{\alpha}_h \overline{p}_h \overline{\beta}_h$ (or $\alpha_h p_h \beta_h$ if h is odd) not equal to a halting id and possibly with the last blank symbol B (or $\overline{B}$) missing from the string of y_i's. That is, any partial solution is either of this form or is an initial segment of a partial solution of this form. Since there will never be a halting id at the end of a partial solution, it will never be possible to use pairs from Group 3 which introduce an E or an $\overline{E}$. Thus it will never be possible to get a complete solution. That is, it will never be possible to get the string of x's to be as long as the string of y's. $\square$

In order to complete the proof of Theorem 10.4, we still must get around the restrictions on the number of symbols and states for the Turing machines mentioned in Lemma 10.5. One way to do this is to show that the size of an alphabet Δ has nothing to do with whether or not the Post correspondence problem for Δ is solvable. This is done in the next lemma.

10.6 Lemma Let Δ be any alphabet with at least two letters. If we have an algorithm to solve the Post correspondence problem over Δ and if Σ is any other alphabet, then we can find an algorithm to solve the Post correspondence problem over Σ.

PROOF Suppose $A = (x_1, x_2, ..., x_k)$ and $B = (y_1, y_2, ..., y_k)$ are two lists of words over some alphabet $\Sigma = \{a_1, a_2, ..., a_l\}$. Let b and c be two distinct symbols in Δ. Code each symbol in Σ as a string in Δ^* as follows:

Code$(a_i) = b^i c^{l-i}$. For any string $d_1 d_2 ... d_n$ of symbols over Σ, define Code$(d_1 d_2 ... d_n) = $ Code(d_1)Code$(d_2)...$Code(d_n). It is routine to show

Claim: The instance $A = (x_1, x_2, ..., x_k)$ and $B = (y_1, y_2, ..., y_k)$ of the Post correspondence problem has a solution if and only if the instance $A_c =$

$(\text{Code}(x_1), \text{Code}(x_2), ..., \text{Code}(x_k))$ and $B_c = (\text{Code}(y_1), \text{Code}(y_2), ...$
$... \text{Code}(y_k))$ has a solution.

By the claim, an algorithm for the Post correspondence problem over Δ can be used to algorithmically solve the Post correspondence problem for any lists A and B of nonempty strings over Σ. $\square$

Proof of Theorem 10.4

Suppose there were an algorithm to solve the Post correspondence problem over Δ. That is, suppose we had an algorithm to compute the function p described in the theorem. Using Lemmas 10.5 and 10.6 we will show how to produce an algorithm to solve the halting problem and thereby will derive a contradiction. Given any simple Turing machine M and any input string w, this algorithm should determine whether or not M halts on the input w. The algorithm proceeds as follows. First it constructs the two lists $A(M, w)$ and $B(M, w)$ as in the proof of Lemma 10.5. Since M is arbitrary and Δ is fixed, these might not be lists of strings over Δ. To solve this problem, the algorithm then constructs list $A_c(M, w)$ and $B_c(M, w)$ of strings over Δ from $A(M, w)$ and $B(M, w)$ as in the proof of Lemma 10.6. We know that M halts on w if and only if the instance $A_c(M, w)$ and $B_c(M, w)$ of the Post correspondence problem has a solution. The algorithm then uses our hypothesized algorithm for the Post correspondence problem over Δ in order to test the instance $A_c(M, w)$ and $B_c(M, w)$. In this way, the algorithm determines whether or not M halts on w. Since we know there is no algorithm to solve the halting problem, it follows that we could not have had an algorithm to solve the Post correspondence problem. $\square$

CONTAINMENT QUESTIONS

In this section we show that a number of containment questions, such as does one cfl contain another or equal another, are unsolvable. In the process we will also show that a number of structural questions are unsolvable. One such unsolvable structural question is: Given a context-free grammar G, is $L(G)$ a deterministic language? Since context-free grammars arise naturally in the design of programming languages and since it is at least desirable for programming languages to be deterministic, this is a natural and important question. Unfortunately, this, as well as a large number of other structural and containment questions, are unsolvable. Hence any such questions must be handled on a more or less ad hoc basis.

The technique we will use to show that these questions are unsolvable is again the reduction technique we discussed at the beginning of this chapter. In all cases we show that if the problem were solvable then the Post correspondence problem would be solvable. The following definition and two lemmas develop the tools we need for this project.

10.7 Definition

Let Δ be a fixed alphabet. Let $A = (x_1, x_2, ..., x_k)$ and $B = (y_1, y_2, ..., y_k)$ be two lists of words over Δ. Let $\Gamma = \{a_1, a_2, ..., a_k\}$ be an alphabet of k symbols which is disjoint from Δ. Let $\mathbb{\phi}$ be a symbol not in Γ or Δ. Finally, let $\Sigma = \Delta \cup \Gamma \cup \{\phi\}$. We now define two deterministic cfl's which are closely related to the Post correspondence problem for the lists A and B. Set

$$C_{AB} = \{x_{i_1} x_{i_2}...x_{i_m} a_{i_m} a_{i_{m-1}} \cdots a_{i_1} \phi a_{j_1} a_{j_2} \cdots a_{j_n} y_{j_n} y_{j_{n-1}} \cdots y_{j_1} \mid m \geqslant 1, n \geqslant 1,$$

and $i_1, i_2, ..., i_m, j_1, j_2, ..., j_n$ chosen from among $1, 2, ..., k\}$.

An element of C_{AB} represents a solution to the Post correspondence problem if and only if it is of the form $w\phi w^R$. With this observation in mind, the relevance of the deterministic cfl we define next should be more or less clear. Let $E_{AB} = \{w\phi w^R \mid w \text{ in } \Delta^*\Gamma^*\}$. Now set $\overline{L}_{AB} = C_{AB} \cap E_{AB}$. Notice that the Post correspondence problem for the lists A and B has a solution if and only if $\overline{L}_{AB}$ is nonempty. We still need to define one more language. Set $L_{AB} = (\Sigma^* - C_{AB}) \cup (\Sigma^* - E_{AB})$. Notice that $\overline{L}_{AB} = \Sigma^* - L_{AB}$.

10.8 Lemma

1. C_{AB} and E_{AB} are deterministic cfl's.
2. L_{AB} is a cfl.
3. $\overline{L}_{AB}$ is nonempty if and only if there is a solution to the Post correspondence problem for the lists A and B.

PROOF We leave it as an exercise to construct deterministic pda's to accept C_{AB} and E_{AB}. Next we proceed to show that L_{AB} is a context-free language. Notice that $\Sigma^* - C_{AB}$ and $\Sigma^* - E_{AB}$ are complements of deterministic cfl's and hence, by Theorem 9.15, they also are deterministic cfl's. So L_{AB} is the union of two cfl's and hence, by Exercise 2-2, it too is a cfl. (3) is clear from the definitions involved. $\square$

10.9 Lemma $\overline{L}_{AB}$ is a cfl if and only if it is empty.

PROOF It suffices to show that, if $\overline{L}_{AB}$ is not empty, then it is not a cfl. Assume $\overline{L}_{AB}$ is nonempty and that it is a cfl. We will derive a contradiction. Let $uv\phi v^R u^R$ be any fixed element in $\overline{L}_{AB}$, where u is in Δ^* and v is in Γ^*. Now $uv\phi v^R u^R$ represents a solution to the Post correspondence problem. Given such a solution, we can repeat the solution to get other solutions. So $u^n v^n \phi (v^R)^n (u^R)^n$ is in $\overline{L}_{AB}$ for all n. Let $L = \{u^n v^n \phi (v^R)^n (u^R)^n \mid n \geqslant 1\}$. In order to pick out these particular members of $\overline{L}_{AB}$ use the finite-state language $R = \{u^i v^j \phi (v^R)^k (u^R)^l \mid \text{any } i, j, k, \text{ and } l\}$. It is easy to check that $L = \overline{L}_{AB} \cap R$. But, by assumption, $\overline{L}_{AB}$ is a cfl and clearly R is a finite-state language. So, by Theorem 9.11, L is a cfl. It is routine to find a finite-state transduction f such that $f(L) = \{a^n b^n \phi b^n a^n \mid n \geqslant 1\}$. So, by Theorem 9.13,

$\{a^n b^n \mathrm{¢} b^n a^n \mid n \geq 1\}$ is a cfl. However, we know by Exercise 2-5, that it is not a cfl and so we have obtained the contradiction that was promised. $\square$

10.10 Theorem All of the following questions are unsolvable. Here G_1 and G_2 are arbitrary context-free grammars and Σ is an alphabet such that $\Sigma^* \supseteq L(G_1)$.

1. Does $L(G_1) = L(G_2)$?
2. Does $L(G_1) \supseteq L(G_2)$?
3. Is $L(G_1) \cap L(G_2)$ a cfl?
4. Is $L(G_1)$ a finite-state language?
5. Is $L(G_1)$ a deterministic language?
6. Is $\Sigma^* - L(G_1)$ a cfl?

PROOF Let Δ be a fixed but arbitrary alphabet and adopt the notation of Definition 10.7. For each question, we show that if we had an algorithm for the given question, then we could produce an algorithm for the Post correspondence problem over Δ. Since we know the Post correspondence problem is unsolvable, it then follows that the given question is unsolvable. For lists A and B, G_{AB}, G_{CAB}, and G_{EAB} will denote grammars for L_{AB}, C_{AB}, and E_{AB} respectively. Notice that we can write an algorithm to produce these grammars given A and B. Let G_* be a grammar for Σ^*. We now consider the questions in order.

Question (1)

Given two lists A and B, there is a solution to this instance of the Post correspondence problem if and only if $L_{AB} \neq \Sigma^*$. This follows from Lemma 10.8 part (3) and the fact that $L_{AB} = \Sigma^* - \bar{L}_{AB}$. To test for a solution to the Post correspondence problem for A and B, we need only test if $L(G_{AB}) \neq L(G_*)$. Hence, if we have an algorithm to answer (1), we can easily produce an algorithm to solve the Post correspondence problem.

Question (2)

Notice that $L(G_{AB}) = \Sigma^*$ if and only if $L(G_{AB}) \supseteq \Sigma^*$. With this observation the proof of the unsolvability of (2) is essentially the same as the proof of the unsolvability of (1).

Question (3)

Let A and B be lists of strings over Δ. Notice that $L(G_{CAB}) \cap L(G_{EAB}) = C_{AB} \cap E_{AB} = \bar{L}_{AB}$. So, by Lemma 10.8 part (3) and Lemma 10.9, there is a solution to the Post correspondence problem for A and B if and only if $L(G_{CAB}) \cap L(G_{EAB})$ is not a cfl. The unsolvability of question (3) now follows by the standard reduction technique.

Question (4)

There is a solution to the Post correspondence problem for lists A and B if and only if $L_{AB} \neq \Sigma^*$. By Lemma 10.9, it is easy to see that $\overline{L}_{AB}$ is a finite-state language if and only if it is empty. So, since $L_{AB} = \Sigma^* - \overline{L}_{AB}$ and the finite-state languages are closed under complement, it follows that $L_{AB} = \Sigma^*$ if and only if L_{AB} is a finite-state language. Hence there is a solution to the Post correspondence problem for A and B if and only if $L(G_{AB})$ is not a finite-state language. The unsolvability of (4) is now more or less immediate by standard reduction techniques.

Question (5)

A proof that this question is unsolvable can be obtained from the proof that (4) is unsolvable by replacing the term "finite-state language" by the term "deterministic language" throughout the proof.

Question (6)

Given lists A and B, there is a solution to the Post correspondence problem for A and B if and only if $\Sigma^* - L(G_{AB})$ is not a cfl. This follows from Lemma 10.8 part (3), Lemma 10.9, and the fact that $\Sigma^* - L(G_{AB}) = \overline{L}_{AB}$. The unsolvability of (6) now follows by the standard reduction techniques. □

AMBIGUITY

Recall that a context-free grammar G is said to be ambiguous if there is a string w in $L(G)$ such that w has two parse trees. The meaning of a programming language is frequently determined in large part by the parse trees for programs. Hence, if we have a context-free grammar for a programming language and that grammar is ambiguous, then it is quite likely that some program will have two different meanings. If we design a compiler using this ambiguous grammar, we can easily produce a situation in which a programmer intends one meaning for the program but the compiler uses a different parse tree from the one the programmer had in mind. In this situation, it can easily happen that the object code produced by the compiler does not do what the programmer intended. To help avoid such situations, it would be nice to have a program that can test any context-free grammar and tell whether or not it is ambiguous. The next result says that, unfortunately, no such program can be written.

10.11 Theorem The following problem is unsolvable: Given a cfg G, determine whether or not G is ambiguous.

PROOF The proof is similar in character to those of the previous section. Suppose we had an algorithm to solve the ambiguity question. We will show how to obtain an algorithm to solve the Post correspondence problem. Since we know this is impossible, it will then follow that the ambiguity question is unsolvable.

Let A and B be two lists of strings and adopt the notation of Definition 10.7. It is routine to write unambiguous grammars G_{CAB} and G_{EAB} such that $L(G_{CAB}) = C_{AB}$, $L(G_{EAB}) = E_{AB}$ and such that G_{CAB} and G_{EAB} have disjoint sets of nonterminal symbols. Let S_C and S_E be the start symbols of G_{CAB} and G_{EAB} respectively. Let S' be a new symbol. Construct a grammar G for $C_{AB} \cup E_{AB}$ by taking all the productions from both G_{CAB} and G_{EAB} plus two more productions $S' \rightarrow S_C$ and $S' \rightarrow S_E$. Take S' to be the start symbol for G. The only way a string $L(G) = C_{AB} \cup E_{AB}$ could have two parse trees is if it is in both C_{AB} and E_{AB} . So, G is ambiguous if and only if $C_{AB} \cap E_{AB} = \overline{L}_{AB}$ is nonempty. By Lemma 10.8, G is ambiguous if and only if the Post correspondence problem for A and B has a solution. Hence, if we could solve the ambiguity problem, we could solve the Post correspondence problem. Since we know the latter is unsolvable, it follows that the ambiguity problem is unsolvable. $\square$

INHERENT AMBIGUITY

Suppose we have a grammar for a programming language and that we somehow find out that it is ambiguous. A natural question to ask is the following: Is there some way to change the grammar so that it will generate the same language but be unambiguous? We would probably want the new grammar to be similar to the grammar we started with. Hence, an answer to this question, even if it is yes and even if it also provides some new unambiguous grammar, may not solve all our language design problems. Still, an answer to this question may be of some help. Again, we will see that no computer program can answer this type of question and so once more we must rely on more or less ad hoc methods to answer the question. Recall that a context-free language for which all possible grammars are ambiguous is said to be inherently ambiguous. For this reason the above question is frequently called the *inherent ambiguity question*.

If there were no inherently ambiguous languages, then the solution to the inherent ambiguity question would be trivial. We start this section by proving that there is at least one inherently ambiguous context-free language.

10.12 Theorem The context-free language $L = \{a^i b^j c^k \mid i = j \text{ or } j = k\}$ is inherently ambiguous.

Before proving Theorem 10.12, we will give a preliminary definition and three preliminary lemmas.

10.13 Definition

A context-free grammar is said to be *clean* provided that for every nonterminal A, there is some derivation $S \overset{*}{\Rightarrow} xAy \overset{*}{\Rightarrow} w$, where S is the start symbol and w is a terminal string.

Given a cfg G_1, we can always obtain a clean cfg G_2 which is equivalent to G_1. To obtain G_2 from G_1, simply remove all symbols and productions which do not occur in any derivation of a string w in $L(G_1)$. Since G_2 has exactly the same parse trees as G_1, this G_2 will be ambiguous if and only if G_1 was ambiguous. Hence when discussing inherent ambiguity we can restrict our attention to clean grammars.

10.14 Lemma Suppose G is a clean cfg for $L = \{a^i b^j c^k \mid i = j \text{ or } j = k\}$. Suppose further that G does not have any nonterminals A such that $A \overset{*}{\Rightarrow} A$. It then follows that every nonterminal A of G satisfies one and only one of the following conditions:

1. There do not exist terminal strings x and y such that $A \overset{*}{\Rightarrow} xAy$.
2. $A \overset{*}{\Rightarrow} xAy$ where $xy = a^l$ for some $l \geq 1$.
3. $A \overset{*}{\Rightarrow} xAy$ where $xy = c^l$ for some $l \geq 1$.
4. $A \overset{*}{\Rightarrow} a^p A b^p$ for some $p \geq 1$.
5. $A \overset{*}{\Rightarrow} b^q A c^q$ for some $q \geq 1$.

PROOF We first show that conditions (1) through (5) are mutually exclusive. Clearly, condition (1) is disjoint from the remaining conditions. Hence, we need only consider conditions (2) through (5). In order to show that (2) and (3) are disjoint, we assume the contrary. That is, we assume there is a nonterminal A such that

6. $A \overset{*}{\Rightarrow} x_1 A y_1$, where $x_1 y_1 = a^{l_1}$, $l_1 \geq 1$ and
    $A \overset{*}{\Rightarrow} x_2 A y_2$, where $x_2 y_2 = c^{l_2}$, $l_2 \geq 1$.

Since G is clean, we also know that

7. $S \overset{*}{\Rightarrow} uAv \overset{*}{\Rightarrow} uzv$,

where S is the start symbol and uzv is a string in the language L. Combining (6) and (7) we see that the following is a valid G derivation for all s and t:

$$S \overset{*}{\Rightarrow} uAv \overset{*}{\Rightarrow} ux_1^s A y_1^s v \overset{*}{\Rightarrow} ux_1^s x_2^t A y_2^t y_1^s v \overset{*}{\Rightarrow} ux_1^s x_2^t z y_2^t y_1^s v = w(s, t)$$

Hence, for all s and t, $w(s, t)$ is in L. We will derive a contradiction by showing that, for some s and t, $w(s, t)$ is not in L. Choose s so that $sl_1 > \text{length}(uzv)$. Then $w(s, t)$ will contain at least sl_1 a's and at most $\text{length}(uzv)$ b's. The number of a's will be greater than the number of b's for any $w(s, t)$ with s so chosen. Similarly, choose t so that $tl_2 > \text{length}(uzv)$. Then $w(s, t)$ will also contain more c's than b's. So for these values of s and t, $w(s, t)$ is not in L and we have the promised contradiction. Thus conditions (2) and (3) are disjoint.

Next we show, again by contradiction, that conditions (3) and (4) are mutually exclusive. Suppose there is a nonterminal A which satisfies (3) and (4). Since G is clean, we again know that A also satisfies (7). Combining (3), (4), and (7) we get that the following is a valid G derivation of some string w in L.

$$S \overset{*}{\Rightarrow} uAv \overset{*}{\Rightarrow} ua^p A b^p v \overset{*}{\Rightarrow} ua^p x A y b^p v \overset{*}{\Rightarrow} ua^p x z y b^p v = w$$

where xy contains a c. So w has a c between an a and a b. Therefore w is not in L and we have a contradiction. Thus conditions (3) and (4) are disjoint.

The mutual exclusion of the other pairs from conditions (2) through (5) are proven in similar ways and we leave these proofs as an exercise.

It remains to show that every nonterminal A satisfies one of the conditions (1) through (5). Suppose A does not satisfy (1). We then know that $A \overset{*}{\Rightarrow} xAy$ for some x, y in $\{a, b, c\}^*$. Since G is clean, there must also exist a derivation $S \overset{*}{\Rightarrow} uAv \overset{*}{\Rightarrow} uzv$, where S is the start symbol and u, z, y are in $\{a, b, c\}^*$. Thus we can form the following derivation in G

8. $S \overset{*}{\Rightarrow} uAv \overset{*}{\Rightarrow} ux^2Ay^2v \overset{*}{\Rightarrow} ux^2zy^2v$.

Since ux^2zy^2v must be of the form $a^i b^j c^k$, it then follows that x consist of all a's, all b's, or all c's and that y consists of all a's, all b's, or all c's. By assumption $A \overset{*}{\Rightarrow} A$ cannot happen. So we also know that at least one of x and y is nonempty.

We now proceed by cases according to which letters make up x and y. In each case we show that either we get a contradiction and so that case cannot occur or else one of the conditions (2) through (5) holds for A.

If both x and y are all a's, then condition (2) holds. If both x and y are all c's, then condition (3) holds.

Suppose $x = a^s$ and $y = c^t$ with $s > 0$ and $t > 0$. We will derive a contradiction and thereby show that this case is not possible. By the same reasoning that yielded (8), we see that

9. $S \overset{*}{\Rightarrow} uAv \overset{*}{\Rightarrow} ux^h Ay^h v \overset{*}{\Rightarrow} ux^h zy^h v$, for all h.

But for large enough h both the number of a's and the number of c's will exceed the number of b's in $ux^h zy^h v$. Hence it cannot be in L and we have a contradiction as promised.

Suppose $x = a^s$ and $y = b^t$ with $s > 0$ and $t > 0$. If $s = t$, then condition (4) holds. To complete this case, we need only show that $s \neq t$ leads to a contradiction. Suppose $s \neq t$. Say $s > t$; the case $t > s$ is symmetric. Again we know that a derivation of form (9) is possible for all h and hence $ux^h zy^h v$ is in L. But, for h large enough, $ux^h zy^h v$ will have more b's than c's. Also, since $s > t$, a large enough h will cause $ux^h zy^h v$ to have more a's than b's. Hence $ux^h zy^h v$ is not in L. Again, we have our desired contradiction.

The other cases are similar and we leave them as an exercise. $\square$

10.15 Lemma Suppose G is a clean cfg for $L = \{a^i b^j c^k \mid i = j \text{ or } j = k\}$ and let S be the start symbol of G. Suppose further that G does not have any nonterminals A such that $A \overset{*}{\Rightarrow} A$. We can then find a constant m such that the following hold. If $S \overset{*}{\Rightarrow} a^N b^N c^{2N}$ and the derivation does not contain any nonterminals satisfying (4) or (5) of Lemma 10.14, then $N < m$. Also, if $S \overset{*}{\Rightarrow} a^{2N} b^N c^N$ and this derivation does not contain any nonterminals satisfying (4) or (5) of Lemma 10.14, then $N < m$.

PROOF We will produce an m which has the desired property for derivations of strings of the form $a^N b^N c^{2N}$. It will then follow by symmetry that m also has the desired property for strings of the form $a^{2N} b^N c^N$. Suppose $S \overset{*}{\Rightarrow} a^N b^N c^{2N}$ and the derivation contains no nonterminals satisfying (4) or (5) of Lemma 10.14.

First observe that the derivation also contains no nonterminals satisfying (2) of Lemma 10.14. To see this note that, if

$$S \overset{*}{\Rightarrow} uAv \overset{*}{\Rightarrow} uwv = a^N b^N c^{2N}$$

and A satisfies (2) of that lemma, then the following is also a valid derivation of G:

$$S \overset{*}{\Rightarrow} uAv \overset{*}{\Rightarrow} uxAyv \overset{*}{\Rightarrow} uxwyv = a^{N+l} b^N c^{2N}$$

where x, y and l are as in (2) of Lemma 10.14 and hence $l \geqslant 1$. But this would be a contradiction, since $a^{N+l} b^N c^{2N}$ is not in L. So there cannot be any nonterminals satisfying (2) in the derivation of $a^N b^N c^{2N}$. Hence every nonterminal in the derivation of $a^N b^N c^{2N}$ satisfies (1) or (3) but not (2), (4), or (5) of Lemma 10.14.

Let n be the number of nonterminals of G and let $s = \max\{\text{length}(\alpha) \mid A \rightarrow \alpha \text{ in Productions}(G), \text{ for some } A\}$. The desired m is $m = s^n$. The relevant property of m is expressed in the claim below.

Claim: Suppose $S \overset{*}{\Rightarrow} w$ for some terminal string w. Suppose further that the parse tree for this derivation has the property that on any path from the root (start) node to a leaf node, no nonterminal is repeated. Under these assumptions, length$(w) \leqslant m$.

To prove the claim, simply note that no such path in the parse tree contains more than $n + 1$ nodes, since it can contain at most n nonterminals plus either a terminal symbol or Λ at the leaf node. Thus the parse tree has height at most n, that is at most n arcs occur on any such path. Also each node branches to at most s nodes below it. So there can be at most $s^n = m$ leaf nodes and so length$(w) \leqslant m$.

We will describe a process for modifying the derivation $S \overset{*}{\Rightarrow} a^N b^N c^{2N}$ in order to obtain another valid derivation $S \overset{*}{\Rightarrow} a^N b^N c^i$, for some $i \geqslant 0$. This derivation of $a^N b^N c^i$ will satisfy the assumptions of the above claim. So, once we obtain such a derivation, it will follow immediately from the claim that $N < m$. It remains to show how the derivation of this $a^N b^N c^i$ is obtained.

If the derivation $S \overset{*}{\Rightarrow} a^N b^N c^{2N}$ already satisfies the assumptions of the claim, it is the desired derivation. If it does not satisfy the assumptions, then there is some nonterminal A in the derivation such that

$$S \overset{*}{\Rightarrow} uAv \overset{*}{\Rightarrow} uxAyv \overset{*}{\Rightarrow} uxzyv = a^N b^N c^{2N}$$

where the u, v, x, y and z are strings of terminal symbols. Hence A satisfies (3) of Lemma 10.14 and $xy = c^l$, for some $l \geqslant 1$. This derivation can be modified to yield the following valid derivation:

$$S \overset{*}{\Rightarrow} uAv \overset{*}{\Rightarrow} uzv = a^N b^N c^{2N-l}$$

If this new derivation satisfies the assumptions of the claim, then it is the desired derivation. If it does not satisfy the assumptions, then we can repeat this process to eliminate another nonterminal satisfying (3). We continue to repeat this process until we get a derivation of some $a^N b^N c^i$ which does satisfy the assumptions of the claim. It then follows immediately from the claim that $N < m$.

A completely symmetric argument shows that this same m also has the desired property for strings of the form $a^{2N} b^N c^N$. So the lemma is proven. □

10.16 Lemma Suppose G is a cfg for $L = \{a^i b^j c^k \mid i = j \text{ or } j = k\}$ and consider a string of the form $a^n b^n c^n$. No G derivation of $a^n b^n c^n$ can contain both a nonterminal satisfying (4) of Lemma 10.14 and a (possibly different) nonterminal satisfying (5) of that lemma.

PROOF Consider a derivation $S \overset{*}{\Rightarrow} a^n b^n c^n$, where S is the start symbol of G. Suppose this derivation contains a nonterminal satisfying (4) and a nonterminal satisfying (5) of Lemma 10.14. It is then easy to see that

$$S \overset{*}{\Rightarrow} a^{n+p} b^{n+p+q} c^{n+q}$$

where $p \geqslant 1$ and $q \geqslant 1$. But this is a contradiction, since $n+p \neq n+p+q$ and $n+p+q \neq n+q$. Hence it is not possible for the derivation of $a^n b^n c^n$ to contain both a nonterminal satisfying (4) and one satisfying (5) of Lemma 10.14. □

Proof of Theorem 10.12

Suppose $L(G) = \{a^i b^j c^k \mid i = j \text{ or } j = k\}$, where G is a context-free grammar. We will show that G is ambiguous. By the remarks which followed Definition 10.13, we may assume that G is clean. Suppose G happens to contain a nonterminal A such that $A \overset{*}{\Rightarrow} A$. Since G is clean, there is some derivation $S \overset{*}{\Rightarrow} uAv \overset{*}{\Rightarrow} w$, where w is in $L(G)$. By inserting $A \overset{*}{\Rightarrow} A$ into the above derivation of w, we obtain a derivation with a different parse tree. So G is ambiguous.

We now turn to the remaining case where G is clean and G does not contain a nonterminal A such that $A \overset{*}{\Rightarrow} A$. In this case, Lemmas 10.14 and 10.15 apply. Let m be as in Lemma 10.15. For each nonterminal A satisfying condition (4) of Lemma 10.14, let p_A be the minimal value of p for which (4) is true for A. Similarly, for each A satisfying (5) of the lemma, let q_A be the minimal value of q for which (5) is true for A. Let P be the product obtained by multiplying all these p_A's and q_A's together. Finally, choose N so that $N > m$ and so that N is a multiple of P. Note that N will then be a multiple of all these p_A's and q_A's.

Consider a derivation of the string $a^N b^N c^{2N}$. Since $N > m$, we know by Lemma 10.15 that any derivation of this string must contain some nonterminal A which satisfies condition (4) on (5) of Lemma 10.14. That is,

10. $S \overset{*}{\Rightarrow} uAv \overset{*}{\Rightarrow} uzv = a^N b^N c^{2N}$

for some strings u, z, v and where A satisfies condition (4) or (5). Suppose A satisfies condition (5). Then, since N is a multiple of a q satisfying (5) for A, we get

$$S \overset{*}{\Rightarrow} uAv \overset{*}{\Rightarrow} ub^N Ac^N v \overset{*}{\Rightarrow} ub^N zc^N v = a^N b^{2N} c^{3N}$$

But $a^N b^{2N} c^{3N}$ is not in $L(G)$. So, A cannot satisfy (5) and hence it must satisfy (4). Now since (10) holds, since A satisfies condition (4) and since N is a multiple of a p satisfying (4) for A, we get

11. $S \overset{*}{\Rightarrow} uAv \overset{*}{\Rightarrow} ua^N Ab^N v \overset{*}{\Rightarrow} ua^N zb^N v = a^{2N} b^{2N} c^{2N}$

where u, v, z are some strings and the derivation uses at least one nonterminal satisfying (4) and hence, by Lemma 10.16, no nonterminals satisfying (5). We will show that there is another derivation of $a^{2N} b^{2N} c^{2N}$ which has a different parse tree from the derivation (11).

Consider a derivation of $a^{2N} b^N c^N$. By an argument which is symmetric to the preceding one, we get that this derivation contains a nonterminal B which satisfies (5). That is,

12. $S \overset{*}{\Rightarrow} u'Bv' \overset{*}{\Rightarrow} u'z'v' = a^{2N} b^N c^N$

where B satisfies (5) of Lemma 10.14. Continuing with the symmetric argument, we see that it is possible to use B and condition (5) to change derivation (12) into the following:

13. $S \overset{*}{\Rightarrow} u'Bv' \overset{*}{\Rightarrow} u'b^N Bc^N v' \overset{*}{\Rightarrow} u'b^N z'c^N v' = a^{2N} b^{2N} c^{2N}$

where u', z', v' are some strings and the derivation uses at least one nonterminal satisfying (5) but no nonterminals satisfying (4) of Lemma 10.14.

Since (11) uses a nonterminal satisfying (4) and (13) does not, (11) and (13) must have different parse trees. Hence G is ambiguous. □

We next use the fact that $\{a^i b^j c^k \mid i = j \text{ or } j = k\}$ is inherently ambiguous as a lemma in proving that the general inherent ambiguity question is unsolvable.

10.17 Theorem There is no algorithm which can decide, for an arbitrary context-free grammar G, whether or not $L(G)$ is inherently ambiguous.

The proof requires two additional lemmas. In order to motivate the first lemma, we will use it in proving Theorem 10.17 and then, after seeing its significance, we will fill in the proof of the lemma. The proof of the second lemma is left as an exercise.

10.18 Lemma If G is an unambiguous cfg and z is a fixed string of terminal symbols, then we can find an unambiguous cfg G_z such that $L(G_z) = \{zx \mid zx$ is in $L(G)\}$, that is, such that $L(G_z)$ is the set of all strings in $L(G)$ which begin with z.

10.19 Lemma Let L be a language and z a fixed string. Define zL as follows, $zL = \{zw \mid w$ is in $L\}$. If zL is an unambiguous cfl, then L is an unambiguous cfl.

Proof of Theorem 10.17

The proof uses the usual reduction technique. Specifically, we will show that if the inherent ambiguity problem were solvable, then the Post correspondence problem would be solvable. Since the Post correspondence problem is unsolvable, it will then follow immediately that the inherent ambiguity problem is unsolvable.

Let A and B be two lists of words of the same length. Let C_{AB} and E_{AB} be as in Definition 10.7. We know, by Lemma 10.8, that there is a solution to the Post correspondence problem for A and B if and only if $C_{AB} \cap E_{AB}$ is nonempty. Hence it will suffice to show that if we had an algorithm for the inherent ambiguity problem, then we could find an algorithm to decide whether or not $C_{AB} \cap E_{AB}$ is empty.

For any lists A and B, let $C'_{AB} = C_{AB}\{\cent a^i b^j c^k \mid i = j\}$. That is, let $C'_{AB} = \{z\cent a^i b^j c^k \mid i = j$ and z in $C_{AB}\}$. Let $E'_{AB} = E_{AB}\{\cent a^i b^j c^k \mid j = k\}$ and let $U'_{AB} = C'_{AB} \cup E'_{AB}$. It is routine to write unambiguous cfg's for C'_{AB} and E'_{AB}. Hence by Exercise 2-2, we can easily obtain a cfg for U'_{AB}. Once the following claim is shown we will have shown that the emptiness problem for $C_{AB} \cap E_{AB}$ is reducible to the inherent ambiguity problem and the theorem will be proven.

Claim: $C_{AB} \cap E_{AB}$ is nonempty if and only if U'_{AB} is inherently ambiguous.

We now proceed to prove the claim. First note that $C_{AB} \cap E_{AB}$ is empty if and only if $C'_{AB} \cap E'_{AB}$ is empty. If $C_{AB} \cap E_{AB}$ is empty, then, by Exercise 2-2, U'_{AB} is an unambiguous language. it remains to show that, if $C_{AB} \cap E_{AB}$ is nonempty, then U'_{AB} is inherently ambiguous. With this goal in mind, assume that $C_{AB} \cap E_{AB}$ is nonempty and that U'_{AB} has an unambiguous cfg that generates it. We will derive a contradiction. Let w be a fixed element of $C_{AB} \cap E_{AB}$ and set $z = w\cent$. Consider $L_z = \{zx \mid zx$ in $U'_{AB}\}$. By Lemma 10.18, L_z is unambiguous. But $L_z = \{za^i b^j c^k \mid i = j$ or $j = k\}$. Hence, by Lemma 10.19, $\{a^i b^j c^k \mid i = j$ or $j = k\}$ is unambiguous. This is a contradiction. Hence the proof of the claim, and hence the proof of the theorem, is completed. □

We now go back and prove Lemma 10.18.

Proof of Lemma 10.18

We will design the grammar G_z to be basically the same as G except that there will be a number of copies of each nonterminal of G. These extra copies will code information that will allow G_z to block derivations which do not yield terminal strings which begin with z. To simplify the notation, we will follow the usual conventions that lower-case letters near the end of the alphabet represent terminal strings and upper-case letters represent nonterminals of the grammar G. Since the nonterminals of G will be a subset of the nonterminals of G_z, these upper-case letters are also nonterminals of G_z.

G_z and G have the same terminal symbols. The nonterminals of G_z are all the nonterminals of G plus all pairs of the form $<A, y>$ and all pairs of the form $<A, y+>$, where A is a nonterminal of G and $z = uyv$ for some strings u and v. In other words, the possible y's are all contiguous substrings of the fixed string z. In particular, one value of y is the empty string. The symbol $+$ is a new symbol. G_z also has one new nonterminal S_z to serve as the start symbol.

The nonterminals of the forms $<A, y>$ and $<A, y+>$ behave like the nonterminal A except that the possible strings that they can derive are restricted. The productions of G_z are designed so that if $<A, y> \overset{*}{\Rightarrow} w$, where w is a terminal string, then $w = y$ and if $<A, y+> \overset{*}{\Rightarrow} w$, where w is a terminal string, then $w = yx$ for some nonempty string x. If $w = yx$ for some nonempty string x, then y is called a *proper* initial substring of w. More precisely, the productions of G_z are all productions of the forms listed below.

1. All productions of G plus the following productions of G_z.
2. $S_z \rightarrow <S, z>$ and $S_z \rightarrow <S, z+>$, where S is the start symbol of G and z is the fixed string mentioned in the lemma.
3. $<A, y> \rightarrow u_0<B_1, v_1> u_1 <B_2, v_2>u_2...<B_m, v_m>u_m$, provided that
   a. $A \rightarrow u_0B_1u_1B_2u_2...B_mu_m$ is a production of G, and
   b. $y = u_0v_1u_1v_2u_2...v_mu_m$

We allow the possibility of $m = 0$. That case is to be interpreted to mean $<A, y> \rightarrow u_0$ is in G_z, provided $A \rightarrow u_0$ is in G and $y = u_0$.

4. $<A, y+> \rightarrow u_0<B_1, v_1>u_1<B_2, v_2>u_2...<B_l, v_l>u_lB_{l+1}u_{l+1}B_{l+2}u_{l+2}...$
   $...B_mu_m$ provided that
   a. $A \rightarrow u_0B_1u_1B_2u_2...B_mu_m$ is a production of G,
   b. $0 \leqslant l \leqslant m$,
   c. y is a proper initial subword of $u_0v_1u_1v_2u_2...v_lu_l$ but is not a proper initial subword of $u_0v_1u_1v_2u_2...v_{l-1}u_{l-1}v_l$.

We allow the possibility of $l = 0$. That case is to be interpreted as saying that $<A, y> \rightarrow u_0B_1u_1B_2u_2...B_mu_m$ is in G_z whenever $A \rightarrow u_0B_1u_1B_2u_2...B_mu_m$ is in G and y is a proper initial subword of u_0.

5. $<A, y+> \rightarrow u_0<B_1, v_1>u_1<B_2, v_2>u_2...$
   $...<B_{l-1}, v_{l-1}>u_{l-1}<B_l, v_l+>u_lB_{l+1}u_{l+1}...B_mu_m$, provided that
   a. $A \rightarrow u_0B_1u_1B_2u_2...B_mu_m$ is a production of G,
   b. $1 \leqslant l \leqslant m$, and
   c. $y = u_0v_1u_1v_2u_2...v_{l-1}u_{l-1}v_l$.

It is routine to prove the following claims and we leave their proofs as an easy exercise.

Claim 1: $A \overset{*}{\Rightarrow} w$ in G_z if and only if $A \overset{*}{\Rightarrow} w$ in G.

Claim 2: $<A, y> \overset{*}{\Rightarrow} w$ in G_z if and only if $w = y$ and $A \overset{*}{\Rightarrow} y$ in G.

Claim 3: $<A, y+> \overset{*}{\Rightarrow} w$ in G_z if and only if $w = yx$ for some nonempty string x and $A \overset{*}{\Rightarrow} w$ in G.

Recall that $S_z \rightarrow <S, z>$ and $S_z \rightarrow <S, z+>$ are the only rewrite rules for S_z in G_z, where S_z is the start symbol for G_z and S is the start symbol for G. It then follows immediately from Claims 2 and 3 that $L(G_z) = \{zx \mid zx$ is in $L(G)\}$.

We still must show that G_z is unambiguous, given that G is unambiguous. However, that follows immediately from Claim 4 below. So once Claim 4 is established the proof will be completed.

In order to state Claim 4, we need to define a function g which maps every G_z parse tree T onto a G parse tree $g(T)$ for the same terminal string. With this in mind, suppose T is a parse tree for some G_z derivation $S_z \overset{*}{\Rightarrow} w$, where w is in $L(G_z)$. The parse tree $g(T)$ is obtained from T as follows. First remove the start node S_z and the arc leading to $<S, z>$ or $<S, z+>$. This still leaves a parse tree but now the top (root) node is either $<S, z>$ or $<S, z+>$. Next replace each node label of the form $<A, y>$ by A and each node label of the form $<A, y+>$ by A. Observe that $g(T)$ is then a parse tree for some G derivation $S \overset{*}{\Rightarrow} w$ of the terminal string w. With the aid of this definition we now state and prove Claim 4.

Claim 4: If T_1 and T_2 are two distinct G_z parse trees for some word w in $L(G_z)$, then $g(T_1)$ and $g(T_2)$ are two distinct G parse trees for w.

In order to complete the proof of the lemma, we need only prove Claim 4. We now proceed to do that. Assume the hypothesis of the claim. We will show that $g(T_1)$ and $g(T_2)$ are distinct. If T_1 and T_2 differ in any way other than in having some nodes labeled differently (that is, if they are "shaped" differently), then clearly $g(T_1)$ and $g(T_2)$ are different. So suppose T_1 and T_2 differ only in node labels. Let N_1 and N_2 be node labels such that N_1 labels a node of T_1, N_2 labels the corresponding node of T_2 and $N_1 \neq N_2$. First observe that N_1 and N_2 do not label the root node, since it is always labeled S_z and $N_1 \neq N_2$. So $g(T_1)$ and $g(T_2)$ contain nodes corresponding to N_1 and N_2 respectively. We now proceed by cases to show that, in all cases, $g(T_1)$ and $g(T_2)$ are distinct.

Case 1: N_1 and N_2 are both symbols of G, either terminals, nonterminals, or Λ.

In this case N_1 and N_2 also label corresponding nodes of $g(T_1)$ and $g(T_2)$. So, since $N_1 \neq N_2$, $g(T_1)$ and $g(T_2)$ are distinct.

Case 2: $N_1 = <A_1, y_1>$ and $N_2 = <A_2, y_2>$, where A_1 and A_2 are G nonterminals and where y_1 and y_2 are terminal strings.

Since $N_1 \neq N_2$, either $A_1 \neq A_2$, or $y_1 \neq y_2$. If $A_1 \neq A_2$ then corresponding nodes in $g(T_1)$ and $g(T_2)$ are labeled A_1 and A_2 respectively. So $g(T_1)$ and $g(T_2)$ are distinct. If $y_1 \neq y_2$, then corresponding subtrees in $g(T_1)$ and $g(T_2)$ have different labels on some of their leaf nodes and so $g(T_1) \neq g(T_2)$.

Case 3: $N_1 = <A, y>$ or $N_1 = <A, y+>$ where A is a nonterminal of G, y is a terminal string and $N_2 = A$.

For this case, recall that the terminal string w derived is of the form zx for some x. By the definition of G_z, it is then easy to see that in T_1 the subtree below N_1 derives a terminal string which includes some subword of the initial z and in T_2 the corresponding subtree below N_2 does not. Since these properties are then also true for the corresponding subtrees of $g(T_1)$ and $g(T_2)$, it follows that $g(T_1) \neq g(T_2)$.

Case 4: $N_1 = <A_1, y_1+>$ and $N_2 = <A_2, y_2+>$, where A_1 and A_2 are G nonterminals and where y_1 and y_2 are terminal strings.

As in Case 2, if $A_1 \neq A_2$, then $g(T_1) \neq g(T_2)$. That leaves the subcase where $y_1 \neq y_2$. For this subcase, recall that the terminal string w derived by both $g(T_1)$ and $g(T_2)$ is of the form $w = zx$ for some x. Using this observation and the definition of G_z, it is easy to see that the derivation represented by T_1 can be decomposed into the form

4. $S_z \overset{*}{\Rightarrow} u_1 <A_1, y_1+> v_1 \overset{*}{\Rightarrow} u_1 y_1 x_1 v_1 = zx_1 v_1 = w,$

for some terminal strings u_1, v_1 and x_1. Hence the derivation represented by $g(T_1)$ can be decomposed into the form

5. $S \overset{*}{\Rightarrow} u_1 A_1 v_1 \overset{*}{\Rightarrow} u_1 y_1 x_1 v_1 = zx_1 v_1 = w.$

Similarly, the derivation represented by $g(T_2)$ can be decomposed into the form

6. $S \overset{*}{\Rightarrow} u_2 A_2 v_2 \overset{*}{\Rightarrow} u_2 y_2 x_2 v_2 = zx_2 v_2 = w,$
for some terminal strings u_2, v_2 and x_2.

By (5) and (6), we get $z = u_1 y_1 = u_2 y_2$. It then follows that, since $y_1 \neq y_2$, that $u_1 \neq u_2$. Now recall that the subtree below A_1 in $g(T_1)$ corresponds to the subtree below A_2 in $g(T_2)$ and hence the symbols in u_1 and u_2 label corresponding leaf nodes of $g(T_1)$ and $g(T_2)$ respectively. But $u_1 \neq u_2$ and hence $g(T_1) \neq g(T_2)$.

Case 5: $N_1 = <A_1, y_1>$ and $N_2 = <A_2, y_2+>$, where A_1 and A_2 are G nonterminals and where y_1 and y_2 are terminal strings.

For this case, we again recall that the terminal string w derived is of the form $w = zx$ for some string x. Also, by claims 2 and 3 and by the definition of G_z, it is easy to see the following. The subtree of $g(T_1)$ which corresponds to N_1 derives some subword y_1 which lies entirely within this initial z. The subtree of $g(T_2)$ which corresponds to N_2 derives some subword y_2x_2 where x_2 is not empty and x_2 lies entirely to the right of this initial z. Hence these two corresponding subtrees do not have corresponding leaf nodes. Hence $g(T_1) \neq g(T_2)$.

All other cases are trivial variants of the above cases. This completes the proof of the lemma. $\Box$

EXERCISES

1. Let M be the simple Turing machine defined as follows. States$(M) = \{q_0, q_1, q_2\}$, Symbols$(M) = \{B, a\}$, Start$(M) = q_0$, Blank$(M) = B$, and Instructions$(M) = \delta$, where $\delta(q_0, B) = (q_1, a, \leftarrow)$, $\delta(q_1, B) = (q_2, a, \leftarrow)$, and δ is undefined for all other arguments. The accepting states of M are irrelevant to this problem and may be anything. Note that M halts on input Λ. Hence, the instance $A(M, \Lambda)$ and $B(M, \Lambda)$ of the Post correspondence problem (Lemma 10.5) has a solution. Find a solution to this instance of the Post correspondence problem.

2. Let M be the simple Turing machine defined as in the previous problem except that $\delta(q_0, B) = (q_1, a, \rightarrow)$, $\delta(q_1, B) = (q_2, a, \rightarrow)$, and δ is undefined for all other arguments. Note that this M also halts on input Λ. Find a solution to the instance $A(M, \Lambda)$ and $B(M, \Lambda)$ of the Post correspondence problem, where $A(M, \Lambda)$ and $B(M, \Lambda)$ are as in the proof of Lemma 10.5.

3. Prove that each of the following questions is unsolvable:
   a. Given cfg's G_1 and G_2, is $L(G_1) \cap L(G_2)$ empty?
   b. Given deterministic pda's M_1 and M_2, is $A(M_1) \cap A(M_2)$ empty?
   c. Given simple Turing machines M_1 and M_2, is $A(M_1) \cap A(M_2)$ empty?
   d. Given a cfg G and a finite-state acceptor M, does $L(G) = A(M)$?
   e. Given simple Turing machines M_1 and M_2, does $A(M_1) = A(M_2)$?
   f. Given a cfg G and a finite-state acceptor M, does $L(G) \supseteq A(M)$?
   g. Given a cfg and a finite-state acceptor M, does $A(M) \supseteq L(G)$?

4. In order to prove Theorem 10.12, we did not need an effective procedure which, given any cfg G_1 would produce an equivalent clean cfg G_2. All we needed to know was that for every cfg G_1 there is an equivalent clean cfg G_2. Still, it is of some interest to know that such a procedure does exist. Prove that there is such a procedure.

5. Complete the proof of Lemma 10.14 by doing the cases omitted.

6. Prove Claims 1, 2, and 3 of Lemma 10.18.

7. Prove: If L is an unambiguous language and R is a finite-state language, then $L \cap R$ is an unambiguous language (*Hint*: Generalize the proof of Lemma 10.18).

8. Prove Lemma 10.19.

Appendix:
The Greek
Alphabet

A	α	Alpha		N	ν	Nu
B	β	Beta		Ξ	ξ	Xi
Γ	γ	Gamma		O	o	Omicron
Δ	δ	Delta		Π	π	Pi
E	ϵ	Epsilon		P	ρ	Rho
Z	ζ	Zeta		Σ	σ	Sigma
H	η	Eta		T	τ	Tau
Θ	θ	Theta		Υ	υ	Upsilon
I	ι	Iota		Φ	ϕ	Phi
K	κ	Kappa		X	X	Chi
Λ	λ	Lambda		Ψ	ψ	Psi
M	μ	Mu		Ω	ω	Omega

References
for Further
Reading

Below is a short list of textbooks and reference books on the material in this book and on related topics. It should provide a tractably short list of references for the reader who wishes to see more material on these subjects. If still more material is desired, the lists of references in these books should be consulted.

A.V. Aho (ed.), *Currents in the Theory of Computing*, 1973, Englewood Cliffs, N.J., Prentice-Hall. Five survey papers on topics that are natural sequels to the subject matter of this book.

A.V. Aho, J.E. Hopcroft, and J.D. Ullman, *The Design and Analysis of Computer Algorithms*, 1974, Reading, Mass., Addison-Wesley. Presents some topics of current research interest in complexity theory. Complexity theory is like computability theory but it refines it to consider questions of efficiency, specifically the time and storage used by procedures.

A.V. Aho and J.D. Ullman, *Principles of Compiler Design*, 1977, Reading, Mass., Addison-Wesley. An introduction to compiler design.

S. Alagic' and M.A. Arbib, *The Design of Well-Structured and Correct Programs*, 1978, New York, Springer-Verlag. An Introduction to proofs of program correctness and to the design of programs so as to facilitate such proofs.

A. Borodin and I. Munro, *The Computational Complexity of Algebraic and Numeric Problems*, 1975, New York, American Elsevier. Some topics on the computational complexity of problems.

W.S. Brainard and L.H. Landweber, *Theory of Computation*, 1974, New York, John Wiley. Another treatment of computability theory which includes some results on efficiency of programs.

M. Davis, *Computability and Unsolvability*, 1958, New York, McGraw-Hill. Turing machines and computable functions from a more mathematically formal point of view.

M. Davis (ed.), *The Undecidable*, 1965, Hewlett, N.Y., Raven Press. A collection of various papers on unsolvability, including Turing's original paper that introduces the Turing machine.

M.A. Harrison, *Introduction to Formal Language Theory*, 1978, Reading, Mass., Addison-Wesley. An encyclopedic work on formal languages and context-free languages in particular.

D.R. Hofstadter, *Gödel, Escher, Bach. An Eternal Golden Braid*, 1979, New York, Vintage Books. Discussion of computability, provability, and related topics aimed at a nontechnical audience.

J.E. Hopcroft and J.D. Ullman, *Introduction to Automata Theory, Languages, and Computation*, 1979, Reading, Mass., Addison-Wesley. A somewhat more advanced and much more encyclopedic treatment of the topics in this book plus a treatment of complexity theory (theory of efficiency of programs).

K. Jensen and N. Wirth, *PASCAL User Manual and Report*, 1974, New York, Springer-Verlag. Description of the PASCAL programming language.

Z. Kohavi, *Switching and Finite Automata Theory*, 1970, New York, McGraw-Hill. A treatment of finite-state machines form a hardware point of view.

M.L. Minsky, *Computation. Finite and Infinite Machines*, 1967, Englewood Cliffs, N.J., Prentice-Hall. An older but particularly nice treatment of finite-state machines and computability theory.

T.W. Pratt, *Programming Languages. Design and Implementation*, 1975, Englewood Cliffs, N.J., Prentice-Hall. An introduction to programming language features which includes discussion of a number of specific programming languages.

H. Rogers Jr., *Theory of Recursive Functions and Effective Computability*, 1967, New York, McGraw-Hill. An encyclopedic work on the mathematical theory of computable functions.

G. Rozenberg and A. Salomaa, *The Mathematical Theory of L Systems*, 1980, New York, Academic Press. *L* Systems are formal grammars that are similar to context-free grammars and that are sometimes used to model biological systems.

A. Salomaa, *Formal Languages*, 1973, New York, Academic Press. Presents more material on grammars and families of languages.

Index
of Notation

(Notation that has a fixed spelling in roman letters will be found in the Alphabetic Index.)

Alphabetic Index

211